Improving Business Intelligence

The Six Sigma Way

Dorothy Miller

HOLT, THOMPSON & ASSOCIATES

Published by Holt, Thompson & Associates

Library of Congress Cataloging-in-Publication data:
Miller, Dorothy.
Improving Business Intelligence: The Six Sigma Way
Holt, Thompson, & Associates
SAN 8 5 3 – 3 7 4 1
ISBN 978-0-9794146-1-9
1. Data warehousing. 2. Business Intelligence

Printed in United States of America

For more information on Improving Business Intelligence: The Six Sigma Way, check the author's web site at www.sixsigmaBI.com

10 9 8 7 6 5 4 3 2 1

CONTENTS

CONTENTS

Defining the X Factors.

The Business Intelligence Asset Base

INTRODUCTION

Improving Business Intelligence

The Six Sigma Way

This book is for you, the owners, the managers, the designers of the data warehouse and business intelligence. This book is for you if you understand the important role of business intelligence in your organization and feel a keen responsibility for making it the best in the industry. This book defines a practical approach for creating and managing business intelligence to get the best product possible.

Six Sigma concepts and practices have been in common use in

the business arena for decades. Product and process improvements have been dramatic and, often, spectacular. However, in large part, Six Sigma has not been adopted by the Information Technology world. Part of the reason may be that the Six Sigma methods were not developed for the highly customized and complex processes involved in most of IT applications. Most likely, though, more of the reason for not adopting Six Sigma has been a lack of time, the rapid pace of IT technology changes and the strong push by the organization for more business intelligence applications at a faster rate than ever.

There are some excellent reasons to stop the mad race to keep up with the ever increasing demand for business intelligence. If we can improve the product which is sitting out there by just 5% to 10%, then the benefits to the organization can be dramatic. The potential is much greater than what could be recognized by any number of new business applications. There are many aspects of the Six Sigma methodology which can be extremely effective for Information Technology. The goal of this book is to provide a foundation and guide for applying the Six Sigma methodology to Business Intelligence.

We have studied the Six Sigma concepts and methods used in the rest of the business world. We have adopted and modified them to provide a framework for applying them to Business Intelligence. The principles are the same and most of the concepts are the same. In many ways, our business intelligence product, however, is not the same as the mass produced products which are the usual subject for Six Sigma analysis and improvement methods. We have made modifications where necessary to incorporate those differences.

The Six Sigma Continuing Improvement Model for Business Intelligence is a customer-focused, metrics based approach to improving business intelligence. Six Sigma refers to a better and smarter way of managing business processes and building products. The Six Sigma Way means putting the customer first and striving for a product that is near perfection. Adopting a rigorous, data based, Six Sigma improvement program for Business Intelligence can provide a dramatic increase in the value of these assets for any organization.

This book describes a practical approach to obtaining breakthrough quality improvement in business intelligence products and performance. The Six Sigma Model for Continuing Improvement of Business Intelligence is outlined and described. The book includes:

- the relevant Six Sigma Concepts, including the Six Sigma *breakthrough* formula, which is the foundation for the continuing improvement process;
- the Six Sigma Continuing Improvement Process, modified for and applied to, Business Intelligence;
- a description of all the primary components involved in the improvement process. This includes identification and descriptions for the Business Intelligence Customer, for each of the Critical to Quality Factors, and all (at least

all that we could think of and document) the factors which cause or influence business intelligence quality;

- metrics for each component;
- data collection and measurement methods; and
- an Action Response Plan for identifying and prioritizing improvement activities.

The goals for the book are to focus on and fully describe:

1. The Business Intelligence Customer;
2. Six Sigma Business Intelligence; and
3. The Six Sigma Continuing Improvement Process.

What the book is NOT about:

This book is not about the details of the Six Sigma statistics. There is a whole world out there of books and publications on Six Sigma Statistics and the application of those statistics. If you want to understand the detailed statistics as, for example, a *sample sign test* (i.e. a test for the probability of a sample median being equal to hypothesized value), this is not the book you need. Those statistics are important and the Business Intelligence Six Sigma Initiative will require that specialized information. You definitely need the resources with statistical expertise on your team. However, you will need to get that knowledge from other sources than this book.

UNIT I

Six Sigma Business Intelligence

Concepts and Structure

In this first Section, we will describe the Six Sigma Way and show the application of the concepts to Business Intelligence. This includes the following:

- Chapter 1: The Six Sigma Way
- Chapter 2: Concepts and Statistics
- Chapter 3: The Business Intelligence Initiative
- Chapter 4: Defining the Y Factors: Customers and Quality
- Chapter 5: Identifying the X Factors

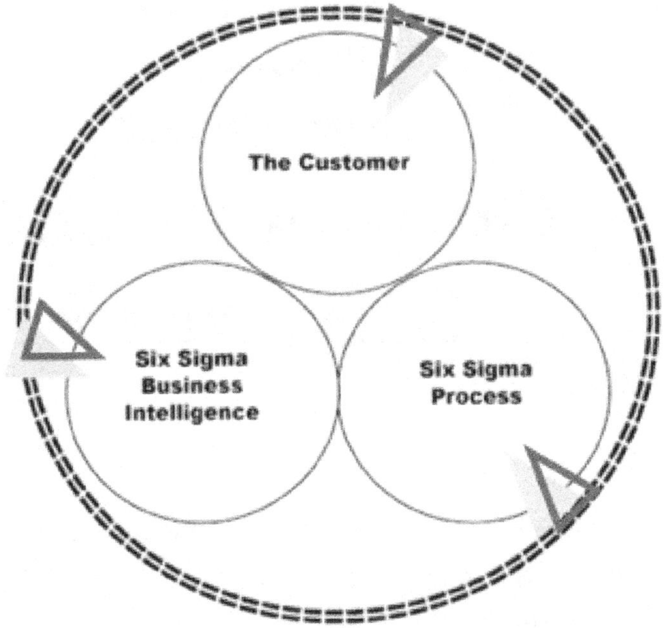

Figure 1-A

The Six Sigma Way

CHAPTER 1

The Six Sigma Way

The goals of Six Sigma for Business Intelligence are:

- to improve the information product
- to eliminate defects and variability, and
- to streamline the underlying business intelligence infrastructures and other components of the asset base.

The methods used by most organizations to create and manage business intelligence are static. Nothing substantive has changed about the process in years. A consultant colleague tells of a data warehouse manager, who was dubious about a Six Sigma program. The manager said, 'I've been doing this job for fifteen years. I know what I'm doing. Why do I need Six Sigma?' Twelve months later that person was leading the program. He was overheard telling his class: "Without improvement, you'll always get what you have always had. You need this program." In the typical organization, the business intelligence applications are created using some standard development methods. The data goes into the warehouse in the established way and the process is essentially complete. There is where the design and creation process ends and support and maintenance begins.

Using the Six Sigma Way, the Business Intelligence product and the whole process of creating and managing business intelligence will change. (*Note: We use the term 'Six Sigma' as a short hand label for all the concepts and experience base which has been incorporated into the Six Sigma methodology for the business product and process improvement over the last few decades.)* Six Sigma has several different aspects:

1. *The quality of the product is measured by the impact on the customer.* How does the customer perceive the product? How is the product used? If we make a change, does it make for a better product for the customer?

2. *The goal for the product is near perfection.* There are two primary reasons for that.

- One: we are striving for excellence in the product.
- Two: we recognize that the product is the result of many complex components and causal factors which must be addressed to impact the quality of the ultimate product. There is a basic concept in Six Sigma called *rolled throughput*

yield. What this means, in practical terms, is that we must establish a very high goal for each of the components and causal factors, if there is to be an expectation of excellence in the final product.

3. *The results and underlying approach to product improvement is data driven.* The metrics are critical. Six Sigma identifies and defines what measures are necessary to gauge the quality of the product for the customer. A first crucial step is to identify the factors which influence the quality of the product. That is to say, if the value for an identified metric, which measures a specific Critical to Quality factor for the customer, changes and/or does not meet specifications for quality, then what is causing the poor quality? Then, the causes for the change in quality are explored. The relevant *causal factor* data is gathered and analyzed to determine what actions and modifications can be made to improve the business intelligence quality.

4. *Six Sigma is proactive.* The Six Sigma methodology is structured and incorporates a definite plan and project management and problem solving tools and concepts. Questions are asked and answered. *How do I use the causal factor data to impact and drive the quality of the product? What do I measure within the product to ensure that any changes for the better or worse are quickly detected? If I make changes in the identified causal factors, how will those changes impact the quality of the final Business Intelligence product for the customer.*

5. *Six Sigma is cross functional, cross organizational, cross applications.* The whole of the organization must be involved and become part of the Six Sigma improvement process.

6. *Six Sigma requires an entrepreneurial culture.* In too many organizations, the cult of the bureaucrat has permeated the workplace. *Cover yourself.* The price for failure is too high, so each person makes the same decision: *Take no risks.* For Six Sigma to work, this attitude must change. In fact, Six Sigma requires risk taking and the possibility of failure. Changing the culture of an organization is difficult, at best. This may be THE primary block to success of any Six Sigma program. Only top down belief, passion and sponsorship will work here.

Six Sigma is a methodology that provides businesses with the tools to improve their business products and processes. The increase in performance and decrease in process variation leads to defect reduction and a vast improvement in the business intelligence product and underlying business intelligence asset base. The employees who use the business intelligence can do a better job. Six Sigma Business Intelligence becomes a ***closed loop of quality*** for the whole organization, where continual improvement in the Business Intelligence product provides more and better information for managing the business.

Applied to Business Intelligence, Six Sigma is a rigorous methodology that is metrics based and allows an organization to measure the quality of their business intelligence product and to systematically improve that product.

Cautions:

We need to approach the Six Sigma process for Business Intelligence in a slightly different manner than is used for general business products and processes. Unlike those processes and products, Business Intelligence is not a mass produced, extremely high volume, uniform and consistent process. Although there are enough common characteristics, there are differences which should be recognized. Therefore, we should approach the improvement process for Business Intelligence with these cautions:

1. Use only the parts of Six Sigma which are of value to the improvement process.

2. Do not get mired in details and data which adds little value to the process and final product quality. Do you really need to know or dwell on some of the more esoteric statistical terms and details? For example, do you need to care about such statistical details as a 2-Sample t Test, which is used for testing hypothesis about the location of two sample means being equal. In most cases, the quality of the business intelligence is obviously good or bad, meets specifications or not. We need to use and understand the statistics in order to be able to determine if our improvement strategy is working, how well, and exactly what effect any changes are making to the quality of the business intelligence. We need to be able to replicate the improvements and processes we used.

3. Don't get lost in the process ---- keep the goal in sight at all times.

Set the Improvement goals. Then, at every point in the process planning and implementation, ask that most pertinent question: ***Do we need to do this to reach the goals.*** Discard whatever ritual and noise of the six sigma dogma which is not essential to your goals.

What do we need to be able to do?

A. Monitor the quality of the Business Intelligence product.

B. Determine whether and when there is a need for improvement.

C. Identify the causal and impacting factors (known as X factors, i.e. from the *breakthrough* six sigma formula) for the critical to quality factors which have changed, i.e. what caused the need for improvement?

D. Audit and analyze those X factors which appear to have been responsible for the degradation in product quality. Determine what needs to be done, i.e. what actions need to happen, to improve quality.

E. Make the identified changes.

F. Measure the product quality to determine whether (and how) the changes to the causal (X) factors have been reflected in quality of the Business Intelligence product.

G. Take whatever steps necessary to 'deploy' and/or expand the product quality improvements.

A/H. Monitor the quality of the Business Intelligence Product.

Remember: **This is an iterative process.** We learn and evolve the product and the process as we continue to use the Six Sigma process.

Business Intelligence - The Six Sigma Way

This Business Intelligence Continuing Improvement Method is based on:

- the Six Sigma methodology for improvement of business products and services;
- the principles and methods integral to good Information Technology project management; and
- some of the best of the principles learned from total quality management.

The Six Sigma Way for Business Intelligence improvement is focused on the following principles and components:

A. *The Customer.* We will identify the customers for business intelligence and define their requirements for the product, i.e. critical to quality (CTQ) needs.

B. *Six Sigma Business Intelligence.* Define and understand the Business Intelligence product, not just as the final perceived product, but also as a complex set of components and infrastructures. We will set goals which reach for a Six Sigma level of quality for the business intelligence product.

C. *The Six Sigma Process*. We define and provide the guidelines for an improvement process which incorporates the most relevant parts of the Six Sigma Methodology, good Information Technology project management and quality management objectives.

This continuing improvement process requires the following:

- Strong management support at the highest levels,
- A focus for quality based on the needs of the customer.
- A process based on metrics, measurement, analysis and control,
- A program which is proactive, iterative and evolutionary, and
- A program which is pervasive across the business intelligence arena and across the organization.

A. The Business Intelligence Customer

Applying six sigma concepts to Business Intelligence requires a new approach, a new way of thinking about business information assets. The focus of attention is shifted to the customer and the needs and perceptions of that customer. Of course, we have always been aware of the people and the systems for which the business intelligence application and information library are created. We always gather requirements from those end users and design around those requirements. However, the focus has been on understanding specific business requirements, the technologies and infrastructures and the methods and processes for producing the business intelligence. Focusing on the customer means much more than gathering requirements from someone. Also, although as critical as ever, the underlying technologies and infrastructures must be redefined and viewed in their role as a means to satisfy the needs of the customer. Focusing on the customer does not mean just talking with Joe Smith about a particu-

Focus on the Customer

Who are they?

1. The Business Intelligence User
2. The Organization

What is Critical to a Quality Product for each?

Identify teh critical to quality factors.

Create Service Level Agreements

lar business intelligence application. There must be some analysis of the organization, as a unit, outside the normal business intelligence application process. Who actually uses the business intelligence? Who is most affected by the business intelligence of the organization. Identifying the customers for operational business intelligence within the organization is an important first step in any Six Sigma initiative.

There are two primary business intelligence customers within the organization.

1. The End Users of Operational Business Intelligence, and
2. The Organization

The direct customer for the business intelligence product is the *end user* of the information. These are the people and the systems who operate and manage the business to meet the needs of the organization customers. If we focus only on this end user, though, the organization does not get the full value of business intelligence. There are also broader, all encompassing, requirements which must be considered. For example, we need to consider such factors as the alignment of business intelligence to business goals. Focusing on the quality aspects for the end user will not highlight the broader needs of the organization.

Therefore, we should recognize that there are many factors that are critical to quality for the organization, but which cannot and will not be addressed at the parochial level of the individual business intelligence end user. We need to treat the organization as a customer also. Only at this level can we begin to envision, define and achieve those overall organization goals that will translate into success in a competitive, global marketplace. We will discuss in more detail in Chapter 4 just exactly how we can virtualize and communicate with the organization customer.

Critical to Quality Goals.

Identification of the customer is the first step. The next step in our Six Sigma Continuing Improvement Process requires that we determine just what business intelligence quality means to these customers. We need to identify and describe quality in short, clear statements using simple common terminology. These quality statements should be in terms of specific goals and objectives which can be documented and measured, as well as, business intelligence goals and objectives that can be monitored. These statements of quality requirements are known in the Six Sigma vernacular as Critical to Quality (CTQ) Factors. These CTQ factors should be carefully documented and widely communicated within the organization. For each business intelligence application project, there should be a continued adherence to Service Level Agreements (SLA) and these SLA's should incorporate the CTQ factors as defined for Business Intelligence.

Note: The Service Level Agreement(SLA) should already be a part of the current business intelligence application development process. These SLA's are signed, formal agreements between Information Technology (IT) and the business intelligence requesting end user group.

Some examples of the critical to quality factors for the organization customers may be related to topics such as:

- Performance (e.g. response time);
- Quality of the Information, (e.g., accuracy, timeliness, clarity);
- Availability and comprehension of the data; and
- Satisfaction of business requirements.

B. The Six Sigma Business Intelligence Product

There are several topics which need to be explored related to the Six Sigma Business Intelligence product.

1. **Exactly what is the product.** It is important that we understand exactly what is being considered as Business Intelligence. There are multiple layers of components and webs of infrastructures and interfaces which make business intelligence easily one of the largest, most complex, and intricate of *products.* The Six Sigma methodology is not usually applied to improve such a *product.* Needless to say, the comprehensive description of business intelligence does not really reflect a workable definition for product. However, we do need to consider the complete package in order to improve quality. In this book, we will define a limited product as the information, interfaces and appearance of business intelligence to the customers. All the complexi-

ties and components of business intelligence will be described and included together under the label of *business intelligence*. This larger set of objects includes the Business Intelligence Asset Base. All the components of the Business Intelligence Asset Base are identified and defined as X Factors. The X factors cause or impact the quality of the business intelligence product. (There are several other components which are also defined as X Factors, i.e. the organization, people, and business processes. These also are considered causal and impacting factors for business intelligence quality.)

2. **Product Quality.** How will we define the quality of the business intelligence product? What are the critical properties and the metrics which capture the essence of quality?

A clear, concise definition of product quality is basic to any methodology which will be used to monitor and improve the product. We need to understand how to analyze and measure quality.

3. **Six Sigma Business Intelligence**. The *Six Sigma* Business Intelligence product is used in this book to refer to one which consistently meets the specifications which have been defined as Six Sigma level quality. That may not actually meet the statistical definition of Six Sigma. The Six Sigma process for continuing improvement is structured, metrics driven and rigorously applied. The quality of the Business Intelligence product is ultimately defined by the standards set by the organization for quality and how well the product conforms to those standards.

Six Sigma has come to have several different connotations and uses. However, the basic statistical term, in effect, translates as "near perfection." A Six Sigma designation indicates that the product (and underlying components) is 99.9997 percent defect free. The statistical significance of this Six Sigma level of performance is important, but not really the most critical part of the rating. The quality rating is the end result of a set of constructs and processes for which the short hand term has been defined as, The Six Sigma Way. This means, essentially, that, at least the following has occurred:

- The product has been carefully defined and described;
- Customers for the product have been identified;
- Metrics have been identified which can represent and define the quality of the business intelligence product to the customers;
- Quality standards and tolerance levels have been set;
- Metrics are carefully monitored;
- The metrics which are used to rate the quality of the product and/or product components show that the defect level is .0003 or less (or at the goal level set by the organization for the business intelligence product).

Striving for Six Sigma quality would mean that if we measure response time for 10,000 queries, we want to find that 9,997+ of those queries would meet the goal of a response time of 3 seconds or less. (The metrics are usually based on defects per million opportunities. There are also other aspects to the measurement process – i.e., short-term versus long-term variations in the data, etc. However, the basic principle is to strive for a near perfect product.)

There are a number of reasons to set a quality goal of near perfection for the business Intelligence product:

1. Setting the goal high means that we will strive to achieve excellence.
2. The business intelligence end product is created from and comprised of a spiderweb of parts. The business intelligence product is the composite end result that is seen by the customer. There are infrastructures, processes, and a myriad of "under the hood" systems that allow for the creation, management and presentation of that business intelligence prod-

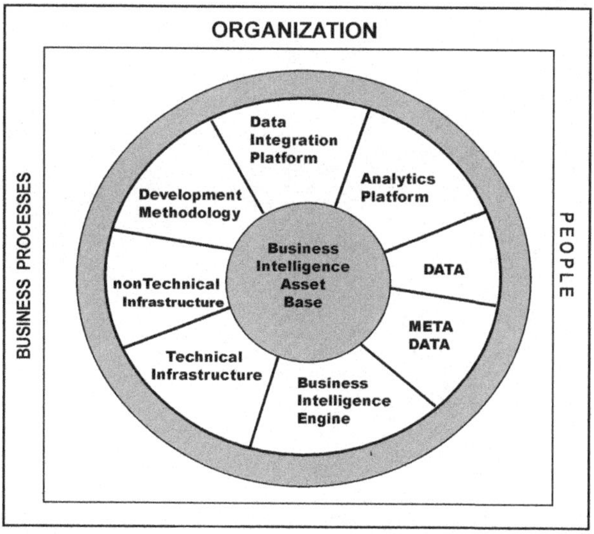

Business Intelligence
Product, Causal and Impacting Factors

uct. Each of these underlying components may have defects that impact the final product. The quality of each of these parts and the resulting combination impact the quality of the business intelligence end product. Setting a Six Sigma goal of near perfection for each component means that there can be a reasonable expectation for the highest quality of the end product.

C. The Six Sigma Process

The Six Sigma *Breakthrough* Formula

There is a single formula which is the foundation for all of Six Sigma. This formula represents the Principle of Determinism. Simply put, a certain set of inputs is transformed into an output. The quality of the Business Information product is dependent on (i.e. a function of) a number of factors plus some degree of error. Creating and managing a Six Sigma Business Intelligence product requires that we fully understand the elements which are represented by each component of this formula. We must identify and describe each notation and keep in mind that the process is rigorous and data driven. Y refers to the quality of the Business Intelligence Product. That quality is dependent on, i.e. a function of, all the inputs. The X factors represent the causal

$$Y = f(X) + E$$

factors which are relevant to the creation and/or impact the outcome. The E represents the 'error' or some uncertainty factor (which we will discount as uncontrollable.) Every variation is caused by something. If you are going to control the output, you must control the cause. That means understanding both the desired results, as well as, the causal factors.

Understanding this basic formula, each of the components, and the deterministic nature of the process is the foundation for creating and managing Six Sigma Business Intelligence. The remainder of the book is an attempt to identify, describe and use this *breakthrough* formula and the factors and concepts inherent in the formula.

Push for Perfection: A Rigorous Process for Continual Improvement

The Six Sigma process is based on a structured program, the application of rigorous rules, and carefully identified and defined metrics and data. This foundation for this book is the *BI Continuing Improvement Model (BI-CIM* $_{6\sigma}$*).* This model includes the methodology and all the components necessary to create and manage a program for the improvement of Business Intelligence assets within an organization.

The constructs and components of the BI-CIM model are outlined below. Each of the parts of the model are further detailed in the remainder of the book.

1. Six Sigma Concepts: The basic formula and Six Sigma Concepts/Statistics
2. Customers: Identification and description of the Customers
3. Business Intelligence Product: Definition of Product, including all the business intelligence assets and components
    - Causal and/or impacting Factors (X Factors)
    - Metrics
4. Product Quality: Definition of Quality of the Business Intelligence Product

- Critical to Quality Factors (Y Factors)
- Metrics

5. Six Sigma Method for Continuing Improvement
    - Detailed plans for a Continuing Improvement Program. The process and steps involved in the umbrella program, including risk assessment and setting priorities for six sigma projects. It also includes the creation and management of a portfolio of six sigma projects - i.e. Action Response Planning.
    - The process and requirements for individual six sigma projects which make up the Six Sigma Continuing Improvement Program.

CHAPTER 2

BI Continuing Improvement Model 68

Six Sigma Foundation and Process

Six Sigma Concepts & Statistics

What is Six Sigma? What are the statistics which are relevant to using the Six Sigma Way for improving Business Intelligence quality. The term, Six Sigma, has become synonymous with a methodology for reducing problems and errors and providing an improved product or process. In this chapter, we will review some of the basic Six Sigma concepts and statistics. Those who wish to study more details on the statistical basis for the Six Sigma Way should refer to any of the industry library of works on the subject. The foundation and premises for this book do not deal with those details. The concepts and basic statistics which we need to describe the Continuing Improvement Process for Business Intelligence are included in this chapter.

We need to emphasize that the real goal should be kept in mind at all times. That goal is breakthrough improvement in Business Intelligence quality. Anything which is not relevant to that goal should be discarded. Use the basic statistics necessary for the job. Keep in mind that getting mired in extraneous or unnecessary details should be avoided. That includes a tendency of some of us to get *carried away* with the beauty of the numbers. A simple rule of thumb should be - don't do it if it doesn't add value. Will it help me answer the important questions about quality and causal factors? Always ask the question, will this help me improve the value of the Business Intelligence product?

Statistics - Yuck!

Why do we need statistics at all? Why not just use the old adage - 'if it ain't broke - don't fix it'? Why not just fix any problems as they occur? Actually, that is what most organizations have been doing with their Business Intelligence assets.

First of all - our business intelligence assets are just too important to take such a *half baked* approach. How do we even know that we have a product which is serving the needs of the organization?

What do the statistics tell us? How do we know how much of this *rigorous approach* we should apply? How much *statistics* is enough -- and when have we 'gone too far'? Can we go too far? We have to measure the value received from the statistics and the *rigor* of the methodology just like anything else. Yes, we can go too far and get lost in the process without adding much value toward our objectives.

In order to get the best Business Intelligence possible - we need to understand what that is.

- What is a quality business intelligence product?
- Who determines quality and utility?
- How do we achieve a quality product?
- How do we prevent problems rather than fight problems?

The questions which the statistics should be answering for us are:

- How do we measure quality? What metrics and data will allow us to measure quality? Are there fluctuations which can be accepted? Can we measure quality? What are the specifications for quality and what are the acceptable, i.e. tolerance levels of deviation from those specifications?
- Is there a product problem? Do we wait for the user of the business intelligence product to complain?
- Just how close or how far are we now from quality?
- If we make changes, how does each change impact the product quality? Are we spending our resources wisely?
- What changes are most effective?

The statistics are key:

1. We need to prevent problems, rather than react to problems.

The Statistics allow us to monitor the product for quality and set tolerance limits which can trigger corrective action.

2. We need to understand what creates product quality and what are all the causal and impacting factors to the quality product.

The breakthrough formula helps us define and understand the relationships between the quality results and the impacting/causal factors. We will set specifications for each of these and manage to those specifications.

3. When we make changes to the product, components, process and/or other assets, we need to understand exactly what is happening - i.e. how those changes are impacting quality of the product. How much are we spending in resources for what kind of return? Have we achieved the desired goals?

Statistics allow us to measure and assess the data.

Six Sigma Statistics

In Six Sigma terminology, important characteristics are referred to as CTXs. This stands for *critical to X, where X* represents whatever the characteristic is linked to. For the Six Sigma Business Intelligence methodology, the X will always indicate QUALITY. Therefore, we will refer to CTQ, or Critical to Quality factors.

Performance Target

The CTQ target values may be depicted graphically as in figure 2-A.

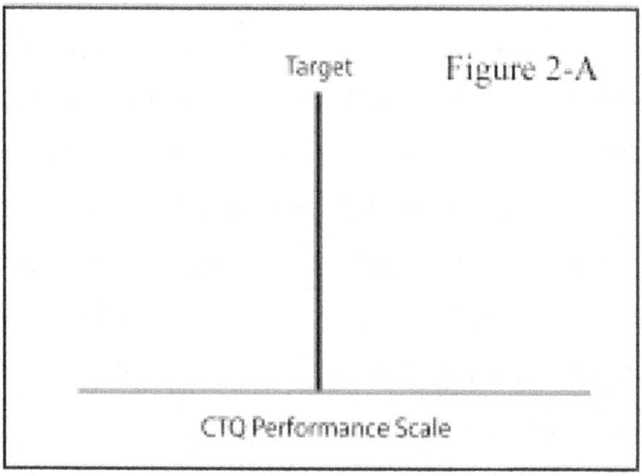

The performance scale is in whatever units are being used to measure the target, e.g. response time in seconds. The Goal of Six Sigma is to come as close to the target metric as often as possible. Thus, the Critical to Quality measurement may be for response time for a simple query to the information library. The target is to consistently (i.e. all queries) keep the time at 5 seconds or less, i.e. from key entry of the request to the response. The customer perceives this as the response time for this application which represents quality. We set the quality target for response time based on what the customer needs to perform the job. (This goal will also be written into a documented Service Level Agreement - so that everyone will understand the response time target.)

Variation

Variation is a deviation from expectations. Variation is the degree to which a part, product, service or transaction differs from all the others in the same class. The reality is that the target will be missed some of the time. No matter how excellent the process and underlying structures are, it is just not possible to hit the target every time. There will always be some variation. The amount of time it takes to process a query varies. This variation shows up as a distribution of actual response times, i.e. performance units, around the target. Normally the distribution is in the form of a bell shaped curve. (See Figure 2-B). This normal distribution is symmetrical about the central line (target). The areas to the left and to the right are equal.

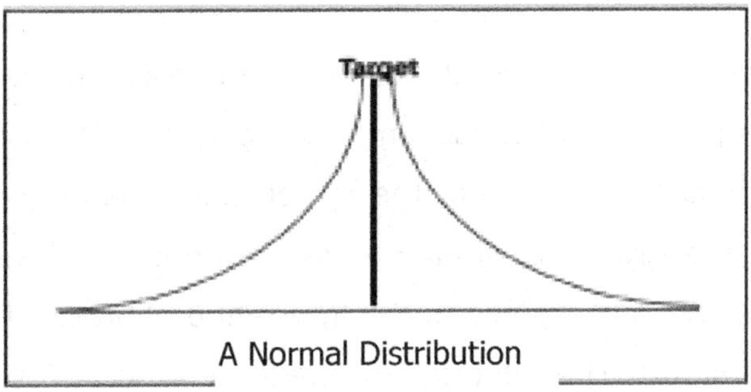

Figure 2-B

Standards and specifications

Since there are always variations, we add the concepts of standards and specifications. Just how much variation can we afford and still maintain the quality standards desired? Once that question is answered and the tolerances are defined, i.e. the upper and lower limits for performance, then we can measure the quality of the performance.

Now there is a way to indicate the acceptable extent of variation which can be allowed and still have a business information product of acceptable quality to the customer. These performance

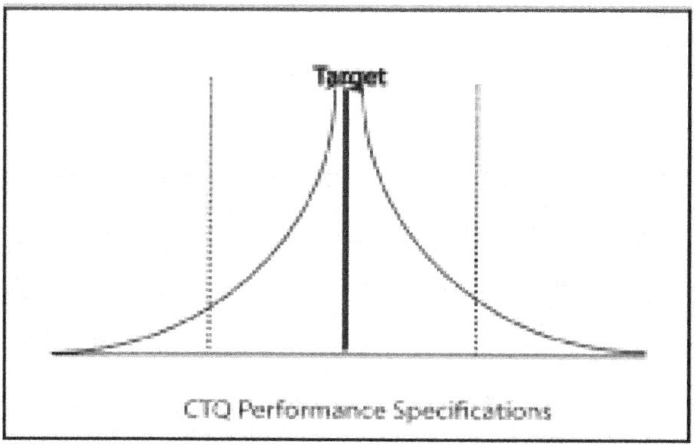

Figure 2-C

specification limits provide the parameters for defining, measuring analyzing, improving and controlling quality.

Quality may be defined as 'getting as close as possible to the target with the least amount of variation', i.e. hit the target and minimize the variation. Quality is essentially defined by conformance to standards/specifications. Any product (i.e. in this case a query/response) which falls outside the preset limits is considered a defect. Thus, if we set the limits as 3 seconds plus 1 second, any query/response which takes over 4 seconds is a defect. (Note: in this case less than 2 seconds for a response time is certainly acceptable. We might track those queries with lower than expected times in order to help determine how to consistently achieve that level of quality.)

The Mean and Six Sigma

If you measure the occurrence of something many times, it is going to vary around some average, i.e. mean value. The mean is the central tendency of the process. If there are enough occurrences of a coin toss, the average will be 50% heads and 50% tails.

Anytime you measure the value of a given occurrence or event, it will almost always vary from the mean. Variation is simply a deviation from expectations. Six Sigma is concerned with this variation of the occurrence from the mean. We study the size, trends, causes, effects of the variation and try to control it.

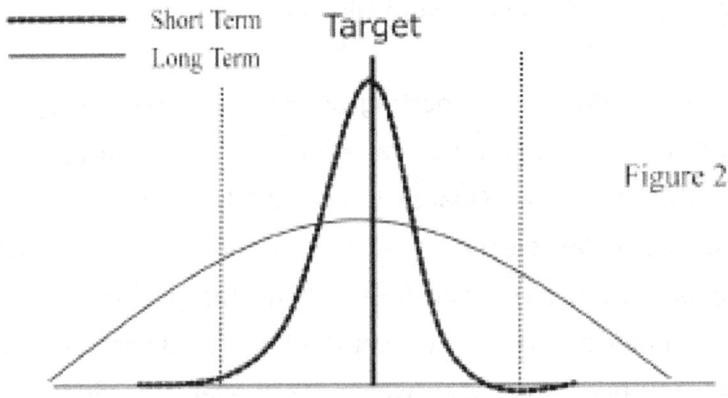

Figure 2-D

Short term & Long term variation

Long term and Short Term Variation

If you measure the variation for a short time versus over a longer period of time, the variance may change. The probability of a defect in the short term does not account for changes that may be occurring in the process/asset base over the long term. Perhaps query response times are being impacted by changes in volumes or new data additions. Whatever performance measure you choose may, and most likely, will become eroded or changed over time. Performance monitoring and analysis must take into account these different variation types.

Roll up of characteristic behaviors

We have defined quality in terms of a single characteristic or component. However, in reality, there are numerous parts to the business intelligence asset base. All the constructs and components must fit together and work in conjunction. Although we may not translate all these components into CTQ's, which we monitor at the customer level, all will impact the quality results which are seen by the customer. All these components and constructs will impact the performance. This multiplies the risk of defects in the product. In much of the statistical documentation, the concept of compounding defect risk is described with the example of rolling a die vs rolling multiple dice. With a single die with six sides, if you assume one side is a defect, you have a five in six change of rolling a 'good' side. However, with each added die, the odds of a successful result decreases. (with two dice - 10 out of 12/69%; three dice - 15 out 18/58%) With 50 to 100 dice, the probability of never getting a defect drops to near non existence, i.e. 1 in millions. This concept of compounding the defect risk is called risk throughput yield. The Business Intelligence Asset Base, which includes the information product, is extremely complex, with myriad parts. That means we need to expect defects. This means in practice that you must establish an extremely high success probability for each characteristic, if you expect the final product or service to be successful and near defect free.

Six Sigma

The Sigma Scale

Sigma	Percent Defective	Defects per Millio n
1	69%	691,462
2	31%	308,538
3	6.7%	66,807
4	0.62%	6,210
5	0.023%	233
6	0.00034%	3.4
7	0.0000019%	0.019

Figure 2-E

The term six sigma is a statistical measure which indicates how well a critical characteristic performs compared to the specifications. The measurement methodology and approach covers the two key concerns discussed in the previous sections, i.e. variation over time and the roll-up of characteristic behaviors.

Using the standard scale for sigma, the higher the sigma score, the fewer defects and the closer to 'perfection' the characteristic being measured. For example, if a characteristic is defective 31% of the time, it is 'rated' at two sigma. The compliance for this characteristic is 69%. If a characteristic operates at three sigma, that means that 67% of the time, the variation in the performance of that characteristic exceeds acceptable levels, i.e. the specifications/goals. The table in Figure 2-E shows some key points on the sigma scale.

Should your goal be Six Sigma?

Selecting Six Sigma as the goal in the original systems work was based primarily on the complexity of the products being measured. Six Sigma was used as a measurement of each characteristic within the whole and only a very tight goal for each of these myriad components would allow for the final product to be acceptable. The Business Intelligence Asset Base is also a very complex system and it is recommended that you use Six Sigma as the goal for each component. The Six Sigma methodology for improving business intelligence includes the monitoring of the Y Critical to Quality factors, i.e. the desired results, along with the analysis of the causal characteristics, i.e. the X factors, using a business intelligence audit and tracking system. The first level, the quality, is based on metrics related to the business information product and interface/interaction with the customer.

These measure business information quality, provide tracking, monitoring and triggering for the second level analysis of X, i.e. the causal and impacting, factors. The second level of metrics involves identifying and analyzing the causal factors and includes an audit of the product, as well as, the underlying infrastructures, software, hardware, systems and processes, i.e. the business intelligence asset base. This business intelligence asset base is extremely complex and there are hundreds of characteristics and impacting factors, i.e. X factors.

Costs vs Reward: Even so, you may find that a product which is of good to excellent quality and acceptable for the customer can be satisfied with a goal less than Six Sigma. The first level of metrics for *six sigma business intelligence*, i.e. the critical to quality (CTQ) characteristics for the customers, are the Y factors. A goal of four or five sigma may be sufficient to satisfy your needs at this level. These Y factors result from the cumulative effects of the X characteristics of the business intelligence asset base. In order to reach the standards of 4 or 5 Sigma, the specifications for the X characteristics must necessarily be set higher. You will need to judge the effects and the specific requirements for your organization. Keep in mind, also, there are some strong psychological reasons to set Six Sigma level goals.

In any case, if you elect to set a Six Sigma goal, then a case must be made to pay the cost and take the risks which are associated with setting the specifications at that Six Sigma level. It is extremely costly to provide for the metrics, the data collection, tracking, analysis and feedback necessary to reach those goals. Remember, these are extremely detailed metrics and processes. You must carefully assess the costs and determine if the incremental gain is worth the additional resources. You should also keep in mind that the process is iterative. You may want to set multiple smaller incremental goals, while planning to achieve an ultimate longer term goal. *(note - the methodology is always identified as a Six Sigma program, whatever the goals established.)*

Whether you meet your six sigma goal or not, you will reap the benefits from the process of defining and understanding all the business intelligence components and iterating through the Six Sigma improvement process. You will see definite improvements and there may be breakthrough changes. You will definitely have a better understanding of the product and the organization.

The Breakthrough Equation

Six Sigma Continuing Improvement Model for Business Intelligence is based on a simple to understand equation:

$$\mathbf{Y = f(X) + E}$$

Y is the outcome, i.e. the result you need

X represents the inputs - the factors which create or impact the outcome;

f stands for function; i.e. y is a function of all the x factors. These X factors create and impact the Y/Quality.

E represents the presence of error. The formula needs to account for the uncertainty factor, i.e. the fact that the X factors combine to produce the Y result has some uncertainty.

Essentially, this basic formula means that a certain set of inputs is transformed by a process into an output. The formula represents the *principle of determination:* The independent variable(s) is operated on by a deterministic function (f) to transform it into the outcome (Y), i.e. the dependent variable. The Y results from, or is a function of, the Xs.

Every variation is caused by something. If you are going to control the output, you must control the cause. That means understanding the causal factors. You may be 25 pounds overweight. You have been diagnosed as a borderline diabetic so you need to lose that weight. The doctor says you need to take vitamins (X1), jog three miles a day (X2), and take in no more than 1200 calories a day. Wow! That will work. But is it ever that simple? There's always some uncertainty about that weight loss. Will you find a piece of cake, a slice of pie and some french fries three days in a row? Maybe you need to push up the jogging to 5 miles to cover that extra food intake. Everything is deterministic. An outcome is the result of inputs and a process which acts on those inputs. No matter how well the inputs and process are designed and executed, there is always some margin of error. There will be some variation.

We use the *principle of determination* to explain cause and effect. The results are dependent on the inputs and the process that acts on them. If you want to get better results, then you analyze the outcome, identify all the inputs and the processes involved in creating that outcome. If the outcome was good, then you will try to replicate the inputs and process. If bad, i.e. needs improving, that analysis should allow you to pinpoint some of the reasons for that less than perfect outcome and try to make it better next time.

CHAPTER 3

BI Continuing Improvement Model 6σ

Describing the Six Sigma BI Initiative

The Six Sigma Business Intelligence Initiative

Where do you start?

Start by considering whether you should even begin a Six Sigma program for improvement of Business Intelligence right now? Do you have (or can you get) the necessary resources and the management buy-in? Do you have the commitment, persistence, and the vision to work through to a successful continuing improvement program? Keep in mind that any successful Six Sigma initiative will require cultural change. Even if the program is limited to the Business Intelligence arena, the changes required throughout the organization will be substantial. Business Intelligence permeates the organization and setting out to improve it the Six Sigma Way will impact every level of the organization, every department and most of the people.

Consider, also, your organization's history and status in regards to the following:

- success with previous and/or current Total Quality Management and Six Sigma enterprise programs;
- level of capability maturity in terms of your Information Technology organization as rated against the industry - i.e. is your organization a leader, about average, not keeping up?
- desire and commitment to the program; and
- the relationship between IT and the Business Community.

You should also consider:

Who is the driving force behind this initiative? An initiator and supporters are important, but even the greatest desire may not be enough to make such an initiative work. This will require a *full court press* by both the Information Technology and the Business teams, including most of the rest of the organization, the business intelligence contributors and all levels of management.

Do you have senior management support? This must be a top down initiative. There are just too many different areas of the organization involved to make it work without full commitment and buy in.

The Six Sigma Way requires persistence and a long term commitment.

What is a Six Sigma Continuing Improvement Program for Business Intelligence?

The Six Sigma Continuing Improvement Model for Business Intelligence is a targeted, rigorous, structured program aimed at understanding and improving Business Intelligence for the organization. The initiative involves an aggressive, broad impact, iterative approach to eliminating defects in the product and in creating and managing the business intelligence assets.

Six Sigma requires a new way of thinking, an approach to daily activities which is energized, even passionate, and focused on the goals. The program should begin with the vision and commitment of top level executives. The individual mindset of each participant must be that of an entrepreneur in search of new ideas and *break through* performance. That term, 'breakthrough' performance improvement, is one of the most used and most useful terms relevant to the Six Sigma Way. That is the best way to describe the goal. The basic formula on which the concepts are built is termed the *breakthrough* formula. The Six Sigma Initiative is the program through which this *breakthrough* strategy for improvement is planned and executed.

Some of the Six Sigma Initiative basic principles, strategies and requirements are defined here. The Six Sigma Initiative is characterized by the following:

- A cross organization program. It must be recognized and

supported and implemented throughout the organization - across departments and various layers of management.

- Based on Six Sigma Concepts. Among these is a goal for breakthrough performance and product improvement.
- Metrics based. Data collection, measurement and analysis are the foundation for the process.
- A rigorously applied. structured process. A step by step proven process which is adopted and integrated into the organization culture, infrastructures, and disciplines. See a description of the DMAIC process in Chapter 6.
- Specialized training. Training must be available to all and mandatory for many of the participants of the initiative.
- Culture Change. The organization, as a whole, i.e. the attitudes, communications, operations, must change as necessary to support the program and adopt the improvement goals.
- Mandatory Management support. The program requires management support at highest levels, as well as, buy-in across the organization. You will not get the buy-in which crosses the organization political and departmental boundaries without top level management support.
- Special Resources. Whether you call them black and green belts, or Six Sigma specialists, you need someone trained to understand the concepts and statistics and capable of applying them to the process
- Special Tools. You need the software and tools relevant to the six sigma process, including project management and the software and tools for data collection, statistics,

and auditing.

- Project based. The whole strategy must be applied using the best of project management methods.
- Knowledgeable and willing participants.
- Persistence and the will to succeed.
- Strong, rigorous iterative approach

The Six Sigma Team

The Six Sigma initiative requires the participation and buy-in of a lot of people, across the organization. The specialized nature of the program means that special training and skills are required. There are some specific needs, which are outside the usual realm of either the business or information technology specialist. Some of these skills include, for example, the understanding and the application of the relevant statistics, the program management, and the rigorous processes involved.

The Six Sigma program requires a strong, cross functional, cross organization approach. The team must reflect this. The roles and responsibilities for the people resources include the following:

Leader of the Initiative -- usually a senior manager, who is responsible for the effective alignment of the organization goals, the business goals, and the information technology goals. This Six Sigma leader is responsible for monitoring the program and ensuring that goals are met. This also includes the development of the plan, the resources, the training and the program dynamics.

The Six Sigma BI Leadership Team

This is the cross-functional team which is responsible for

- Driving the program and ensuring organization recognition and commitment
- Installation and leadership of the process, metrics and other program requirements
- Providing the Virtual persona of the Organization Customer for development of Critical to Quality Y factors for the business intelligence product
- Development and implementation of the support infrastructure necessary to sustain the Six Sigma Continuing Improvement program
- Monitoring and assessment of the program - i.e. goals and level of achievement.

The Six Sigma Operations Team

This is the hands-on team and will include members of the business and information technology groups, a team leader, and the specialists who are trained and skilled in the Six Sigma concepts and statistics.

The Martial Arts Specialists

Who are they?

Martial arts terms have been used to describe the specialists who are skilled in applied statistics for the program. The persons with the highest level of skill are called *Black Belts*. These are the hands-on experts who can teach and mentor the other participants, as well as, act as team expert and consultant. Those with a medium level of skill are *Green Belts* and those with the every day skill level are the *Yellow Belts*.

Do We Need them?

Your organization may or may not elect to refer to your statistics specialists with the martial arts terms. You may also elect not to 'buy into' the whole mystic-like approach which has characterized some of the Six Sigma dogma. However, there is no doubt that you will need the skills represented by these specialists. Collecting and analyzing the data, which are at the core of a successful Six Sigma program, requires specialized statistics and analysis knowledge on a day to day basis. In most cases, you will find that selecting and training those interested participants already involved in the program will be most advantageous. However, the bottom line is, include these specialists in your program.

Six Sigma Initiative LIfe Cycle

There are five stages to the Six Sigma Initiative:

1. Initialize the program. We establish the goals and infrastructure and the team management.
2. Roll out the initiative by establishing and training the team and providing the tools which are necessary to the program.
3. Implement the program - as shown in the remainder of this book.
4. After the first iterations of the program with specific business intelligence applications, the program may be more fully established and structured and applied to other business intelligence applications and products.
5. The program is re-assessed and modified as necessary to sustain a continuing improvement for Business Intelligence.

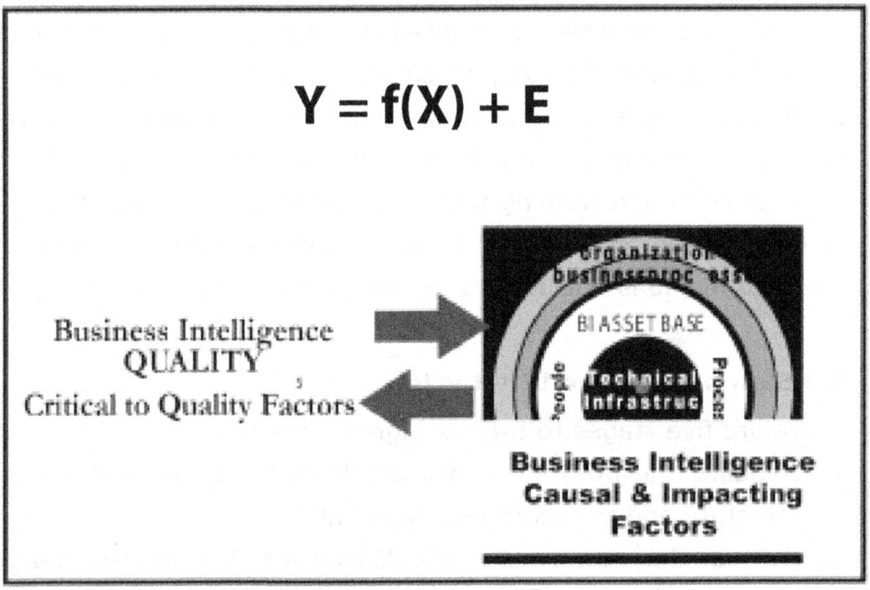

The Six Sigma Formula

Foundation for Continuing Improvement of Business Intelligence

CHAPTER 4

BI Continuing Improvement Model 68

Identifying Critical to Quality Y Factors

Customers and Quality

The focus of attention of the Six Sigma Methodology is the customer. Defining a quality product means determining what the customer perceives as quality. In order to do this, we must first understand the customer. Who is the customer? What are the characteristics which will define what is important in their specific business intelligence product set? How does each customer relate to the product? Understanding and defining the customer base should provide a foundation for describing the factors which represent quality to the customer.

The objectives for this chapter are to provide a clear understanding of the customers of business intelligence and the Critical to

Quality Factors which can be used to monitor business intelligence quality. This will include the following topics:

- Identify the customers.
- Identify the Business Intelligence used by the customers - describe the Business Intelligence product used by specific customers.
- Identify and define the factors which represent quality to the customer. Make sure we understand how and why these factors are the essential ones, i.e. why and how do each of the factors represent quality to the customer.

Who are the customers for Business Intelligence?

In the Six Sigma approach to improving business intelligence, the customers play a pivotal role. The focus of the improvement process is based on the needs of the customer. The success of Business Intelligence is defined in terms of how well the customer perceives the product. Therefore it is crucial that we identify and clearly describe the customer(s), locate that customer in their working environment, and build a picture of their requirements for the business intelligence product. We need to identify these customers and clarify their roles and responsibilities.

From the perspective of the Six Sigma process, there are two classes of customer who are crucial to the quality improvement process:

1. The end user of the business intelligence product.

These are the people and systems within the organization who create, use, or in some way, interface with business intelligence in doing their jobs.

2. The Organization.

The organization, viewed as an entity, has a strong interest in the successful use and effectiveness of business intelligence assets.

The Category 1 Customer: The End User

The end users of the business intelligence product are the people within the organization who rely on the information to do their jobs. This class of customer may also include people outside the organization who use the business intelligence in ways that have been designated by the organization. For example, they may check their account information, pay bills, and update personal information. The customer could also be an automated system which uses the information to manage and/or control some set of functions for the organization. Each of these customers will have specific requirements for their business intelligence product.

The Category 2 Customer: The Organization

The organization is also an important customer, with very specific and crucial requirements. There are many factors that are critical to quality for the organization which cannot and will not be addressed at the parochial level of the business intelligence end user. Treating the organization as a separate customer provides a focal point to envision, define and achieve the overall, i.e. umbrella, organization requirements which cannot be addressed at any other level. These requirements include, for example, alignment of the Business Intelligence assets to the organization strategic and tactical goals.

In order to clarify, understand and meet these requirements, we must translate and treat this customer as a tangible entity, an entity which can speak for the organization. The most helpful way will be the formation of a team of management, business and information technology specialists who can define and clarify the organization requirements.

Special Requirements Customers

We need to define and categorize any customers who have important special needs which will not be met by the general end user and organization customer CTQ factors.

In most cases, the two groups of customers defined above (i.e. end users and the organization) are sufficient to provide all the relevant *critical to quality* requirements for Business Intelligence. However, we should still carefully analyze categories of business intelligence; users of the business intelligence assets; and the specific business intelligence products they use ... ... to determine whether we should provide for additional customer categories. For example, are there special sets of characteristics which identify a customer group, i.e. are there some specific needs which mean one group of customers will perceive the quality of a business intelligence product in a different manner. A primary reason for this exercise is to determine whether we need more than one set of *critical to quality* factors and metrics for the Business Intelligence improvement process. Do we group all the end users into a single category or do we need, for example, to identify more specifically the 'forecasting/analytics team'? There may be some groups of end users who may have special requirements which need to be addressed to ensure that these customers get a quality Business Intelligence product.

Defining special categories of customers requires that we take a closer look at the business intelligence products in use. We need to know whether some customers have special product needs. The most visible component of a Business Intelligence product is the associated sets of data and meta data, i.e. the management and decision support information. That Business Intelligence product also includes the nature and relationship of the information to the user, i.e. the people or systems which interface with and use the information. Look also at the business intelligence applications which were responsible for the development of the information and reporting structures and access. The applications should not be a deciding factor. They should merely be one of the items which will be reviewed. The components of the product include the data sources and information subject matter, the delivery formats, including reporting, query and analysis capabilities, infrastructures, and much more.

Special requirements customers may be identified and segregated by determining any specific customer characteristics, along with the relevant business intelligence product characteristics.

How do we measure Quality? (The Y Component)

Business Intelligence quality is based on customer requirements and perceptions. Quality must be measurable. An intuitive understanding and a *fix it if it breaks* attitude is not sufficient. We need to be able to set objectives for quality and to determine when those objectives are met. Improvement of the Business Intelligence product can best be accomplished when we can identify what the customer perceives as critical to product quality and describe and measure those requirements.

The Six Sigma Foundation Formula is:

$$Y = f(X) + E$$

The Y Component is Quality. Quality is dependent on all the causal and impacting factors defined as X, i.e. the independent factors. We need to identify and be able to measure the quality of the Business Intelligence product --- before we can identify and study the relationships of the X factors which cause and/or impact that quality. We quantify the product quality through the identification of specific factors which make up and reflect the product quality to the customer.

Identify the critical to quality factors.

Focusing on the customer requires that we describe the business intelligence product and identify those factors which are critical to quality for each customer. What are the most important factors of the business intelligence product to the customer? Improvement of the product can best be accomplished when we can identify what the customer perceives as critical to product quality. If we (a Six Sigma BI team) believe that five characteristics of the business intelligence product need improvement, but the customer believes that only one of these characteristics is important – then we will know where to concentrate our efforts for the best results for the customer. We also will need to monitor these 'critical to quality' factors in a program which seeks to both improve the product quality and to ensure that the product continues to meet the defined level of quality.

One of the most crucial of the jobs of the Six Sigma team is to determine what are the factors inherent in the Business Intelligence product which reflect what is Critical to Quality for the customer. The goal of the team should be to identify and define five to eight core level factors which reflect quality as perceived by the customer. These factors must be in a form which can be measured, i.e. they will be translated into metrics which can be used to monitor customer satisfaction and the quality of the

Business Intelligence.

In defining these factors and associated metrics, we should keep in mind several critical points:

1. The product quality is represented by all the Critical to Quality (Y) factors which are defined during this stage of the six sigma process.
2. Product quality is defined in terms of the customer - i.e. what does the customer perceive?
3. The CTQ factors must be realistic, intuitive and measurable.

The Six Sigma team needs to identify a set of these factors which can be generally used within the Business Intelligence continuing improvement program. The identified factors must then be tested to ensure that they do, in fact, capture the Critical to Quality requirements for the Business Intelligence customer. Critical to Quality factors should be identified and defined for each of the customer categories.

How do we know what the customer perceives as necessary to business intelligence quality? The simplest way is to ask. There are some preliminary analysis steps which may be helpful. Providing some draft ideas will shorten the process. However, finding some representative people and using surveys and discussion groups will be the most simple and get the fastest answers. You may have some of these quality answers already available. If you have routinely written Service Level Agreements for your Business Intelligence applications, then that experience and those SLA's are an excellent first step. If your organization has not used Service Level Agreements prior to this Six Sigma Program, then you should definitely start now.

Service Level Agreement

The Critical to Quality factors which are identified should be documented, and there should be a signed, formal agreement between Information Technology (IT) and the business intelligence customer. In most cases, there are already some clear best practices and industry standards that support a service level agreement (SLA) for individual business intelligence applications between IT and customers. In the Six Sigma business intelligence initiative, the CTQ factors within these SLAs will be rigorously monitored.

CTQ Factors: Category 1 Customer (ie. the End User)

We have identified a preliminary set of CTQ (Y) Factors for the end user category of customer. The Six Sigma team may find that some of these are not exactly reflective of your organization. You should use the concepts and the process. Change the CTQ factors based on specific needs of your organization. (Also, you should define the special needs of any additional groups of customers based on your analysis of their requirements.)

1. Performance. Response time is probably the most relevant performance factor for the customer, i.e. time from request/query for information to receipt of the information.
2. Reliability. Is the product always there when needed?
3. Quality of Information. Is the information accurate, timely and clear?

4. Meets Business Requirements. Does it satisfy the requirements which were defined initially; and we might also ask: can it meet expanded requirements with minor enhancements?
5. Format and Delivery. Is it intuitive and easy to use, from simple reports to power user analytics?
6. Velocity. How soon is the data available i.e. from data entry into the system to user accessible?
7. Availability and Comprehension. Is the desired information available? Do we have all of it?
8. Support and Training. Do the users get help when they need it?

Critical to Quality (Y) Factors
Level 1 Customer - the End User

Performance
Reliability
Quality of Information
Meets Business Requirements
Format
Velocity
Availability & Comprehension
Support and Training

For the Category 2 Customer (ie. the Organization)

The following CTQ (Y) Factors have been identified as a list you may consider for the Organization customer. The Quality Factors associated with the Organization should reflect the wider scope and overall business requirements of this customer. Some of these CTQ factors are:

1. Satisfaction of Business Objectives. Do the available information and analytics satisfy the Organization Business Goals i.e. alignment with Business Goals?

Critical to Quality (Y) Factors
Level 2 Customer - the Organization

Satisfaction - Business Objectives
Quality of Information
Velocity
Availability & Comprehension
User Understanding and Satisfaction
Cost to Benefits Received

2. Quality of Information. What are the expectations of management? Is the information accurate, timely, integrated and up to date?
3. Velocity. How soon is the data available i.e. from data entry into the system to user accessible?
4. Availability and Comprehension. Is the desired information available when it is needed? Do we have all of it? i.e. the data warehouse - comprehension and accessibility of 'integrated information'.
5. User Understanding and Satisfaction. Are the Service Level Agreements for end users accomplishing the goals? Are users being trained? What is the Category 1 Customer satisfaction level?
6. Cost to Benefits Received. Can we afford it? Is it worth it?

$$Y = f(X) + E$$

The Six Sigma *Breakthrough* Formula

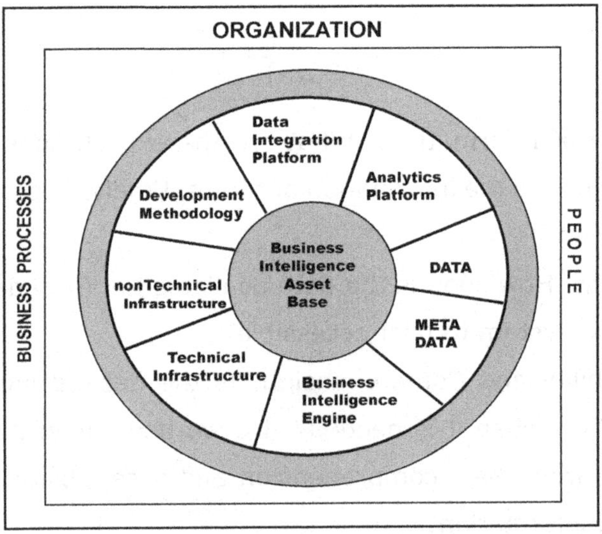

Business Intelligence
Product, Causal and Impacting Factors

CHAPTER 5

BI Continuing Improvement Model 68

Defining the Causes for BI Quality

Identifying X: the Causal Factors

Identifying, and ultimately, assessing, the factors which cause and, in some way, impact the quality of the business intelligence product are not a simple tasks. A primary difficulty is the sheer complexity and volume of the organization elements, infrastructures and relationships which impact business intelligence and which must be considered. Those factors within the organization which are involved with and drive the creation, management and state of the business intelligence assets are myriad and complex.

In the analysis of product fluctuations and of product quality issues for business intelligence, we have identified the following components:

- The Organization;
- The People of the Organization
- Business Processes (external to the Business Intelligence Asset Base)
- The Business Intelligence Asset Base

We will describe and define each of these in this chapter. Metrics and assessment procedures will be discussed in the remainder of the chapters in this unit.

The Causal (X) Factors

Causal (X) Factors

These may impact the quality of the Business Intelligence Product

Organization

People

Business Processes

Business Intelligence Base

Data Integration Platform
Analytical Platform
Data
Meta Data
Business Intelligence Engine
Technical Infrastructure
nonTechnical Infrastructure
Development Methodology

THE ORGANIZATION as an impacting factor on Business Intelligence product quality

The organization has a primary and, in many ways, a very direct impact on the business intelligence product. Some of the major characteristics of the organization which are important aspects in the study of the Organization as a cause and/or impacting factor on the Business Intelligence product quality are:

- Integration of Business Intelligence
- Organization Planning and Goals
- Understanding and support for Business Intelligence
- Communications and Training
- Organization Structure
- Organization Culture

These characteristics will be used as metrics to assess the effectiveness of the organization in the success of the Business Intelligence product. Each is defined in Chapter 10. The methods for assessment and rating the organization using these metrics are discussed.

PEOPLE as an impacting factor on Business Intelligence product quality

People are an integral part of the business intelligence asset base. In considering the people of the organization as an impacting factor on the business intelligence product, we need to recognize that the individuals who use the information are also a critical component of the business intelligence product. People access the information, combine it with their special expertise and use it in the operations and management of the organization.

We will consider in later chapters how to assess the impact and relationships of the people of the organization to the success of the business intelligence product. Some of the important elements are discussed below. We identify each of these as metrics and will describe them in more detail and provide some assessment suggestions in Chapter 10.

- Number of people within the organization who use business intelligence. Level of the use, in terms of, for example, how often each accesses the business information library and reporting structures; and what is the nature of their business responsibilities.
- Awareness and involvement in the Six Sigma Business Intelligence initiative, i.e. involvement, attitudes and general behavior patterns.
- Willingness to Change. What is the attitude toward change? Inflexible? Ready for change? Aggressively pushing for better ways?
- Levels of competency. Are there a few experts who run the business based on hard won experience and who jealously guard that expertise? Everyone else depends on their knowledge base? Is the expertise more widespread, with more depth of knowledge across the organization?

BUSINESS PROCESSES as a cause of Business Intelligence product quality issues

The ultimate and most desired foundation for Business Intelligence would be an ideal business world where there is a common, integrated business language; a common set of data which is used by all business processes, whether transaction based or for business information/decision support activities. There would be no need for a secondary library of information, i.e. the data warehouse. There would be only a single source and creation point for any set of data.

Since that ideal world does not exist in most organizations, then we must appraise and rate the impact of those areas within the business process arena which affect and interface with the Business Intelligence operations and product quality. The most critical of these interface/impact points and the metrics which will be further described in later chapters are:

- Source Data Quality
- Number of data sources and level of uniformity.
- Level of feedback and closed loop use of business intelligence in operational business processes.
- Level of interface and integration for transaction processes and for business intelligence and operational processing.
- Information Quality
- Master Data Management or similar program(s)
- Development Methods, Standards, Guidelines.

- Integration of business intelligence into transaction/operational processing - feedback and closed loop processing.

THE BUSINESS INTELLIGENCE ASSET BASE as a cause of Business Intelligence product quality issues

The Business Intelligence Asset Base includes everything which is directly related to the creation and delivery of the Business Intelligence product. The parts of the Business Intelligence Asset Base are numerous and complex. These assets are spread and interwoven like a spider web throughout the organization. Perhaps the simplest way to understand the full nature of Business Intelligence is to step back and look at the whole picture. There are three levels which comprise the Business Intelligence Asset Base.

1. Level 1 – the platform architectures. These are the Data Integration Platform and the Analytical Platform.
2. Level 2 – the nonTechnical Infrastructure. This is the whole set of guidelines, standards, training and communications, governance and a myriad of other topics and constructs which provide the glue and makes for successful Business Intelligence.
3. Level 3 – the Technical Infrastructure. The hardware, toolsets, middleware, communications, data base management systems, meta data management systems and other such tangible constructs and components.

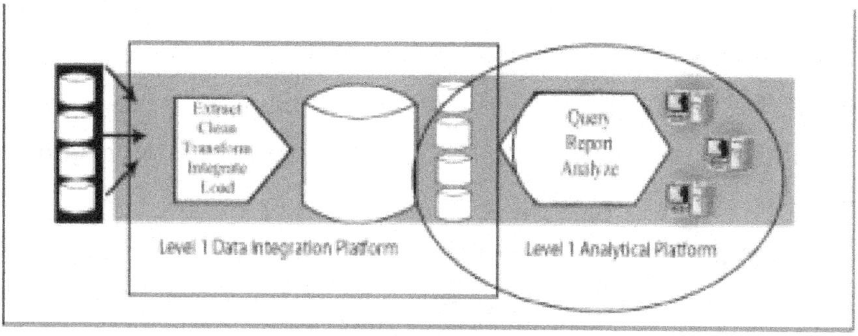

Business Intelligence Platform Architectures

In addition to these three levels of the Business Intelligence architecture foundation, there are several other components which are essential parts of the Business Intelligence Asset Base. The Business Intelligence Engine is the driving force which collects, transforms, and moves the product across the Business Intelligence platforms and infrastructures. The Business Intelligence Engine incorporates and expands upon those constructs which are usually labeled Extract, Transform, and Load. The Business Intelligence Asset Base also includes the Business Intelligence product. In assessing the quality of the product, we will assess not only all the other parts of the Business Intelligence Asset Base, but also, the components of the product. The Business Intelligence Product is considered, for audit purposes, to begin with the 'raw' data and moves through several transformations to Information and then to Business Intelligence.

The Development Methodology for creating the Business Intelligence Assets is also a key part of the Business Intelligence Asset Base. How these assets are planned, designed and developed shapes the entire nature and the contents of the Business Intelligence Asset Base. Understanding and assessing the Development Methodology is crucial to understanding and realizing the Business Intelligence potential and capacity within an organization.

The components of the Business Intelligence Asset Base are identified in the following chart. Each of these components will be briefly defined in this chapter. In later chapters, we will decompose each component and describe the metrics which will be used to assess them.

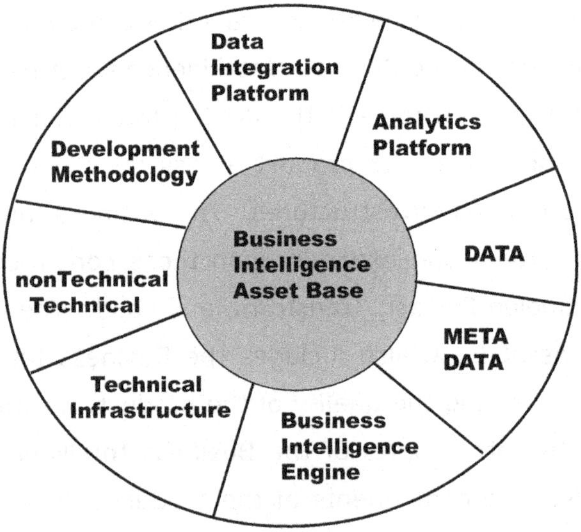

Audit Wheel
The Business Intelligence Asset Base

The Data Integration Platform

In most of today's more mature organizations, the data integration platform is, in fact, the Enterprise Data Warehouse. The Enterprise Data Warehouse provides the architecture for collection and integration of data from multiple sources, and the establishment of a library of business information which is a *single source of truth* for the organization. There are other integration methods, like federation of data, which refers to the virtual integration of multiple data sources. However, the Data Integration Platform is most often an Enterprise Data Warehouse. The primary roles of the Data Integration Platform are to collect the *raw* product, Data, and to transform and integrate it into a unified and uniform library of quality Information.

The Analytics Platform

The Analytics Platform provides the user access and interface to the Business Information. This includes all the analytical tools, delivery mechanisms, formatting, and user interface. The presentation library of the Enterprise Data Warehouse is where all the cleansed, translated, unified information is stored. The Analytics Platform provides access to this information.

The query, reporting, and analysis of the data and the interface with the end users is the province of a myriad number of vendors and toolsets. There are several primary categories for these business intelligence end products.

The tools and activities may be categorized as

- query and reporting
- on line analysis processing (OLAP) along with the different forms of the data models and processing which support variations - i.e. relational on line analysis processing (ROLAP); multidimensional on line analysis processing (MOLAP).
- data mining and statistical analysis
- forecasting and simulation

The Product

For our purposes, we will identify the end product as part of the complex of assets which is Business Intelligence. It is also a given that the business intelligence product is defined as that part of the asset base which is recognized as business intelligence by the customer. For this discussion, we define the product as the Business Information which has been integrated with human resources or automated systems in order to better understand and manage the organization. Accurate information, which is complete, timely, and easily accessible can make the difference in success or failure for any organization.

Data is the initial, i.e. *raw*, product. Data is collected from a myriad different sources and is gathered into a library within the Data Integration Platform That data is the basis for the business information and the final Business Intelligence product which can be used by the organization to understand, manage and plan for the operations of the business. A distinction is made here between business information and Business Intelligence. In much of the current industry language, the two terms are synonymous or blurred. However, there continue to be some valid reasons for remembering the difference. Business Information is the passive form. It is created and exists in isolation within the computer or whatever the communications form. Business Intelligence requires the interface with the mind of a human or a computer system which has been programmed to accept and use the business information and provides automated interface and response.

Note: Security of the product is addressed as a primary Key Assessment Feature for Data and other Business Intelligence Asset Base Components.

The nonTechnical Infrastructure

The secondary layer in this virtual Business Intelligence blueprint includes the infrastructures which support and provide the cohesion for the Data Integration Platform and the Analytics Platform. The nonTechnical Infrastructure layer is composed of all the *soft* or *intangible* glue components. This includes features and functions such as standards, guidelines, processes, initiative and governance.

These are the components which overlay and provide the cross organization framework for Business Intelligence. The non technical components of the Business Intelligence Asset Base are defined as anything necessary to the operations and success of the Business Intelligence for an organization which can NOT be included in any of the other Business Intelligence Asset Base components. As noted, this includes the standards, policies, procedures, and special initiatives and programs which are layered and integrated into the structure of the Business Intelligence Asset Base.

The Technical Infrastructure

The Technical Infrastructure includes Hardware, Middleware, Database Management Systems, Meta Data Management Systems, Networks and communications plus all the software and other tools. This Technical Infrastructure provides the architectural base and support for both the Data Integration Platform and the Analytics Platform.

Some of the important aspects of the Technical Infrastructure are:

- How well is it designed and built to match the requirements for Business Intelligence for the organization, and
- Does it meet the standards described by the Business Intelligence Key Performance Indicators.

The Business Engine

This is the construct used in our model to describe and clarify the collection, transformation, and movement of data across the various parts of the Business Intelligence Asset Base. This Business Intelligence Engine includes all of the Extract, Transform and Load (ETL) activities and expands on the functions and features. This Business Intelligence Engine also includes the access and delivery of the integrated information into the hands of the final users.

Meta Data

Meta data is Information about Data. Meta Data is a part of several components within the Business Intelligence Asset Base. The product, the infrastructures, the Business Engine - all have meta data aspects and these Business Intelligence Asset Base components include a meta data Key Assessment Feature. Meta Data is reviewed during any audit of those components. However, Meta Data is also treated as a separate and unique component. The major reason for this is to ensure that the importance and place for meta data is understood and documented. Meta Data is all the information about DATA - both technical and business. In fact, without a considerable amount of Meta Data, there can be no transformation of Data into Business Information and Business Intelligence. Therefore, the importance of Meta Data needs to be highlighted. A second reason for concern and for special treatment of Meta Data is that it is so easy to overlook it. For decades, information systems developers have considered 'documentation', which is to a great extent, what Meta Data represents, to be on the lowest rung of their priority lists. The job of documentation most often was assigned to the lowest ranking team members and then usually only as a 'wrap-up' assignment for the project. The current frequently poor state of the Meta Data within an organization is, at least partially, the result of these decades of neglect.

Meta Data may be divided into two categories:

- Business Meta Data - all the definitions and information necessary to understand the Business Language of the organization; and
- Technical Meta Data - all the information necessary to understand the underlying data structures and data movement within and across the Business Intelligence Asset Base.

Development Methodology

This is the component of the Business Intelligence Asset Base which includes all the processes, guidelines, standards and governing rules and characteristics used in creating the Business Intelligence systems and information for the organization. Following a consistent and tested set of processes and methods is important in successfully and consistently providing top value for the expenditures made by the organization. It is important that the guides and standards for development are in place and that they are followed in every case. That means that there should be some check points and governance inherent in the development process. A well designed Development Methodology is of critical importance in creating the assets and ultimately the success of Business Intelligence for an organization.

UNIT II

The Continuing Improvement Process

This section focuses on the Six Sigma Process, guidelines for measurement of the X and Y Factors and planning and implementing an action plan for improvement of business intelligence.
This includes the following:

CHAPTER 6

BI Continuing Improvement Model 6σ

Six Sigma Foundation and Process

The Six Sigma Improvement Process

The Six Sigma Way for continuing improvement of Business Intelligence is based on the following concepts. The process is:

1. Customer focused. Customer requirements and perceptions are key. Improvements depend on a clear understanding of who the customers are, their information requirements and their perceptions of what they are receiving from the business intelligence product.
2. Metrics driven. Metrics to evaluate performance must be identified and clearly defined. They should be simple to understand, i.e. intuitive, and easy to collect.
3. Proactive. Directed to the whole product and infrastructure

of Business Intelligence. In the general business arena, the six sigma methodology is directed at the design, characterization, optimization and validation of processes. At the surface level, that may also be said about improving business intelligence, which, in many ways, may be viewed as a set of general business processes of the organization. However, at the working level, the six sigma methods are directed at the whole of the business intelligence assets and impacting factors. The asset base is composed not only of processes, but also, major infrastructures and other constructs and components.

4. Based on *Project Management* principles. The Six Sigma Business Intelligence Continuing Improvement process incorporates the same project management fundamentals which are necessary to any other Information Technology program or project. Opportunities for improvement are identified and a project is structured to effect a resolution. All the tools and processes, including management and assignment of specialists and close monitoring of resources and output, are applied to the improvement opportunities.
5. Requires some basic and specialized *Tools and Technology*: The institution and management of a Six Sigma Business Intelligence initiative is complex and difficult. Managing training, multiple projects, data and people require all the tools and technologies which can be identified and integrated into the initiative. This may include at least the following areas:

   Process design, modeling, and management.

   Management of projects across multiple organization

units.

Data collection, analysis, results distribution and monitoring.

Training and communication.

Assessment and analysis of the business intelligence asset base and feedback into the overall initiatives/projects.

The Six Sigma Foundation Formula

The Six Sigma *Breakthrough* formula was defined in Chapter 2. This formula provides the basic structure around which the Continuing Improvement Process is built. Essentially, this formula means that the quality of Business Intelligence (Y) is a result of, and dependent on, all the components (X) which go into the creation, management and structures of the final result, i.e. the Business Intelligence product.

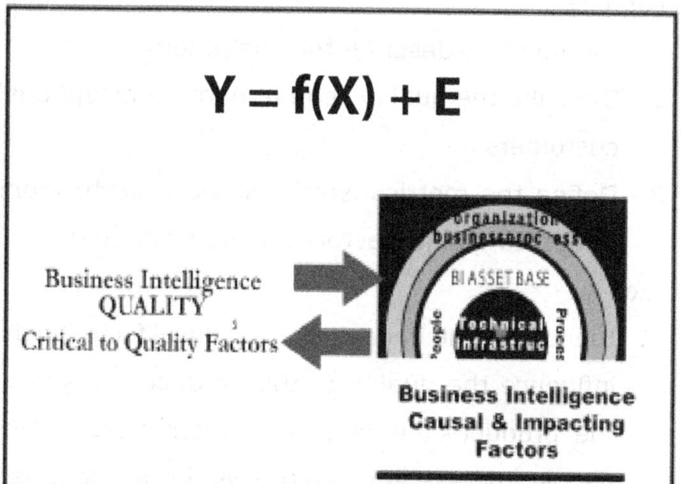

The Six Sigma Formula

Foundation for Continuing Improvement of Business Intelligence

In the remainder of the book, we will identify each of the components of the formula, as well as, identify and describe the customers who are the focus of the Six Sigma process and whose perceptions we will use to determine the quality of Business Intelligence for the organization. In addition, we will define metrics for each component and make recommendations for the collection and measurement of relevant data.

The Structured Improvement Process

The process for continuing improvement of the business intelligence product requires the following:

Clearly identify and define all components of the foundation formula.

- For Y --
  1. Identify and describe the customers
  2. Describe the quality requirements (perceptions) of the customers
  3. Define the metrics which will be used to monitor the critical to quality factors for the customers
- For X --
  1. Identify all the impacting, i.e. causal factors, which may influence the quality of the product. This includes all the product components, infrastructures, constructs, people and systems, culture and other features of the organization.
  2. Define the metrics which will be used to measure the

capability maturity of the causal and impacting factors/ components.

As noted, once the components have been identified, each must be carefully studied. Metrics must be defined which will allow the measurement of success, i.e. capability maturity, for the component. The metrics must be simple to understand and relevant data should be easy to collect and interpret.

Also critical to the Six Sigma Continuing Improvement process is the analysis and understanding of the relationships among the X Factors and between those X Factors and the Critical to Quality (Y) factors. A full understanding is necessary to creating and implementing a successful Action Response Plan which will define the activities which are needed to improve the Business Intelligence product. For example, how will we assess the risks and potential success for specific corrective actions unless we know (or can easily learn) what the effect might be on the quality of the product. In other words, exactly which of the identified business intelligence critical to quality (Y) factors will be impacted by the proposed action. How does that X component relate to the Critical to Quality Factors and the customer?

The methods and processes which will be used for such activities as measurement of the components must also be determined and carefully described.

The DMAIC Process

Six Sigma, in many organizations, simply means a measure of quality that indicates that we strive for near perfection. However, Six Sigma also is used as a short hand term for a disciplined, data-driven approach and methodology for eliminating defects (i.e. Six Sigma level of defects) in any process, from manufacturing to transactional and from product to service. The statistical representation of Six Sigma describes quantitatively how a process is performing. To achieve Six Sigma, a process must not produce more than 3.4 defects per million opportunities. A Six Sigma defect is defined as anything outside of customer quality specifications. Six Sigma opportunities are the total number of chances for a defect. The fundamental objective of the Six Sigma methodology is the implementation of a measurement-based strategy that focuses on process improvement and variation reduction through the application of Six Sigma improvement projects. There are two Six Sigma methodologies: DMAIC and DMADV. The Six Sigma DMADV process (define, measure, analyze, design, verify) is an improvement system used to develop **new** processes or products at Six Sigma quality levels. We will concentrate on the DMAIC process. The Six Sigma DMAIC process (define, measure, analyze, improve, control) is an improvement system for existing processes.

The DMAIC process is a rigorous, data based, structured and iterative set of steps which have been proven highly effective. The name is derived from the steps of the process. This DMAIC process is the guide for the methodology which is the foundation iterative process model for the Six Sigma Business Intelligence Continuing Improvement Model *(BI-CIM $_{6\sigma}$)*. That DMAIC process is described in this chapter.

Note -- Don't let the process become the focus. We need to use the process and not let the details of the process drive or become the objective.

The process name (DMAIC) is derived from the steps of the process:

Define: In this step, we define the context and set the objectives for the Six Sigma project. In effect, here is where the goals are defined and fully described. These must be specific and measurable. It has been said many times that picking the right problems and goals is the most critical step in the whole Six Sigma process. This is the step which includes full documentation of the problem and the goals of the project.

Measure: This step involves the identification of relevant metrics and using those metrics. It is critical that we fully understand the current process and that is the initial priority. We choose the metrics and get a baseline performance. At other points in the Six Sigma project, we will validate the data accuracy, and determine the capabilities of the varying components and processes and then roll through the measurement process repeatedly as we make changes, review results, make additional X level changes and adjust the process. It is important that objectives and results are documented with specifics, using numbers and as much detail as possible. For emphasis, we repeat: The metrics must be simple, easy to collect and easy to understand. The goals must be tangible and measurable.

Analyze: This is where we use the data to understand more about the process and the cause and effect relationships. Here is where we use the data to understand the Y and X factors and their relationships in the base formula: $Y = f(X) + e$. We will audit the X factors and assess them to determine their impact on product quality. The BI Continuing Improvement Model (BI-CIM $_{6\sigma}$) is based on a set of identified metrics for the critical to quality factors (Y) and the X - causal and impacting factors.

Improve: Develop the modifications that lead to a validated improvement in the process or system. Determine, validate and implement solutions to achieve the objective statement

Control: Establish plans and procedures to ensure the improvements are sustained. Implement process control methods and monitor performance to sustain results.

The Six Sigma Continuing Improvement Process

The Six Sigma Umbrella Program and Portfolio

The BI Continuing Improvement Model *(BI-CIM $_{6\sigma}$)* includes a foundation process layer, which is essentially an umbrella project for the Continuing Improvement of Business Intelligence product/assets. This foundation process includes the creation of a portfolio of Six Sigma Action Response Projects. These individual Six Sigma Projects will be launched as part of the overall program to provide corrective actions and product improvements. Each part of the program, including all the definitions, metrics, and process steps are included in the detail information in the remaining chapters of this book.

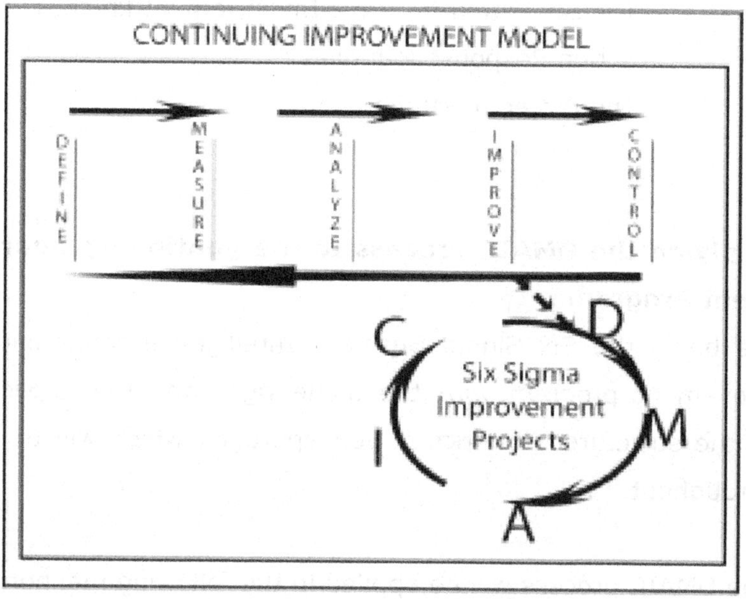

The Umbrella Program. This umbrella program is essentially the first, i.e. foundation, project of a multiple project, iterative approach to the Continuing Improvement of the Business Intelligence assets for the organization. The objectives of this foundation project include identification, definitions and descriptions of all the foundation elements and descriptions of all the preparatory work of the Six Sigma Continuing Improvement methodology. This includes the following:

The Break Through Equation
The Program Strategy
The Customers
The Product
Product Quality and the Y Critical to Quality Factors
Causal and Impacting Factors (the X Factors)
The Six Sigma Iterative Improvement Process
Action Response Planning
The Project Portfolio

Applying the DMAIC Process to the Continuing Improvement Program

We begin the Six Sigma Business Intelligence continuing improvement program with the same rigor and the application of the structured, metrics driven approach which will be used throughout.

The DMAIC process will be applied in the following manner:

1. Define

In this first 'umbrella' project, we will define

- the elements of the Six Sigma Program -- including each of the program elements defined earlier. Each of those elements and program components are discussed in detail in the remainder of the book. The customers, the product components, and the critical to quality Y factors have been identified, defined and carefully described. During the first stage of the program, you should validate these definitions and descriptions for your own organization.

- Define the Quality Objectives for the product - in terms of each of the CTQ Y factors which have been defined.
- Define the relationships between the CTQ (Y) factors and the causal and impacting (X) factors.
- Define some first level industry standard based objectives for capability and maturity levels of the X Factors. You may use the standards and rating scales presented in this book. You should make sure they are relevant and modified as necessary for your organization.

2. Measure.

Measurements will include:

- The Critical to Quality (Y) factors. Begin the monitoring program for the quality of the product. During this initial phase of the umbrella program, we will begin the monitoring (data collection and review) of the identified Critical to Quality Y factors. These are the metrics which have been identified as critical to the customer's perception of the quality of the product. CTQ factors have been identified in Chapter 4. You may wish to use these as your first iteration CTQ factors. The initial stage of the program should include a review and assessment of these factors, modified where necessary to reflect the special needs and characteristics of your organization, e.g. what is important to your customers.

- The causal and impacting factors: The measurement of the Causal and Impacting X Factors should also be a part of the stage one umbrella program. This will entail an audit of the Business Intelligence Assets and impacting factors. The Six Sigma team may elect to concentrate on a more limited audit which will focus on some elements which are known issues. Use your common sense here. Assess the value and costs of a full audit versus what you can gain from a modified, limited version. Keep in mind, also, that this audit and the CTQ Y factor monitoring process are the measurements which will provide you with the information you need for development of your portfolio of Six Sigma Projects (for improving the Business Intelligence product.)

3. Analyze

This analysis involves a study of the results of the audit of the X Factors. You should have some measurements of the maturity and capabilities of whatever X Components you chose for your initial audit. Review these results, as well as, the relationships between the X and Y components. Some of this preliminary relationship work has been included for you in Chapter 9 in this book. This was compiled using information based on industry experience. (See Chapter 9, also, to learn more about the Action Response Planning and the preliminary relationship maps.) Remember: We should expect to start with some initial understanding, then expand that knowledge base as we iterate through the Six Sigma continuing improvement process. In other words, we will use the iterative nature of the process to produce more complete answers for the organization as we grow. During this Analysis phase, we will develop an *action response plan,* with an accompanying program folder which includes

- a portfolio of the possible Six Sigma projects for improvement
- a list of corrective actions
- an assessment of each set of corrective action(s) in terms of risk, potential value vs time, costs, scope, other potential constraints. These are called, in program management jargon, the 'triple constraints' (OK, there's more than three - but that's still the term). These assessments should help in prioritizing the work involved in the corrective action program.
- a suggested prioritization of the Six Sigma projects

Keep in mind a couple more things here:

1. The definition of a project - *A project is a temporary endeavor with a beginning and an end. A project creates a unique product, service, or result. A project is 'progressively elaborated'. That means that the details for the project will be added as the project is better understood.*

2. You will end up with a set of projects, i.e. a portfolio.
3. You will need to decide which to tackle first, so pay careful attention to the 'triple constraint' assessment. You want to get the most value up front. (You can read more about this assessment in Chapter 9, which includes the Action Response Plan.)
4. The Six Sigma initiative is a cross organization program. The team will not be operating in the 'closet'. Decisions will impact a lot of people, even though some of those people may be involved only peripherally.

4. Improve

Here is where we will launch the Six Sigma Project(s) for improvement. There should be strong plans and milestones, with feedback into the umbrella program and team. Corrective actions must be tied to continued measurements of the CTQ quality factors. Follow up audits should be planned for those portions of the Business Intelligence assets and other impacting factors which are included.

5. Control

The Control phase of this process should include:

- Documentation of results from projects
- Impact analysis -- by action/activity - i.e. what happened when we made a change?
- Rework of the basic concepts on cause/effect, selected metrics, monitoring activities.

Follow up with continued quality monitoring and targeted audits of the X Business Intelligence components.

Six Sigma Project Portfolio

The business intelligence audit results are compiled and assessed. We will use these results to develop a list of actions which should be taken to modify and improve the quality of the business intelligence. The primary goal of the Action Response Plan is to identify and describe sets of responsive activities; to categorize these activities into a list of action response projects; and to prioritize those projects for action.

The audit results and the suggested responsive actions are defined and further expanded to describe what each project might include. A project portfolio is created as a result of these measurement and assessment activities. This project portfolio starts with a list of all the possible corrective actions and modifications which are identified during an audit of the business intelligence assets. Those assets are, essentially, the X Factors which cause and impact the quality of the business intelligence product.

These projects are prioritized and managed much like any information technology portfolio is managed. We define the goals; assess the risks, the time and resource requirements, and the value to be received. Of critical importance in the assessment process is a knowledge of how the X Factor and the corrective actions are correlated to the quality of the product -- i.e. which

CTQ factor will be impacted by any changes and how much of an impact can be expected. We validate the estimated costs, i.e. review and reaffirm the costs in terms of money, resources and client satisfaction. We re-estimate the potential impact of the modifications to be made on the identified critical to quality (CTQ) factors.

Six Sigma *Action Response* Projects

The six sigma projects which result from the business intelligence audits also are managed using the Six Sigma DMAIC process. For each project, the initial work of the selected project team will be to:

- Define the problem to be addressed.
- Write the objective statement.
- Recruit the project team, obtain final approvals and launch the project.

The DMAIC process for each of these Six Sigma *Action Response* projects is described below.

Define

Project Definition. The project will be defined in a skeleton fashion during the Portfolio creation process. In chapter 9, the relationships between the Y-Quality factors and the X-Causal factors are described. In the initial definition of the project, we need to make a preliminary judgment about that relationship(s). What specifically needs improvement and is there a reasonable chance that some particular set of activities will result in that improvement.

As we plan and launch the project, then we will begin to elaborate on and complete the definition of the project. Some of these steps should have been covered in the Analysis stage of the umbrella project. We will need to revisit them to provide a more complete understanding of the individual project. The steps of the definition process will include:

- Identify exactly which of the CTQ factors will be impacted (improved, we hope). Identify, define and validate the metrics to be used to measure success.
- Identify exactly which of the X Causal Factors will be modified; define them in relationship to the organization and the business intelligence assets. Identify, define and validate the metrics which will be used to measure the changes to be made.
- Review and validate the baseline performance. We should already have this baseline performance from the initial/ previous iteration of the Six Sigma Continuing Improvement process.
- Write the Project Plan - exactly what actions will we take to correct the problem, i.e. modify the X factors.
- Recruit the project team, obtain final approvals and launch the project.

Measure

- Take the actions which have been defined as part of the project plan.
- Measure the Y factors which have been identified. Keep a monitor on all CTQ factors - and recheck the expected correlations between the X and Y factors.
- It will also be necessary usually to take another audit of the X factors being modified - to determine that the modification has actually occurred.

Analyze

The data which is collected before and after the project planned actions should be reviewed and analyzed. The logging of the CTQ Y factors should be continuous. Regular checks of those CTQs which are not continuous should be made. Has the product quality, in fact, been impacted? For the better or worse? Have the X Factors actually been modified as planned? Which CTQ Y factors were impacted? Were they the ones which were identified in the preliminary plans?

Improve

The Improvement actions which have been identified for this project are taken. As we take action, we also document and carefully review the process and results. We expect to be learning more about the components, the X and Y factors, as well as, how to make the process work better.

Control

We need to keep the gains which are made as a result of each Six Sigma project. There should be a follow up and regularly scheduled re-measurement and validation of results. The changes to the causal factors especially need to be reviewed, a re-audit at least for those X components within the limited scope of the individual project. Make sure that modifications are not removed or discarded as the project team completes their mission. Periodic reviews and continued monitoring are critical.

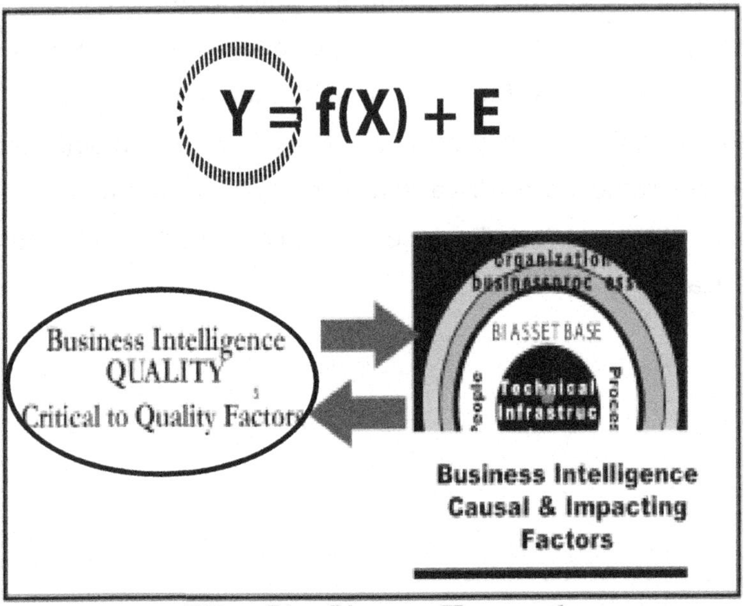

The Six Sigma Formula

Foundation for Continuing Improvement of Business Intelligence

CHAPTER 7

BI Continuing Improvement Model 6σ

Measuring Y: Critical to Quality Metrics

Measuring Y: Business Intelligence Quality

Customers and associated Critical to Quality (CTQ) Y factors for those customers have been identified in a previous chapter. In order to use the *critical to quality* factors in any monitoring and improvement process, they must be stated in tangible, measurable terms. The CTQ factors must be associated with metrics which are relevant and reflect the requirements which have been identified by the customers. In other words, we need to translate the customer requirements for quality of the product into measurements which can be used to monitor that product quality. For example, we can measure a response time, which we may describe as a number which identifies how long it takes from a query/request (e.g. key strokes into a computer or transaction entry) to a reply (screen response).

Not only must the Critical to Quality metric reflect the customer perception of quality, ***it must be simple to understand, and relevant data must be easy to collect, monitor and track.*** Selection of the response times metric would be acceptable, since we can rather easily collect the data, track and report on it with currently available operations software.

Thus, the metrics, i.e. those numerics which will be used to measure quality, for the CTQ Y factors must meet the following criteria:

1. Easy to collect,
2. Simple enough for general understanding by both the customer and the IT, Business and Six Sigma specialists;
3. Provide a clear and understandable basis for research of causal factors and monitoring of feedback/corrective actions back into the Business Intelligence Base and product.

Measuring Quality.

How do we design the metrics and collect the data? That will depend on the specific metric and the unique characteristics of the data. The data may be collected as a logging process, usually by operational software already in place. In this case, we will monitor the quality on a relatively continuous basis. In other metrics, however, it may be necessary to take periodic audits or measurements using different techniques. For example, if the metric '*meets business requirements*' is selected, then you may decide to quantify and measure some set of descriptive attributes at various stages of the implementation and utilization life cycle.

Level 1 Customer: The End User

Critical to Quality Y Measurement Factors

The metrics which have been identified for the level 1 Customer, i.e. the end user, are shown in Figure 7-A. Each of those metrics will be further defined and described here.

Figure 7-A

Critical to Quality (Y) Factors
Level 1 Customer - the End User

Performance
Reliability
Quality of Information
Meets Business Requirements
Format
Velocity
Availability & Comprehension
Support and Training

These Y Measurement Factors are attributes which identify and define as exactly as possible what product quality means for the customer. These are the factors which will be monitored in order to provide a basis for continuing improvement of the Business Intelligence product. Tolerances for the metrics will be set in such a way that the quality of the product will be monitored and any variances will trigger some review and action for improvement.

Performance

Speed and response of the system. For example, response time for queries is probably the most obvious performance factor for the customer.

Metrics: Response times - e.g. time from query entry to reply, report request to report viewing. Report 'on time' delivery.

Metrics source: These response times are most likely already being logged within operations software.

Data Collection: These metrics are logged continuously.

Data Specifications and Tolerances: Set Specifications based on customer requirements and formal agreements (Service Level Agreements) for the Business Intelligence application. Capture and set triggers and follow-up/review responsibilities and times.

Reliability

Is the product available when needed?

Metrics: Down times for system, data bases, and other impacting components; problems with software or data bases; other outages which impact customer access.

Metrics Source: Operations software will log downtimes and outages. Databases are also monitored by software within the operations arena. Be sure these are logged and reported. Assign a responsible person for monitoring and reporting of results.

Data Collection: Log all incidents and outage times.

Data Specifications and Tolerances: Specifications and tolerances should be set based on customer requirements and the current level of technology. Expectations must be set accordingly.

Quality of Information

Is the information accurate, timely and clear?

Metrics: number of reported inaccurate data/information occurrences; number of data quality issues which reach the customer. Severity of these should be noted by number and level within the organization of the people impacted.

Metrics Source: The metrics collection will depend on the level of maturity of the organization in creating quality information. At the lowest end of the maturity spectrum, there is no collection mechanism and you will have to depend on setting up a basic reporting system which will depend directly on customer response and problems. For organizations which have a formal Information Quality Initiative, there should be information quality metrics collection methods already in place.

Data Collection: All incidents of poor quality information should be collected. Consequences in terms of people/systems impacted, times and resources. Be sure to keep a running log of all the problems - even if just a manual documentation process.

Data Specifications and Tolerances: There is NO tolerance level to be set for these information quality issues. Each should be noted, researched and causes documented and included as part of an Action Response Plan (with the specific problem corrected immediately or as soon as possible.)

Meets Business Requirements

Does it satisfy the requirements which were defined initially? We should also ask: can it meet future expanded requirements with minor enhancements?

Metrics: These metrics should be based on the Business Application at a minimum of three different milestones in the development life cycle:

1. Set up check points at various stages within the development, including formal design and data base reviews; as well as, at the point of implementation and roll out. The questions and metrics here are based on how well the development and implementation system meets the requirements as agreed upon at the project initiation - i.e. pre and post design sign off. Design and development methodology for Business Intelligence applications should always follow an iterative methodology. This means, at the very minimum, that there will be a prototype during design and pilot systems during implementation stages. (For specific business intelligence applications, it is not acceptable to consider these kinds of *post-implementation* issues as a support and maintenance issue.)

2. A check point should be set for a time after the working applications and information base has been *evolved* into a form which is considered final by both the customer and IT specialists. This is also after Service Level Agreements have been established. There should also have been sign off by the specific business customers that the system meets their preliminary specifications.
3. Finally, take a check when new requirements become known which are directly and closely related to the relevant business intelligence application functions. Can these new requirements be easily satisfied?

The metrics are based on specific functional requirements. These are to be judged for the overall application functionality; as well as, at the lowest complete 'component' possible.

Metrics Source: Customer and IT specialists must document and agree on the satisfaction of the requirements and on any missing requirements.

Data Collection: Document all issues brought by either customer or IT. Note: An audit of business intelligence resources should highlight the relationship of this CTQ Y factor to the *development methodology* component.

Data Specifications and Tolerances: Specifications and tolerances should be set based on customer requirements and the current level of technology. Although Information Technology groups usually wish to have a documented set of functions and sign off by the customer, the reality of Business Intelligence application development is that it is an iterative process of design and development. The prototype and the pilot systems will be the customer decision points. Every issue must be documented, researched, with the cause clearly determined. This might be, for example, a lack of common understanding among the development team (customers and IT); or there may be some design or development flaw or just something which was overlooked.

Format

Is it intuitive and easy to use, from simple reports to power users analytics? Ease of Use. Easy to understand. Complexity level based on the current/standard user.

Metrics: This factor is measured by the satisfaction level of the customer and the alignment of the presentations and delivery formats with what is possible at current levels of industry expertise and technology, current organization constraints, as well as, the customer input. Measure this Factor using these metrics:

1. Number of customer complaints and problems with the product and presentation.
2. Satisfaction level based on survey of customers.
3. Number of points which align with current levels of industry expertise and technology. For example, there are now many instances of the use of analytical Business Intelligence, which provide guided walk through of the process for the user. This analytical type business intelligence system actually 'grows' with the customer, in terms of complexity and presentation.

Data Collection: This is not a factor which can be continuously monitored. This is a point in time related measure. Data should be collected for new products and anytime there is a change in the format of delivery of the product to the user. There should also be periodic reviews to check the current status of customer satisfaction.

D*ata Specifications and Tolerances*: Although this metric is not one which fits the standard six sigma methodology, it is still important that we include it. We will set the specifications and measure based on the rating of the customer per report/analytic product. Capture and set triggers and follow-up/review responsibilities and times as for other metrics. We may wish to correct and revise immediately. We need, also, to feed the information back into the Business Intelligence creation/management processes for improvement .

Velocity

How soon is the information available i.e. from data entry into the system to user accessibility?

Metrics: The metric for this factor is the length of time required to collect the data from sources, transform it into a unified information product and make it available for access.

Metrics source: You should find the data you need for the Velocity metrics are being collected within the data warehouse operations. There should be logging of the various activities, e.g. data sourcing, ETL operations, and database loading. There may be a need to combine these into a single 'velocity' figure. However, keep in mind that a combined figure is not sufficient. You need to know the statistics for each of the interim stages from sourcing to availability. You will need to analyze those to determine exactly where the time issues exist.

Data Collection: Operations, ETL, and database software should be able to automatically log the movement of data across the data warehouse.

Data Specifications and Tolerances: Set Specifications based on customer requirements and formal agreements (Service Level Agreements) for Business Intelligence application. Capture and set triggers and follow-up/review responsibilities and times.

Level 2 Customer: The Organization

Critical to Quality Y Factor Measurements

The organization customer is complex and has many facets. We have suggested that a team be identified to represent the interests of the Organization. The responsibilities for that team should include the oversight of those aspects, standards, concepts and constructs of the organization which must be reflected in the Business Intelligence product. This *virtual organization*

Figure 7-B

Critical to Quality (Y) Factors
Level 2 Customer - the Organization

Satisfaction - Business Objectives
Quality of Information
Velocity
Availability & Comprehension
User Understanding and Satisfaction
Cost to Benefits Received

team should include members of management, as well as, business and information technology specialists, who will represent the various aspects, goals, and expertise necessary to speak for the organization. This Virtual Organization team should take on the responsibility for identifying and describing the relevant critical to quality Y Factor metrics. The team will also review, rate, and follow-up on those metrics. This team may also be the group which acts as the leadership team for the Six Sigma initiative. However, because of time or other constraints, you may wish to limit their responsibility to recommendations and review of individual Six Sigma projects.

The Critical to Quality (Y) Factors which have been identified for the Organization Customer are noted in Figure 7B. The Metrics for each of these Critical to Quality Factors are discussed in the remainder of this chapter.

Satisfaction of Business Objectives

Do the available information and analytics satisfy the Organization strategic and tactical goals?

Metrics: The Business Objectives for the organization are not limited to the end user goals for individual business applications. The metrics should reflect an organization view of all the business applications and business intelligence. On the whole, do they meet the overriding needs of the organization - in terms of information availability and analytical functions.

Metrics Source: The information which is collected at

the application level for Business Requirements satisfaction should be reviewed for relevance to the Organization Goals.

Data Collection: The data should be collected and documented for review by the Virtual Organization team at the same check points noted for the End User customer. However, there should also be a review of the business intelligence application requirements when each specific business intelligence application is funded.

Data Specifications and Tolerances: What does the organization expect and what goals have been set for such topics as the alignment of the business intelligence with the short and long terms for the organization? The organization requirements will determine the specifications and tolerances within each business intelligence application and for the overall business intelligence asset base. Part of the tolerance issue will be driven by any divergence of goals between the organization and those perceived to be critical for the specific business intelligence application and end user group.

Quality of Information

Is the information accurate, timely, integrated, up to date and clear?

Metrics: number of reported inaccurate data/information occurrences; number of data validation issues which reach the customer. The level of severity of these should be noted by number of incidents, how many people and systems were affected, and the level of impact, i.e. severity, of each quality issue. For the organization, we should also include the response times for correction of the information, as well as, customer satisfaction with the corrections.

Metrics Source: The metrics collection will depend on the level of maturity of the organization in creating quality information. At the lowest end of the maturity spectrum, there is no collection mechanism and you will have to depend on setting up a basic reporting system which will depend directly on customer respondents. For organizations which have a formal Information Quality Initiative, there should be information quality metrics collection methods already in place.

Data Collection: All incidents of poor quality information should be collected. Consequences in terms of people/systems impacted, times and resources.

Data Specifications and Tolerances: There should be a NO tolerance policy for these information quality issues. Each incident should be noted, researched and causes documented and included as part of an Action Response Plan. At the organization level, there should be some specifications set for the number and level of severity of the reported information quality problems.

The *Virtual Organization* team should be responsible for initiating and implementing a Quality Information Initiative, if there is none. They should also oversee anything which is already in place. What this means, in practice, should be that, if there is already a team in place to handle some of the critical initiatives, like Quality Information - that team should be assigned to act as the Virtual Organization team for the Six Sigma BI initiative.

Availability and Comprehension

Is the desired information available when it is needed? Do we have all of it? In other words, we need to know exactly what is in the data warehouse, i.e. the comprehension and accessibility of 'integrated information'. Comprehension should be interpreted as how much of the data required by the organization (both current and planned) is included in the current library. There are two primary aspects: 1. What percentage of the business intelligence applications have had the information they need? 2. Does the organization have a complete information library which meets the organization goals?

Metrics: Maps and inventories of available data and information analytics capabilities should be the base for measuring this CTQ Y Factor. In addition, questions about the requested and delivered *required* information for each application should be documented.

Metrics Source: These metrics are the result of documentation of application final and other reviews, of inventories of information, and comparisons to goals for information.

Data Specifications and Tolerances: Goals need to be set based on the organization stated desires for information availability.

The Virtual Organization team needs to focus on overall results.

Each application team will know whether their information and analytic needs have been satisfied. There will be no one else to determine how the organization is doing on a longer term and more comprehensive basis.

User Understanding and Satisfaction

Are the Service Level Agreements for end users accomplishing the goals? Are users being trained? What is the Category 1 Customer Satisfaction level?

Metrics: Number and use of education products and web sites and other communications tools should be part of the metrics base. Incidents involving Service Level Agreements should also be documented along with support and maintenance logs and responses. Are there Service Level Agreements? The percentage of SLA's to the number of Business Intelligence applications should be considered as a metric worth review.

Metrics Source: Sources are logs of support and response; logs of Service Level Agreement complaints and training availability and number of participants and feedback questionnaires. These are some of the sources to look for measurement data.

Data Collection: Collect and analyze logs and information above.

Data Specifications and Tolerances: The organization team needs to set the specifications based on where you are in the growth and maturity of the organization.

Velocity

How soon is the information available, i.e. from data entry into the system to user accessibility?

Metrics: The metric for this factor is the length of time required to collect the data from sources, transform it into a unified information product and make it available for access.

Metrics source: The data collected for the end user customer should satisfy the needs for the organization team. As with the end user customer statistics, the data should be compiled and analyzed in two different ways.

1. For the individual parts, i.e. or stages, of the data collection and movement process.
2. The combined 'velocity' figure.

For the Organization Customer, we will need to compile figures for all the business intelligence applications and to take a look at the overall statistics for data movement.

Data Collection: Operations, ETL, and database software should be able to automatically log the movement of data across the data warehouse.

Data Specifications and Tolerances: The specifications for the Organization Customer should be set based on organization capabilities, constraints and goals for data availability. There should be a correlation to the needs of the end user customers and applications. Expectations need to be set and communicated for reasonable, meetable goals.

Cost to Benefits Received

Is the organization getting the best value for the resources being spent on business intelligence? This is not relevant to the end user customers. They know their specific business needs and goals. This CTQ Y metric measures just how well the resources of the organization are being expended.

Metrics: The metrics are the relatively standard financial ones -- costs of resources, time, some estimates or actual numbers for benefits received. The resulting metric is essentially a cost to benefit ratio for business intelligence.

Metrics Source: These are organization level metrics which should be collected from operational sources. Where they are not being collected, the Virtual Organization team should initiate a process for data collection, analysis and reporting.

Data Collection: There should be periodic reviews of the metrics. In particular when an audit of X Factors is scheduled, these figures should be collected and analyzed along with the other X and Y factor data.

Data Specifications and Tolerances: Specifications/tolerances should be set based on organization goals as set by the Virtual Organization team, along with the organization management.

$$Y = f(X) + E$$

The Six Sigma *Breakthrough* **Formula**

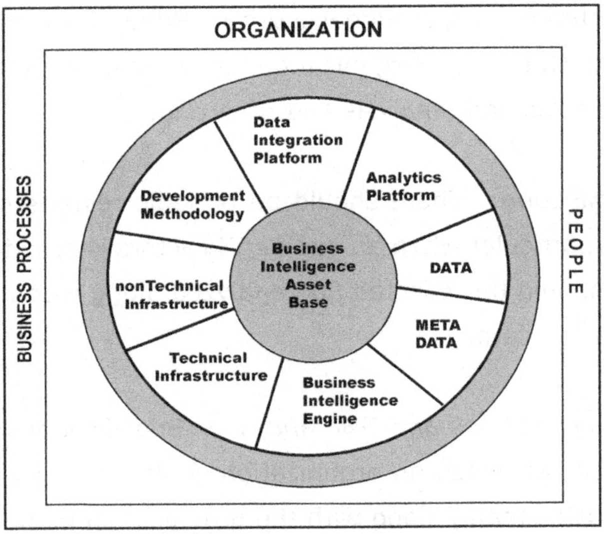

Business Intelligence
Product, Causal and Impacting Factors

Figure 8-A

CHAPTER 8

BI Continuing Improvement Model 6σ

Measuring the X Factors

Measuring X: **The Business Intelligence Audit Process**

The X factors in the foundation Six Sigma equation are those independent components which impact the quality of the business intelligence product. These X factors are identified in Figure 8-A. As might be expected, all the closely associated business intelligence assets, e.g. the technical infrastructures, may cause or influence business intelligence quality. In addition, however, almost every other part of the organization may also play a role in the quality of the business intelligence product. Each of these X factors has been identified and described in Chapter 5. In this chapter, we will describe a process for measuring them.

Critical to Quality Factor (Y) Metrics and Measurement:

The Y Critical to Quality factors have been identified and, in Chapter 7, we discussed data collection and measurement of these Y factors. The results of the monitoring of these Critical to Quality Y factors will drive the audit and resulting action response plans for the X factors. In measuring product quality, we focused on:

- ensuring that each Critical to Quality factor and metric is based on a clear understanding of the product, the customer and the customer relationship and interactions with Business Intelligence.
- data collection and measurement as a continual process. Wherever possible the data is collected as a log or stream of data. When the method of data collection is not handled as a continuing log or data stream, there are still certain audits and specific time or event points for collection of the data.
- setting of specified tolerances and triggers for action response and improvement.

Measuring the X Factors?

There are two primary questions regarding the measurement of the Causal X factors for Business Intelligence.

1. What are the X Factors?

   Exactly what is the nature and composition of these components and factors which may cause or impact the nature and quality of Business Intelligence?

2. What will we measure?

The goal is to determine just how well each X factor is performing. Are we getting the best contribution possible from each of the components? The metrics descriptions include a scale of reference to determine the performance level of each X factor.

Causal (X) Factors

These may impact the quality of the Business Intelligence Product

Organization
People
Business Processes
Business Intelligence Base

- Data Integration Platform
- Analytical Platform
- Data
- Meta Data
- Business Intelligence Engine
- Technical Infrastructure
- nonTechnical Infrastructure
- Development Methodology

Figure 8-B

The Audit Process

We will measure the effectiveness and maturity of the X factors by conducting an audit. The goals of this audit (or series of audits) are multiple:

1. To understand the nature and extent of the business intelligence assets for the organization.

A primary goal of the Business Intelligence audit is to better understand the organization components and constructs which influence the quality of the business intelligence product. Whatever the level of improvement achieved through the process, the advantages inherent in such an increased knowledge base should pay long term dividends.

2. To measure the effectiveness, capability and maturity of each of the components.
We need to be able to assess how well these components are performing. That is, we need to be able to measure the performance level and to have a way of judging changes in this performance level. These performance levels will give us an indication of the impact on the quality of the business intelligence product.

3. To understand the relationships among the X components and between each X component and the quality of the business intelligence product. This should include both the product quality as a whole and product quality in terms of each of the CTQ metrics.
The relationships between each of the X Components and the Critical to Quality (Y) factors will allow us to estimate and measure more definitively how a change in X will produce a consequent effect in Y. Just as critical, we can use the knowledge of which quality factors will be impacted by a change in specific X components to help select and prioritize the Action Improvements which will follow the audit. The Continuing Improvement Model is based on an iterative

Auditing Business Intelligence Components

1. Determine business intelligence asset base component to be audited.

2. Identify specific constructs within the organization which correlate with the BI-CIM model definitions.

3. Identify each of the Key Assessment Features as it appears within the organization.

4. Decide which of the Key Performance Indicators is relevant in measuring the relative success of the Key Assessment Feature.

5. Measure each Key Assessment Feature for the organization using the guidelines established for each KPI.

6. Measure the business intelligence asset base component, as a whole, for the organization using the guidelines established for each KPI.

7. Establish a rating for the business intelligence asset base component by combining the results from the audit of the individual Key Assessment Features and the Business Intelligence Asset Base component:
   a. Summarize and determine an average for the results for the Key Assessment Features for the component.
   b. Combine the audit ratings from the summarized average of the individual ratings for each of the Key Assessment Features *and* the rating for the business intelligence component.

process. Fine tuning our knowledge of these relationships should mean that we can more quickly provide adjustments for quality in future iterations.

4. To obtain enough information to assess and make modifications which will lead to improvements in business intelligence for the organization.

This goal is perhaps the most critical. We can learn a lot about the X Components and all that we learn will be helpful in understanding the business intelligence assets. However, we need to ensure that the goals and results of the audit are focused on providing specific information which will lead directly to a better quality business intelligence product. Thus, the questions and goals for the audit are not just 'how does this work and what is included?'. The question is 'how does this work, what is included, and how will this knowledge allow us to make a better quality business intelligence product?'

X Factor Metrics

There are several categories of metrics which will be used to measure the performance of the Causal Factors. Individual metrics which are specific to each component have been identified for the Organization, the People, and the Business Processes. These are described in Chapter 10.

The metrics which are used in the audit of the Business Intelligence assets are the Key Performance Indicators. (See Figure 8-C) These Key Performance Indicators are described in Chapter

11. The details of the metrics are defined, along with guidelines for applying them to the business intelligence X components.

The Audit Process

An audit of the business intelligence X components is planned and conducted in much the same way as an accounting audit. The audit process includes collection of relevant data about each of the X components. The data is collected through various means. This may entail study of the operations, available documentation, interviews, surveys, and whatever other means of data collection might be available plus the specific requirements for the

Figure 8-C

Key Performance Indicators

Management Support
Business Goals/Requirements
Business Alignment
Business - IT Partnership
Integration
Scalability
Adaptability
Performance
Ease of Use
Comprehension
Product Quality
Velocity
Value

audit. The results are studied and analyzed, and more data, as necessary, is collected. This data collection is accomplished under stringent rules with specific data to be collected about each component. Then, we assess the audit results to determine how well the component performs against industry and organization standards. This will require:

- a clear understanding of the component;
- careful analysis of the current state;
- guidelines for assessment of the X component; and
- a scale for rating of the X component.

The resulting performance ratings are based on the metrics and guidelines for measuring and rating of the performance and capabilities of the specific component(s) being audited.

Note: Organization, People, Business Processes. The audit, including metrics, assessment and measurement of the first level X components, i.e. the organization, people, and the business processes is discussed in Chapter 10. The remainder of this chapter refers specifically to the components of the Business Intelligence Asset Base.

Complexity. Critical points which must be understood about any audit of Business Intelligence assets is that the assessment is complex and time consuming. The assets are spread across the organization like a spider web and each of the components is multi-structured and, not necessarily, well understood. The audit must be undertaken as a well structured, iterative, 'one bite at a time' process.

Comprehension of the audit.

The audit may be full or partial, i.e. all the components may be assessed during the same audit project or they may be done as partial audits. With a partial audit, a limited subset of the X factors are chosen for assessment. You might choose a partial audit for a number of reasons. There may be resource or time constraints. You may have limited the goals of the audit to specific results. For initial iterations of the Six Sigma Continuing Improvement process, it may just make more sense to limit your risks and make some pilot efforts. This will allow the teams to grow in their understanding of the process, the components, and the necessary actions. Understanding the relationships between the Y and the X causal components will allow some discretion in applying the audit process. That is, do we know that a specific Critical to Quality Y Factor has been triggered and are we relatively sure about which X factor(s) have caused the quality issue. This could indicate that we do a partial audit for specific results. We can audit those particular components, assess the capability, and make a correction in a shorter time period with fewer resources.

Relationship Maps.

Preliminary *relationship maps* have been included in chapter 9. These maps may be treated as an initial guide and starting point for clearly identifying the cause and effect relationships among the critical to quality Y Factors and the X Factors and components. If we wish to make a change to an X component which will impact a specific CTQ Y factor, then the map will suggest the most likely area for analysis and action. These preliminary relationship maps are only a first step in understanding the X/Y relationships.

The Audit Tools and Guidelines

Audit Wheels.

Audit Wheels will be used to drive the audit process. These wheels are simply graphics which depict each of the X Components. There are two primary levels of Audit Wheels. The first level identifies all the components and constructs of the Business Intelligence Asset Base. (See Figure 8-D) Each of the components in this first level audit wheel has been identified and briefly described in Chapter 5.

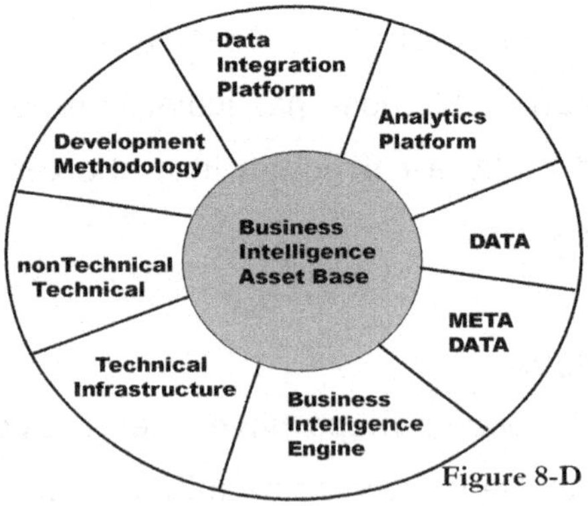

Figure 8-D

Audit Wheel
The Business Intelligence Asset Base

The second level Audit Wheel identifies each of the Key Assessment Features of a component. (See Figure 8-E).

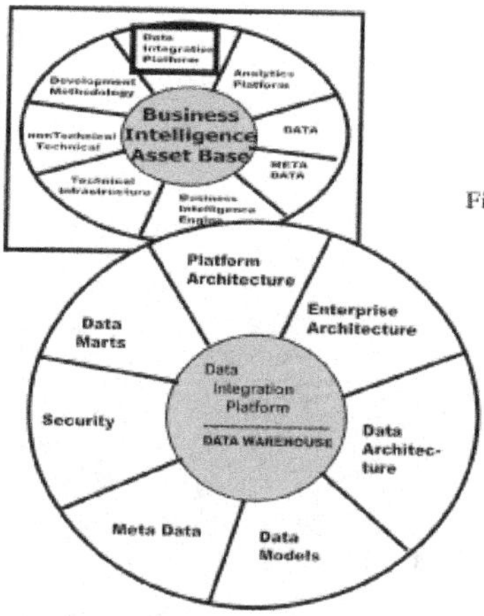

Figure 8-E

Key Assessment Features. These Key Assessment Features are the parts which comprise the identified Business Intelligence Asset Base component/construct. The data collection process for the audit begins with the study of each of these Key Assessment Features. Each of the components is covered in a separate chapter in the last section of the book. Those chapters provide more detail for the relevant audit wheels, the related Key Assessment Features, as well as, specific audit guidelines.

Audit Scorecards.

The Audit Scorecards are a simple spread sheet template which guides the metrics collection and the assessment process for the audit. Each of the Key Assessment Features should be rated using each of the Key Performance Indicators and the scores are noted in the relevant scorecard. The Key Performance Indicators are identified in Chapter 11.

In that chapter, we also provide detailed definitions and descriptions of how to use these KPI's to measure the X Factors (i.e. the components) of the Business Intelligence Asset Base.

Figure 8-F

Rate each Key Assessment Feature for each of the KPI's. Rating should be 1 to 5, with 5 as highest rating. See the appropriate chapter for audit and rating guidelines.	KEY PERFORMANCE INDICATORS: Management Support	BUSINESS ALGNMNT	PARTNER SHIP	Business Goals	Scalability	INTEGRATION	ADAPT ABILITY	PERFORMANCE	USER FRIENDLY	COMPREHENSION	QUALITY	VALUE
Platform Architecture												
Analytical Categories												
Analytical Applications												
User Expectations												
Service Level Agreements												
User Interface												
Security												
The Analytics Platform												

$$Y = f(X) + E$$

The Six Sigma *Breakthrough* **Formula**

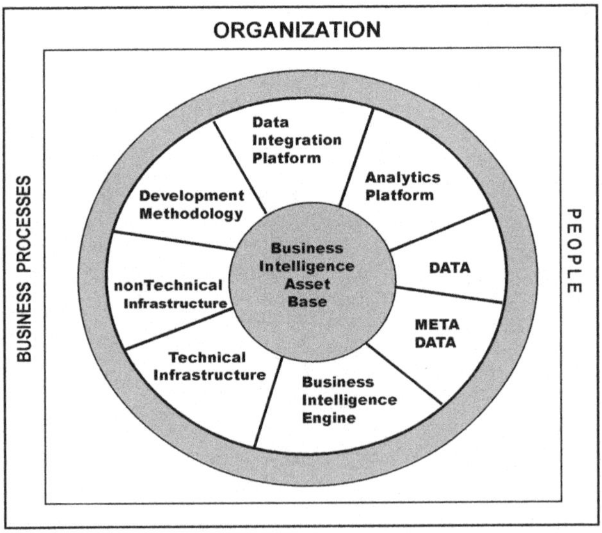

Business Intelligence
Product, Causal and Impacting Factors

CHAPTER 9

BI Continuing Improvement Model 6σ

Planning and Driving Improvement

The Action Response Plan

The results of the audit process for the X components should include an identification of strengths and weaknesses for each X Factor (component). In this chapter, we provide some guidelines for turning these audit results into an action plan for the improvement of business intelligence. We will describe the Action Plan, the X/Y relationship maps and provide a step by step process for assessing and prioritizing the improvement actions.

We have identified and described those factors which indicate quality within the Business Intelligence product (Y Factors) as well as those factors which may impact the quality of the product. We have also defined a set of metrics and processes which will allow us to monitor the quality factors and to audit the underlying causes of any quality deviations. The objectives for this chapter are to provide some guidelines for:

1. correlating the audit results with the product quality factors; and
2. using the monitoring and audit results in the most effective manner for improving the quality of the Business Intelligence product.

The Action Response Plan

In order to use the audit results most effectively, we will need to formulate a plan which includes

1. Identification of those causal (X) factors which
    - need improvement;
    - those which are effective; as well as,
    - those which are exceeding expectations.
2. Detailed Actions necessary to correct and/or improve those factors which are identified as 'needs improvement' or other factors for which auditors have recommended action.
3. Develop a list of actions recommended to take advantage of any lessons learned from those 'exceeds expectations' areas.
4. Anticipated costs, resources, and time requirements for each Action Response, i.e. potential project. set of activities.
5. Some assessment of the degree of impact of the actions.
6. Setting of priorities in the implementation of corrective

and improvement action response projects.

The Six Sigma Project Portfolio

Develop a project portfolio by grouping the improvement actions into activities and goals which are related and which can be tackled as a single project. *Reminder. A project is:*

> *a temporary endeavor with a beginning and an end. The project creates a unique product, service or result and is progressively elaborated.*

The last phrase means that we may not have full clarity or details for the project initially. What we will have are the audit results which show the assessment of the performance of the components. We will also have a set of improvement actions and goals which have been determined by the Action Response Team.

Assessing and Prioritizing the Six Sigma Project list

We have to decide exactly which set of actions and goals to tackle first. How will we do this?

You may want to consider priorities based on some initial goals, such as:

- Make the most improvement as fast as possible.
- Make that improvement visible and as dramatic as possible
- Make the best use of resources
- Provide tangible measurable quality improvement

Note - Develop goals which are most relevant and important to the organization.

What do we need to know and do?

Identify least cost, greater return projects.

Identify fastest return projects.

Determine which critical to quality factors will be impacted by the actions to be taken.

What are the risks for each project and how do we assess them.

The umbrella project team should:

Identify and describe goals.

Assess Risks for each project.

Determine resource needs, time and expected results for each project.

Prioritize the projects.

Select the project teams.

Launch the project(s).

X/Y Factor Correlations

The Improvement Planning process requires that we understand the relationships between the quality factors (Y) which are monitored for the business intelligence product and the X factors which provide the foundation for creation and management of business intelligence. Each of the X factors (Business Intelligence Asset Base components) are described in individual Chapters 11 through 19. We analyze and rate the effectiveness of each of these factors through the audit process. If there is a quality issue as indicated by the results for one or more of the Y Factors being monitored, then we need to be able to identify the specific X Factors which are the most likely causes of the identified problem. In other words, we need to be able to correlate specific quality issues with a limited number of the X factors. This will allow us to focus on making changes in those areas which are most likely to effect improvement in the area of concern.

The audit results will give us some rating of the operational effectiveness, ie, the capability maturity level, for each X factor. Thus, out of this multitude of X Factors, we define as specifically as possible what are the most probable causes of any quality issues with the Business Intelligence product. This can be a complicated and time consuming process. There are number of things to consider in making some decisions about what is causing the identified quality issues. The correlation of the Y and X factors are a start. You may have to make some preliminary trial changes to an X factor(s) and check the results,i.e. the impact to the quality metric.

By first correlating the most likely 'cause and effect' factors, we can then apply the audit results to an Action Response Plan which will focus on those areas we wish to treat as a priority.

In the remainder of this chapter, the X/Y Factor correlations are identified and described. The Y Factors, which are monitored to assess the quality of the business intelligence product, included in our set of correlations are: Performance, Reliability, Quality of Information, Meets Business Requirements, Format, Velocity, Availability, Comprehension, Support and Training. For each of these Y factors, the X Factors which are most likely to impact that specific aspect (i.e. as represented by the CTQ Y factor) of business intelligence product quality are identified. In each case, some commentary on the rationale for the correlation is described.

Using the X/Y Factor Correlations

Prioritizing the improvement actions. Use the X/Y factor correlations to assist in the planning process. Some quality issues are more critical than others and require more immediate attention. If you can isolate the basic reasons for the quality problems, then activities and resources can be concentrated on modification to those X Factors.

Use as a guideline, only. In each set of correlations described in the following section, the most likely X Factors are identified. However, this is not to say that the remainder of the X Factor categories have no impact on the Y Factor under review. In any case, study the materials as presented and then review your own organization constructs for an expanded view. You may decide that other factors are more likely to impact the Y quality factor under consideration within your organization.

The Relationship Maps: The X/Y Factor Correlations

X Factors: The Organization, People and Business Processes

The Organization, People, and Business Processes. Each of these may be reasonably correlated to any, and all, of the quality (Y) factors. In fact, because of the pervasive nature of these areas, they should be the first areas for audit and assessment. Any changes here could impact any of the CTQ Y factors. Problems in these areas (i.e. the Organization, People, and Business Processes) may mask or exacerbate any quality issues from other impacting factors. There also may be common problems which have an influence on multiple aspects of quality for the business intelligence product. Strong consideration should be given to placing a first priority on any corrective actions which seem necessary in these areas.

X Factors: The Business Intelligence Asset Base

The X/Y Factor Correlations in this section identify the relationships between the Business Intelligence Asset Base components and those Y factors which are specific to the Level 1 customer, the end user. (Note: two categories of customers have been described in earlier chapters: the end user and the organization.)

Each of the Y Factors and the relevant metrics for monitoring and accompanying alerts are discussed in chapter 7. The X Factors are discussed as part of the individual chapters included for each of the Business Intelligence Base Components.

The remainder of this chapter covers each of the Y Factors which have been identified as Critical to Quality for the End User Customer.

X/Y Factor Correlations for **Performance**

Performance is defined here as the speed and response of the system. For example, response time for queries is probably the most obvious performance factor for the customer. The Y Factor *Metrics are based on* response times, e.g. time from query entry to reply, report request to report viewing.

Those X Factors which are most likely to be of primary importance in the performance aspect of the business intelligence product are: the Data Integration Platform; the Analytics Platform; the Technical Infrastructure and the Development Methodology.

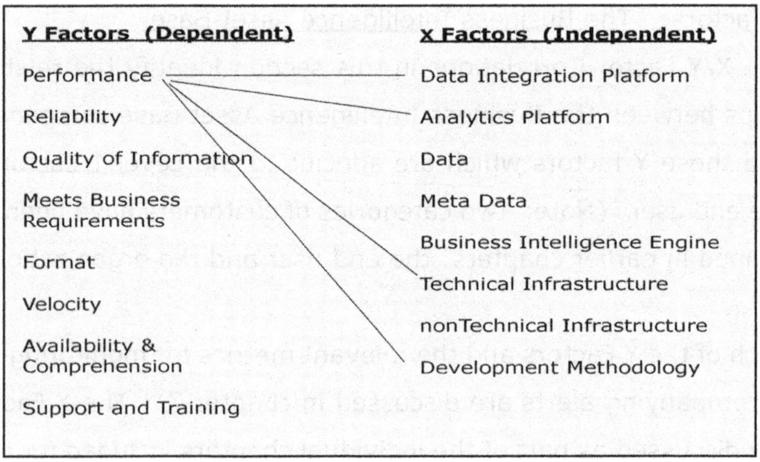

The Data Integration Platform has been identified here because architecture, enterprise and data structures are very relevant to the speed of data access. For example, how the data has been modeled and stored will directly influence performance. How many layers of data and indexing must be retrieved and read in order to access the primary required information?

The Analytics Platform - The paths and methods for query of the data are also key to the response time for information within the system. The analytics platform includes all the architecture and mechanics for the retrieval of data. For example, if queries have been written in a way which most effectively allows access to the data, then, of course, the response time will be better.

The Technical Infrastructure - This includes all the software and hardware of the information technology system. This means we consider:

- Whether we have chosen a 'state of the art' hardware base.
- What the communications and middleware routing and software includes.
- What kind of retrieval and data base software/hardware is in use.

All these are critical factors for response time, i.e. performance - for the business intelligence product.

Development Methodology - How the business intelligence application has been designed and created may have very real consequences in the performance quality of the product. Since here is where the decisions are made related to key topics like placement, retrievals, architectures, and availability, some of the continuing and most persistent quality issues may be perpetuated in the development process. Therefore, this is an area which could cause not only the current quality issues, but, unless corrected, could continue to cause the same issues across applications and time.

X/Y Factor Correlations for **Reliability**

Is the product available when needed? Is the system running and are the data and analytics software available? Some of the metrics which are used to monitor this product quality factor are:

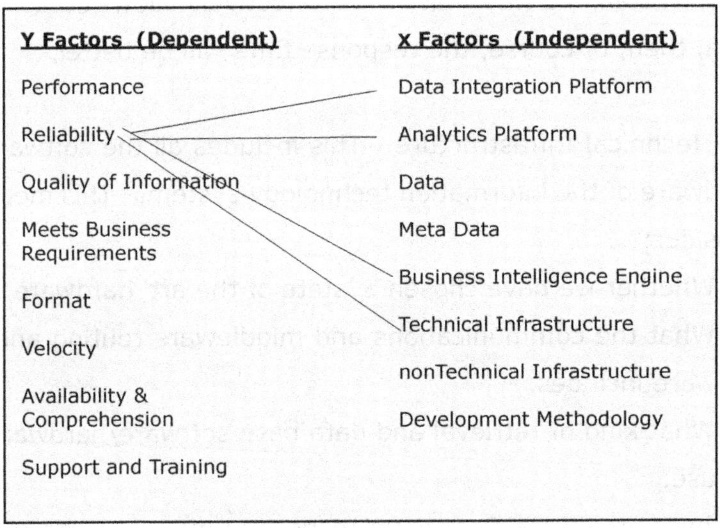

Down times for systems; problems with software or data bases; other outages which impact customer access.

The causal (X) factors which should be considered as the most likely and primary impacting agents are the Data Integration Platform, the Analytics Platform, the Technical Infrastructure and the nonTechnical Infrastructure. In this case, the most likely cause of problems is the Technical Infrastructure. The

Technical Infrastructure includes all the software and hardware of the information technology system. If the system has been working and suddenly has problems, then it is most likely that there is a problem with some part of the Technical Infrastructure. The audit results from the other areas noted should also be carefully reviewed, since there may be related problems.

(It should be noted that any single problem, i.e. a single occurrence, of the non availability of one or more of the system components, [e.g. data, analytics, other] should not be considered as an action required trigger.)

X/Y Factor Correlations for **Quality of Information**

Is the information accurate, timely and clear?

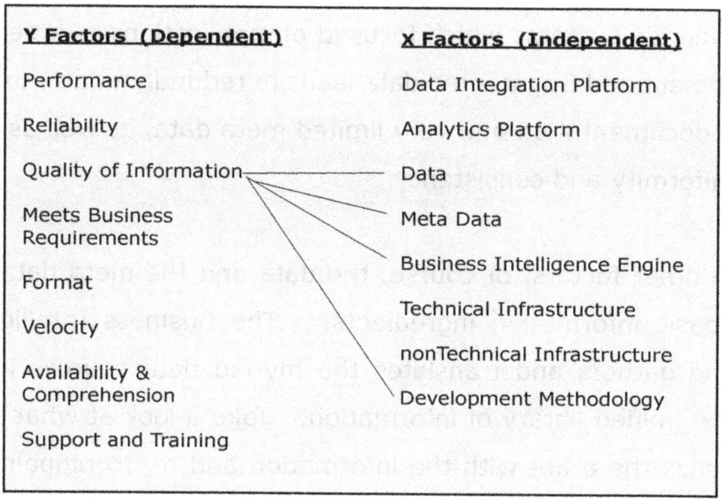

Those metrics which are usually associated with the quality of information are:

- the number and severity of reported inaccurate data/information occurrences; and

- the number and severity of data validation issues which reach the customer.

The most likely causal factors are related to the Data, the Meta Data, the Business Intelligence Engine and the nonTechnical Infrastructure.

nonTechnical Infrastructure. We have placed this X factor first in the discussion because this is the area which should include any Information Quality Initiatives or special programs like Master Data Management. Take a careful look at what the organization is doing in these areas and how much management support, communications, and training are available. If there is little emphasis on the quality of the data within the organization, then there is much more risk from data quality issues. The history of information systems which focused on applications oriented development and fragmented data leads to redundant data, usually poor documentation and very limited meta data, as well as, lack of uniformity and consistency.

As in other factors, of course, the data and the meta data, are the basic information ingredients. The Business Intelligence Engine gathers and translates the myriad data sources into a single, unified library of information. Take a look at what kinds of issues there are with the information and try to pinpoint the issues to specific problems with the data. For example, are there particular data issues like timing or accuracy? Also, for the meta data, are there uniform and up to date definitions and methods for updating? See the relevant chapters for more details on each X Factor.

X/Y Factor Correlations for **Meets Business Requirements**

Does the product satisfy the objectives and business functionality which were defined and agreed to initially; and can it meet potential expanded requirements with minor enhancements?

The X Factors which have been identified are Data, Meta Data, and the Development Methodology. The basic business intelligence product is information. A crucial factor in meeting the business requirements is to have the available data and meta data in a usable format and accessible when needed. Several of the relevant points are made in the chapters which describe these components of the Business Intelligence Asset Base. The content of the information libraries must support both the specific business application needs, as well as the organization busi-

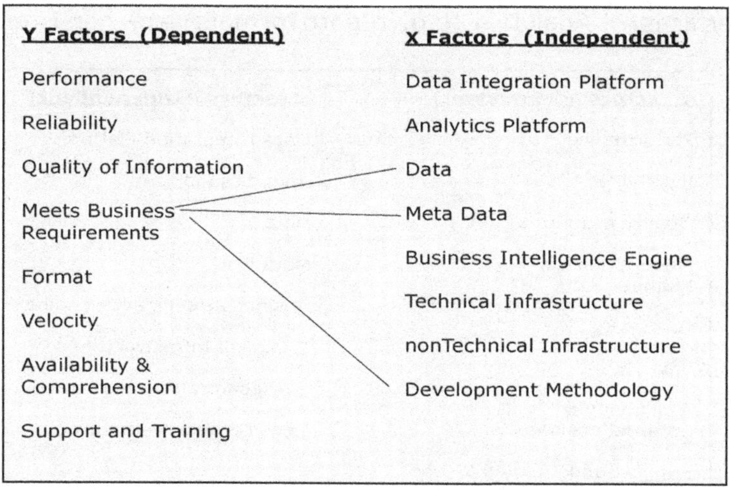

ness needs. The Development Methodology which is used to create and manage the business intelligence applications must incorporate all those actions and concepts which will ensure the information availability, its form and timeliness.

X/Y Factor Correlations for **Format**

Is the business intelligence format intuitive and easy to use? This applies to everything from simple reports to power user analytics? They should be easy to use and easy to understand. The level of complexity should be based on the user who is interfacing with the business intelligence, at the time.

For any CTQ Y factor issues here, take a look at the results of the audit results for the Development Methodology and the Analytics Platform. How the application is designed and developed is crucial to the satisfaction of the users with the final reports and interfaces. Analytics (e.g. report formats) are persistent and

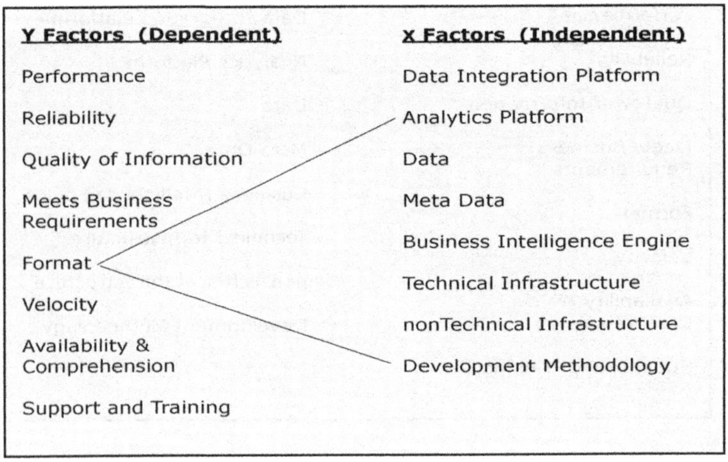

usually derive from the initial design. Correction of any problems here will impact the future quality of business intelligence across time and applications. There may be actions necessary to correct general issues, e.g. in the development process. It will most likely be necessary to implement more immediate actions to correct some of the specific problems. In other words, if there is a problem with a specific report, it may need to be corrected as a standalone activity.

In addition, the Analytics Platform provides a foundation for both delivery and interface with the user. Taking appropriate action for any issues in this area may also give some longer term positive changes needed for the user satisfaction.

X/Y Factor Correlations for **Velocity**

How soon is the information available, i.e. from data entry into the system to user accessibility?

There are four primary Business Intelligence Asset Base components (X Factors) which are most likely to have the greatest impact on the Velocity of Information movement within the system. These are: the Data Integration Platform; The Business Intelligence Engine; the Technical Infrastructure; and the Development Methodology. The results of the audit of each of these areas should be carefully reviewed for any evidence that data translation and movement issues are involved.

The Data Integration Platform provides the architectural foundation. The design and implementation of that architecture may very well impact the data movement. For example, the data may be extracted from data sources on a regularly scheduled basis or there may be an arena for streaming data which provides for

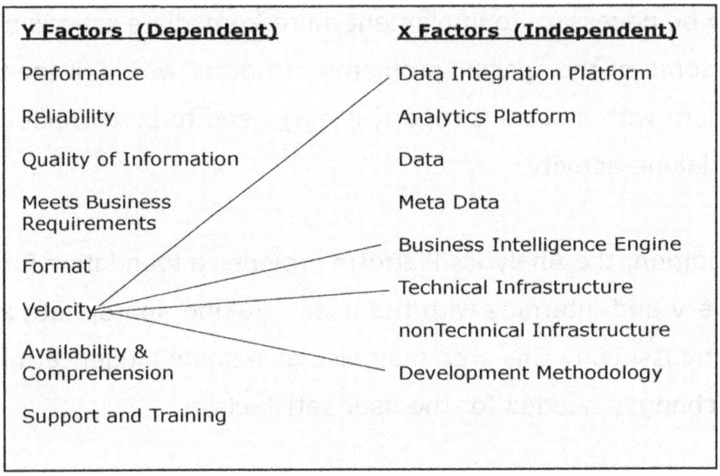

'real time or near real time' access. There may be issues which are built into the architecture. For example, if the design follows the approach which mandates a normalized data model with the associated architecture, with dimensional data marts as a spin off, then look carefully at the possibility that there are requirements for multiple passes of data through the system.

The Business Intelligence Engine includes an expansion of the functionality provided by the Extract, Load and Transform (ETL) tools. Take any actions necessary to correct any issues found with how well these tools and the design of the flows across the system work areas.

The Technical Infrastructure includes all the hardware and software which provides the foundation and operability of the whole of Business Intelligence. Review the audit results for any obvious tie-in with data movement.

Development Methodology, of course, is a major determinant of how the application system is architected and designed. Look at the audit results here for both the documented development methodology, as well as, the identity and approach of the developers and the process used for those specific applications where problems have occurred.

Factor Correlations for **Availability and Comprehension**

Availability. Is the desired information available? In other words, is the data in a data source (usually the data warehouse) which can be easily accessed and can the user find it and retrieve it.

Comprehension. Do we have all of it? Is everything which might be considered part of the set of data available and easily retrievable by the customer. For example, the user may have a need for a full range of data across time, e.g. the time of transaction occurrence or creation and update of the entries. If five years of data is needed - is 5 years available?

These two Y Quality Factors are being considered together because both are usually impacted by the same Business Intelligence Asset components (X Factors), i.e. Data, the Technical

Infrastructure, and the Development Methodology.

Specific issues to look for in the results from the audit of the Data component are width and depth of the available information. The questions are:

- Is the data limited strictly to specifics relevant to finite business applications? or

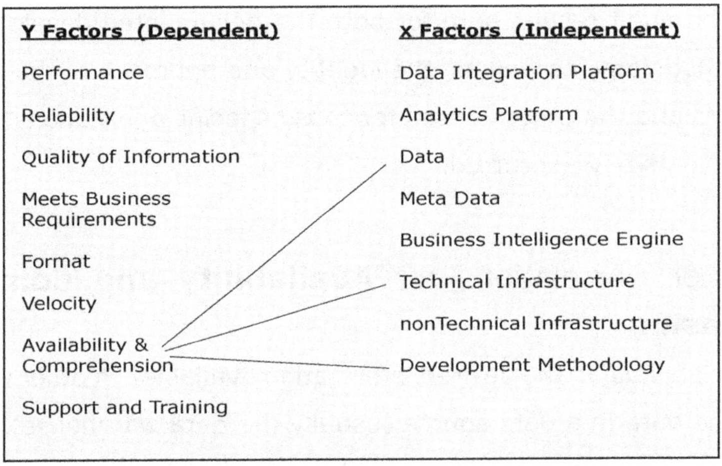

- Has there been some desire and design to expand the information library based on such factors as organization strategic and tactical plans?

Also take a look at specific application data and ensure that the data planned to be available was actually included in the library.

We do not include the Meta Data component for these Y Factors. Essentially, we are trying to ensure here that the data is available and complete. However, you may wish to include a review of the meta data, since there will obviously be a cross relationship. For example, how can we locate the information if we do not have correct or complete meta data?

Of course, the Development Methodology, or how the applications are designed and developed will impact whether the data is available and complete. Review the audit results here for relevant issues which could impact the product quality results.

X/Y Factor Correlations for **Support and Training**

Support and Training. Do the users get help when they need it? Is there easy access training, including on-line and classroom - plus books and materials.

All the communications and support programs are included as a part of the nonTechnical Infrastructure. Review the audit results for this component carefully. You may have to return to the audit process to research more carefully the programs, if there are obvious problems which are not seen in the initial audit results.

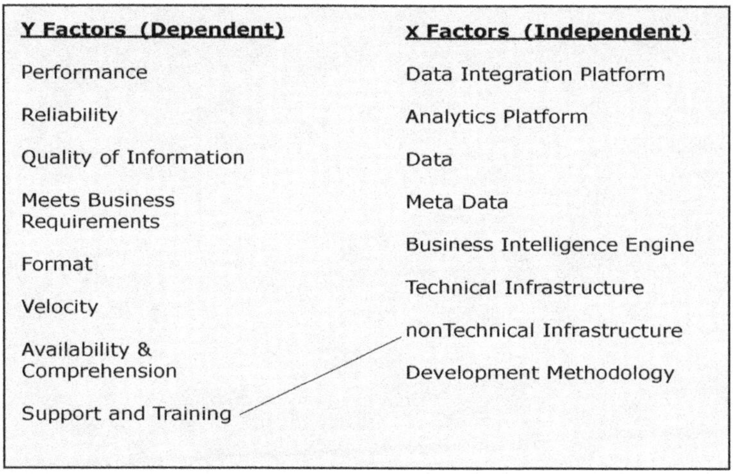

UNIT III

Defining & Measuring The X Factors

The objectives for Unit III are to define and describe all the X components, the metrics for the X components, and to provide some guidelines and ratings for application of the metrics. This includes the following Chapters:

- Chapter 10: Defines and describes the X Factors and the relevant metrics for The Organization, People and Business Processes
- Chapter 11: Defines and describes the metrics to be applied to the X Factors of the Business Intelligence Asset Base.
- Chapter 12 - 19: Defines and describes each of the Business Intelligence Asset Base components and the subsidiary Key Assessment Features.

$$Y = f(X) + E$$

The Six Sigma *Breakthrough* Formula

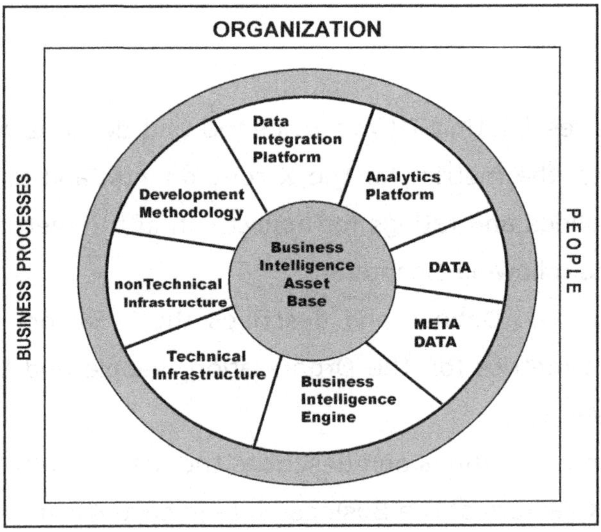

Business Intelligence
Product, Causal and Impacting Factors

CHAPTER 10

BI Continuing Improvement Model 6σ

Measuring the X Components

Organization, People, and Business Processes

We have identified those factors in the product which are considered to be critical to quality for the two identified categories of customers. We will measure and monitor these CTQ Y Factors to determine a continuing level of product quality. The next steps in the improvement process are to identify those factors within the organization which have an impact on and may, in fact, be the cause of any variance in quality of the product. In the analysis of the causes for the product fluctuations and quality issues, we have described a first level of causal factors as the Organization, the People, and the Business Processes.

In this chapter, we will further define and describe these causal (X) factors. How could the quality of the business intelligence product be influenced? We need to understand and define these X factors and determine any characteristics which may play a role.

In doing this, we will define and apply all the relevant metrics. However, we need to keep in mind, as in all other aspects of the Business Intelligence Continuing Improvement Model, the cost and return from using specific metrics. In other words, in every case, we need to assess whether it will cost more to collect the data than the value which will be received. Can we get the same results with less rigorous methods? Our premise in using the Six Sigma methodology is that the metrics and the strict adherence to a rigorous improvement process is that the return is well worth the costs involved. We need to ensure that we weigh the costs against the returns.

Previously, we have identified the Organization as a customer for the business intelligence product. In this chapter, we will be analyzing the organization in a different way. We will define organization characteristics which may influence business intelligence quality.

Identifying the metrics; collecting and measuring the data. The metrics which will be used for each of the components are identified in the sections related to that component. For most of the relevant metrics, the collection methods will include available documentation, surveys and interviews. In many cases, questionnaires for the employees are the most simple way to collect the metrics about the factors related to the organization and the people. In most cases, the data which needs to be gathered is not process oriented. We will be auditing the current state. Questionnaires may include all the areas of interest and the questions should be in the third person form.

Sample Question: Which do you think applies to the ABC organization - It is ______________ to make a change to policy or procedures ---- *1. extremely difficult 2. difficult 3. worth trying 4. fairly easy 5. systems and management are supportive of change for the better.*

For some of the other factors, such as the business plans, the Six Sigma team should just draw up a list of direct questions and ask the appropriate people within the organization.

THE ORGANIZATION **as an impacting factor on Business Intelligence product quality**

How do we determine whether there are issues in the organization, as a whole, which may be causing quality issues for the business intelligence product? In this section, we have identified those topics of interest which need to be researched and evaluated. Once an audit and evaluation of each factor is made, then we can assess the possible impact on the business intelligence product. These are the metrics which will be used to focus attention on the probable causes of product quality issues in the business intelligence product. The most critical of the metrics for the Organization are identified in the table below. In this section, each of these metrics will be described in more detail, along with a rating scale. The scale should be used to evaluate and focus the search for the causes of variation in the business intelligence product.

THE ORGANIZATION
Six Sigma X Factor Metrics
Integration of Business Intelligence
Organization Planning & Goal Focused
Understanding & Support for Business Intelligence
Communications & Training
Organization Structure
Organization Culture

Integration of Business Intelligence into the Organization

The effectiveness and success of business intelligence may be directly correlated to the extent to which the Organization incorporates the business intelligence into daily operations and management. There are a number of aspects to defining and using the associated metric. Basically, we measure the extent (i.e. level of integration) to which business intelligence is available and integrated into the normal business of the organization.

In order to use this Integration characteristic as a metric for business intelligence quality, we need to define the attributes and create a rating scale which may be used in auditing the Organization.

Defining and Using the Attributes as Metrics

The attributes are the unique descriptors which tell what we mean by the term, integration. In other words, 'How do we describe how Business Intelligence is integrated into the Organization?'

We need to be able to describe how we will judge the effectiveness of the identified attribute. That is, if the Integration of Business Information is to be rated at a Level 5 or excellent, what does that mean? Then we will use those attributes and effectiveness ratings in developing an overall rating for the organization as an impacting X Factor for Business Intelligence quality. For each attribute, we will define the levels of effectiveness. Level 1 is the lowest and Level 5 represents the most effective. (We will assess the organization against these scales. The results will be used to develop an Action Response Plan for improving business intelligence quality.) The Attributes and the Rating Scales for the Integration characteristic are shown below:

Availability of the business information. Is the Business Information library and Business Intelligence product base available to everyone in the organization? From any work station can we access and view all the available business intelligence information and access the full range of business intelligence functionality, i.e. reports, query, analytical programs, etc. Any limitations should be security related only.

Rating Scale:
Level 1. Any Business Intelligence is limited to departmental or small group availability.
Level 2. There is some Business Information available across departments or functions for limited applications.
Level 3. Most Business Information is available to most people across the organization.
Level 4. Business Information is available and is widely used.
Level 5. There are documented and mandated standards for cross organization accessibility.

Analytical Applications and On-line Help plus other support. Are there Business Intelligence products in the form of analytical applications and is on-line help generally available to walk users through business processes and functions and information gathering. The questions for the audit team here are:

- How well does the business intelligence product conform to the patterns of the business operations? and
- How well does the business intelligence product conform to the level of sophistication of the user?

Rating Scale:

Level 1. Only the creating department knows the information and how to use it.

Level 2. There are some limited on-line help facilities.

Level 3. Much of the business intelligence is easily understood and usable by those with little expertise as well as the most experienced power user.

Level 4. There are analytical applications which will walk the user through specific operations.

Level 5. Business Intelligence is used to tie the operations of the organization into a coherent whole. There are analytical applications and an integrated flow of information which can guide the user through and across business operations.

Common business language. Is a business language library of common business terms available to all? This should include, for example, common terms, alias names, abbreviations, locations, availability of data and reports. There should also be a closed loop for update of terms by anyone in the organization. This common repository should be available to people and systems across the organization. There should also be interfaces with and automatic updates from business intelligence and other systems.

Rating Scale:

Level 1. There is no common repository or accessibility to a common library of business terms.

Level 2. There are pockets of information available within functional groups and perhaps limited access to some of the tools within the data warehouse which house meta data.

Level 3. There is a common repository of terms which may be accessed by most users within the organization.

Level 4. There is a common repository which is accessible across the organization. The repository may be updated by the users. So we see an evolving business language.

Level 5. Level 4 plus the repository is tied to the systems and data stores. Updates, communication of changes and triggers for management are automated and incorporated into the workflow of the organization.

A Six Sigma Business Intelligence initiative? Is there a business intelligence improvement program. If so, how well integrated into the organization are the elements of the initiative?

Rating Scale:

Level 1. No Business Intelligence Improvement Program. Also no recognition or communication of business intelligence common goals.

Level 2. Limited standards and documented processes to increase the quality levels for Business Intelligence.

Level 3. There are documented methodologies, standards and

processes for Business Intelligence.
Level 4. Level 3 plus there is strong management support for quality Business Intelligence.
Level 5. A working program is in place to manage the quality of Business Intelligence. There is strong management support for the initiative.

The pervasive use and incorporation of Business Intelligence goals and applications.

Business Intelligence should be used to change and optimize the operations of the organization. Business Intelligence should not just be used by the current operations, as is. There are many ways that the current operations can be made better by the incorporation of business intelligence. Some of the other questions to ask here are: Are the Business Intelligence efforts limited to departmental use? Does management use Business Intelligence to drive organization goals? Is the Business Intelligence cross organizational and an integrating factor for operations?

Rating Scale:
Level 1. Business Intelligence is limited to departmental utility with no modifications to operations.
Level 2. Some cross departmental and operational level business intelligence. No integration or modification to operations.
Level 3. Business Intelligence is used effectively in cross organization operations and some integration of business intelligence to change operations for the better, e.g. customer service.
Level 4. Business Intelligence is an integrating factor in the op-

erations of the organization.

Level 5. There is a closed loop of Executive level strategic and tactical goals with management and operations of the organization. Business Intelligence is the key ingredient which management uses and stresses to get the job done. Business Intelligence is aggressively aligned with strategic, tactical and operational goals and activities.

Overall Rating – the Integration Metric

We can combine the assessments for all the attributes into a single metric for Integration for the Organization. An example of such a rating is shown here. You may choose to present the assessment and rating in whatever terms are relevant for your needs. The definitions of the levels may reflect those attribute assessments specific to your audit and assessment. The objective to keep in mind is that you will need to be able to use this metric to plan and define any actions which are necessary to improve Business Intelligence quality.

Planning and Goal Oriented - Strategic Thinking

Is the organization management a thinking, plan ahead and goal oriented working unit? Do they carefully research and plan for

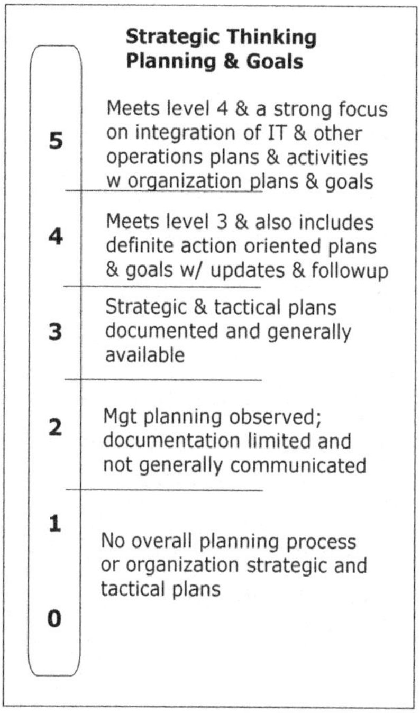

the future? How do they carry out, document and implement their long term plans and do they clearly understand and measure their success in reaching toward organization goals? Do they have short term plans (usually one year or less in duration) which have clearly defined actions with assigned roles and responsibilities and review and follow-up? Are the short term plans tied directly to the long term goals?

This strategic thinking tied to action oriented tactical plans is critical in the development and effectiveness in creating and managing business intelligence assets for the organization. For example, the business decision data which must be available to the first and second line management and operations staff should be part of a long term plan, with the development of Business Intelligence applications tied directly to the organization plans.

There are a number of tangible items to look for in rating the effectiveness of the organization in this area:

1. Documentation of the strategic and tactical plans.
2. Communication and availability of the plans and goals

- across the organization.

3. Review, follow up and update of the plans on a regular basis.
4. Clear, action oriented activities and goals.
5. Methodology for integration of the organization plans into the development and implementation of business intelligence applications. General information availability.

The audit team should look for such programs as

- a Six Sigma Initiative for improvement of Business Intelligence; and
- the creation and management of data and decision support information guided by the requirements of the planned goals of the organization.

Market Awareness

Market analysis should be part of a the basic research for the Strategic and Tactical planning process. Because each of these

Market Awareness
& Analysis
Targets of Interest

Customers
Competitors
Vendors
Raw Materials
Environment

Market Awareness

Level	
5	Meets level 4 & there is a strong focus on integration of mkt analysis & activities w/ org plans & goals.
4	Meets level 3 and also includes definite action plans which reference mkt analysis
3	Recognition of need for & defined competitive analysis. Results are shared x org.
2	Market analysis is limited & retained only at the executive level or by specific department
1	
0	No Market and Competitive Analysis

targets of interest may directly impact the quality of the business intelligence, they have been highlighted and treated separately. Market awareness and analysis involves understanding and clear descriptions of the customers of the organization; the competitors; the vendors and raw materials and, in general, the organization external environment. Assessment should be based on research, documentation and incorporation of that analysis and understanding of the market and specifics about these topics into the planning and goal setting process.

This is important to the quality of the business intelligence product because the ultimate goal of all the business intelligence is the success of the organization in the chosen marketplace. Without an understanding of all the *targets of interest*, which are included in such a market analysis, the organization is operating without a guide. The targets of interest and just a few of the analysis & research questions and topics are described below:

- Customers of the organization - Who are they? (what are the demographics - e.g. age range, socioeconomic levels, etc.) What do they view as a quality product? Where are they?
- Competitors - We need a clear definition of the market and the competition. Otherwise, management cannot properly

guide the development and use of the business intelligence product.

- Vendors - Expectations, relationships, reliability, stability.
- Raw Materials - What do we need to make the organization products and services and run the operations? What is the current and future availability? Are there substitutions, if necessary?
- Environment - what are the general external conditions in which the organization operates? Local environmental factors? Political and global impacting factors?

Management needs to clearly understand, value and incorporate a market understanding and vision.

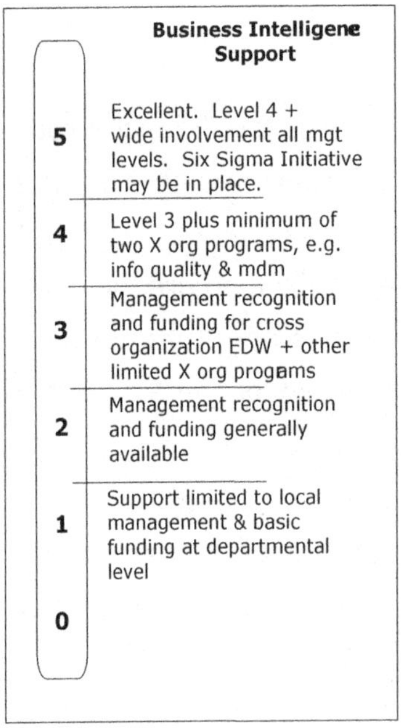

Business Intelligence Support

How well the organization recognizes and meets the needs (with funds, allocated resources, tools and acknowledgement and more) for creation and management of the business intelligence assets is critical to the final quality of the business intelligence product. Look for the following in rating Business Intelligence support within the organization:

1. Funding and other resources are available for business intelligence

assets.

2. Management at all levels understand and provide support for business intelligence - for an integrated whole across the organization, as well as, project by project.
3. Cross organization programs which further the goals of Business Intelligence. This will include, for example, a quality data/information initiative, a master data management program, and a continuing improvement program through an organization wide Six Sigma Business Intelligence initiative.

Communications and Training

Everyone in the organization should be aware of the business intelligence efforts and product. Most will have a need to access and use the business intelligence product in some form. Most will be involved in creating, supporting, and/or managing some part of the business intelligence assets. What they do and how they approach the interface and support for the creation, management and use of the business intelligence resources depends on communications and training within the organization.

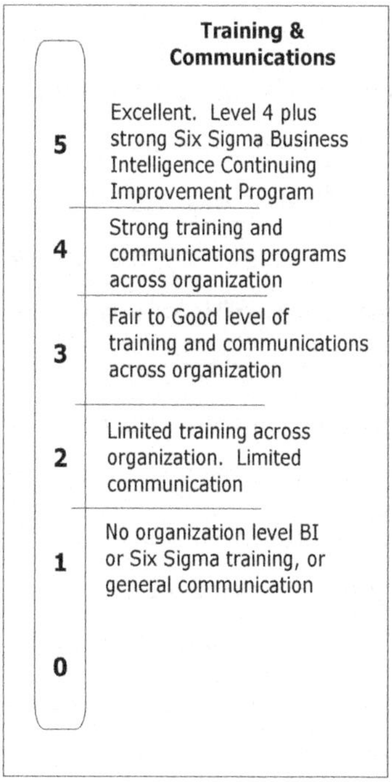

In rating the communications and training for business intelligence within the organization, assess at least the following aspects:

1. Formal and informal training programs in place. Includes classroom, on-line, and computer based training programs. How good (effective) are they? Do they cover all aspects of six sigma and business intelligence.
2. Communications. Clear line of communications from highest level of management related to support and use of business intelligence and the Six Sigma Way. Informal and formal communications channels in place throughout the organization
3. Easy to use lines and methods of communication among and across teams and the organization.

Organization Structure

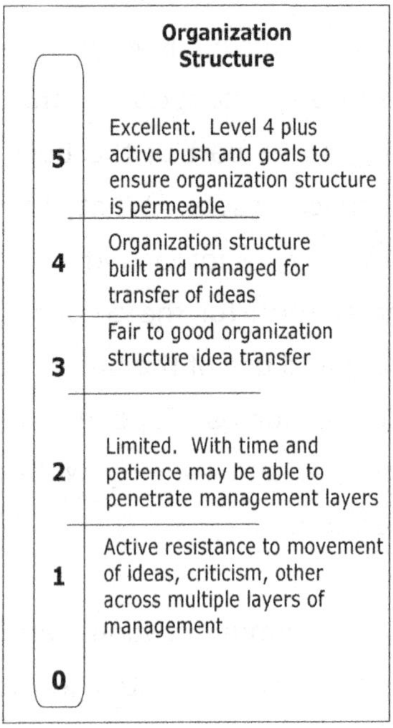

In many organizations, there may be multiple levels of a non working, non workable management structure. There may be pockets at various levels where ideas, commentary and criticism become locked in apathy and neglect. This can happen whether the number of management layers is 3, 5 or 15. It is more likely, however, as the number of middle management layers increases. An organization must be able to quickly absorb and transfer new ideas, criticisms and actions both across the organization and up and down the management structure. Look for the following in assessing the organization structure:

1. Organization hierarchy allows and encourages communication across levels of management.
2. Boundaries up and down management hierarchies provide easy to use communications lines and clear support from management for creative ideas and comments. Note the number of layers of management. The higher the number, the more likely (but not absolutely) the possibility of slow reaction and transfer times.

Culture

Every organization has a feel and ambiance which is understood by all its participants. This may not be a recognized or acknowledged aspect of the organization, but everyone could describe it. Is the organization large, cumbersome and overly burdened with bureaucrats and bureaucracy? How fast can an individual with ideas get things done? What is the dress code (stated or unstated)? What is the 'common language' - fast, easy and 'in your face' or measured, carefully planned and 'respectful'? Are the bosses called Mr or Ms or Rick and

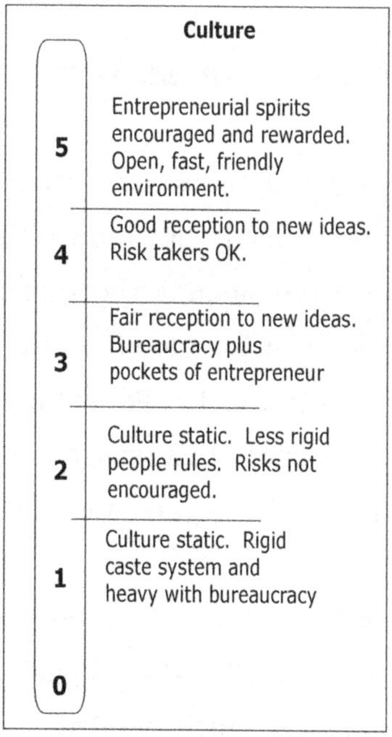

Jen? Are there flex time and child care and good benefits? All these are part of the culture of the organization? Most impact the enjoyment and passion for their jobs which the employees bring to the work place. Indirectly and, in fact, in many cases, directly, the culture of the organization impacts the quality of the business intelligence product.

Look for some of the following characteristics:
1. Entrepreneurial vs cultured rock -- change and new ideas encouraged.
2. Administration/Bureaucratic -- takes a lot of time patience, and persistence to get actions approved and actualized. Organization is bound by rules and bureaucrats.

PEOPLE as an impacting factor on Business Intelligence product quality

People are an integral part of the business intelligence asset base. In considering the people of the organization as an impacting factor on the business intelligence product, we need to recognize that the individuals who use the information are, indeed, a critical component of the business intelligence product. People access the information, combine it with their special expertise and use it in the operations and management of the organization.

We will consider, in this section, some of the other ways in which the people of the organization impact the quality of the business intelligence product. Some of the questions which need to be

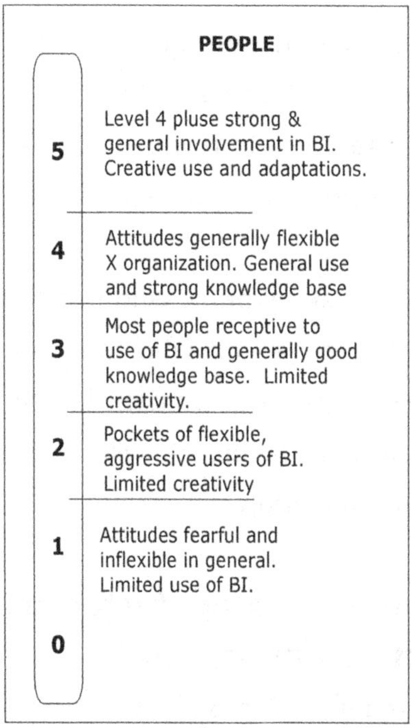

addressed are, for example:

- How broad and deep is the business intelligence use by individuals throughout the organization. In other words, how much do they use it, depend on it and incorporate the business intelligence products into their own work - of their own volition and accord? Do they go after the decision support information and make it a part of their own jobs and responsibilities. As with other metrics in this chapter, we might measure the people aspects using questionnaires. We may also use the operations/data warehousing and data base logs to determine use and number of users, how and when used.
- Six Sigma Awareness and involvement. Who knows about the six sigma, i.e. or other business intelligence improvement, initiative? Who is involved? How are they involved? Are there documented metrics which report how many people and levels of involvement in such an improvement program. If not, can we collect that data and calculate a number or percentage of the organization which is involved in any established improvement program for Business Intelligence, eg. A BI Six Sigma Initiative?

- Attitudes and General Behavior patterns. How is the business intelligence used? Is it the same small percentage of people, all the time? Are there some new ways being tested?
- Willingness to Change. What is the attitude toward change? Inflexible? Ready for change? Aggressively pushing for better ways?
- Levels of competency. Are there a few experts who run the business based on hard won experience and who jealously guard that expertise? Everyone else depends on their knowledge base? Is the expertise more widespread, with more depth of knowledge across the organization?

BUSINESS PROCESSES **as an impacting factor on Business Intelligence product quality issues**

The ultimate and most desired foundation for Business Intelligence would be an ideal business world where there is a common, integrated business language; a common set of data which is used by all business processes, whether transaction based or for business intelligence utility. There would be no need for a secondary library of information, i.e. the data warehouse. There would be only a single source and creation point for any set of data.

Since that ideal world does not exist in most organizations, then we must appraise and rate the impact of those areas within the business process arena which affect and interface with the Business Intelligence operations and product quality. The most critical of these interface/impact points are:

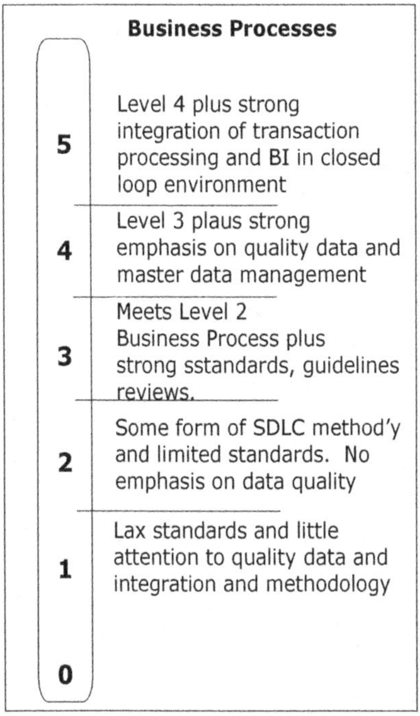

- Source Data Quality - how is the transaction data collected and validated and is it quality data? Is there sufficient and up to date documentation?
- Number of (Silos of data?) data sources and level of uniformity and integration.
- Level of feedback and closed loop use of business intelligence in operational business processes.
- Level of interface and integration, as documented in the formal or informal SDLC methodology, for transaction processes and for business intelligence and operational processing.
- Information Quality - Awareness, initiatives, level of competency
- Master Data Management - Enterprise Information Architecture and strong program for common reference data.
- Development Methods, Standards, Guidelines. How well are they documented and implemented?
- Integration of business intelligence into transaction/operational processing - feedback and closed loop processing.

$$Y = f(X) + E$$

The Six Sigma *Breakthrough* **Formula**

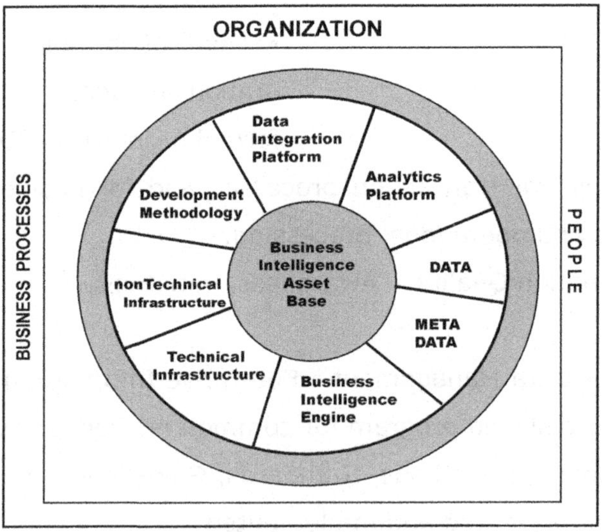

Business Intelligence
Product, Causal and Impacting Factors

Figure 11-A

CHAPTER 11

BI Continuing Improvement Model 6σ

Defining the Metrics for X Factors

Metrics *for the* Business Intelligence Asset Base

The Key Performance Indicators described in this chapter are metrics which may be used in auditing and measuring those X components which are considered part of the business intelligence asset base. (See Figure 11-A) These are the metrics which will be used for the measurement of the business intelligence technical infrastructure, i.e. the business intelligence asset base X components which are described in Chapters 12 through 19. We measure these BI Asset Base components using audit procedures which are described in chapter 8. These Key Performance Indicators (KPI's) are the metrics which are used in the audit process to assess the X factors (Business Intelligence Asset Base components). The

Key Performance Indicators are used to determine the level of maturity and success (i.e. how well does it meet the objectives) for each of the constructs measured.

Using the Key Performance Indicators

Audit and Rating. During the audit process, each of the Business Intelligence Asset Base components (and associated Key Assessment Features) will be reviewed and analyzed and a rating will be determined. Two ratings are recommended. Each of the KPI's will be used to assess each of the Key Assessment Features. The same KPI's will also be used in an overall assessment of the business intelligence asset component. The results of these two assessments will be combined to obtain a capability rating for the business intelligence asset base component.

Key Performance Indicators

Management Support
Business Goals/Requirements
Business Alignment
Business - IT Partnership
Integration
Scalability
Adaptability
Performance
Ease of Use
Comprehension
Product Quality
Velocity
Value

Note: Rating the organization - You may wish to take advantage of the results obtained from a full audit to rate the ***overall organization capability and maturity*** *in the creation and use of business intelligence. This will give you a better idea of how the organization compares to the rest of the industry. This may be useful in setting goals and general action plans for improvement. Organization ratings and how to measure and use these ratings are discussed in the book - Measuring Business Intelligence Success.*

If you plan to determine a rating for the Business Intelligence Asset Base, as a whole, then you may also use these Key Performance Indicators as a ruler for the organization assets. Component ratings and the overall rating for the Business Intelligence Asset Base may be used to rate the organization and to determine the Level of Maturity for Business Intelligence which should be assigned to the organization.

Identifying the KPI's. Some Key Performance Indicators are relatively obvious during a review of Business Intelligence assets. These are usually easy to measure. Some Key Performance Indicators, however, may not be so easily recognized. Whether obvious or not, it is critical to identify *all* the Key Performance Indicators which are relevant to the Business Intelligence Asset Base component being audited. Each needs to be clarified in relationship to the organization assets. This means that we need to understand how the component and key assessment features are manifested in the organization.

The rating should include at least the following for each Key Performance Indicator and each part of the Business Intelligence Asset Base:

> some definition of the objectives for that Key Performance Indicator for that part of the Business Intelligence Asset Base, i.e. how should that Key Performance Indicator be reflected in the part of the Business Intelligence Asset Base under review. For example, scalability is reflected in the existing hardware base as the capability to rapidly increase data access rates and performance as users and volumes increase.

Key Performance Indicators - Definitions and Standard Metrics

The metrics to be used in the assessment of the business intelligence assets are key to rating and using the results. The guidelines described here will allow the audit team to assess and measure each component and relate the organization results to industry standards. These guidelines may be enhanced or modified to meet any special requirements or circumstances encountered for the organization assets. However, any modifications should be specifically limited to special organization requirements and should be consistent across time, asset structures, and audits. This is, if you make a change in a KPI, use the modified version for all measurements, i.e. across the various components and over time.

The Key Performance Indicators, i.e. measurement factors, are identified and defined below. Each business intelligence ***Key Asset Feature*** should be evaluated using the relevant Key Performance Indicators which have been identified for that X Factor. The chapters (Chapters 12-19), which describe the business intelligence components, indicate the relevant metrics, i.e. Key Performance Indicators, for each feature and component. For each of these, some standardized metrics are described. There are details related to exactly how the KPI metrics may be applied to the business intelligence features. In addition, the levels for rating and ranking of the metric are defined.

Each of the Key Performance Indicators is described in this section. For each KPI, the standards and guidelines for measurement are identified and described.

KPI: Management Support

KPI Definition: What is the level of management support, in the form of recognition, funding and allocation of resources?

Description. Is there recognition, acceptance and communication at the appropriate level of management? Are funding and resources allocated, as necessary for the requirements of the project? Keep in mind that this may be management support for any component, feature or expanded topic which is being assessed during the Business Intelligence audit. Management may give verbal support to a data warehouse. Then that same management may refuse to fund some of the hardware or enforce the development standards.

Also, judge the level of management support which is required. For example, the creation of an enterprise data warehouse requires support at the CIO level for the IT group and a similar level of management for the Business arena. Once the data warehouse is a functioning entity with all necessary tools, procedures, and infrastructures in place, then the addition of a data mart may not require sponsorship and support at the highest levels, i.e. perhaps the director and local management would be sufficient.

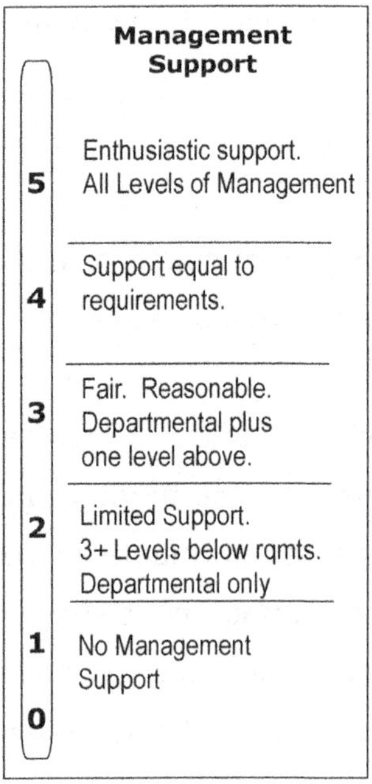

<u>Standard Metrics:</u>

We will measure

- the available level of support versus that level which is necessary to make the project successful.

<u>Rating Scale:</u>

The scale for rating the Organization Structure of Management Support is based on both the requirements for the business intelligence asset feature/component and the recognized support base.

1. There is no management support.

2. The management support is only local and the requirements are for at least three levels above the sponsoring manager.
3. Resource and funding allocations are adequate for specific projects. Management Support is at least one level above the first line management; however, there is a requirement for higher level management recognition.
4. Management Support is appropriate and meets the requirements necessary to the 'job'.
5. Management is extremely enthusiastic and all levels are involved as necessary. Resources, funding, communications and recognition are excellent.

KPI: Business Goals and Requirements

KPI Definition: Business Goals and Business Requirements are two separate constructs. However, we will use both of these KPIs as metrics to assess each of the Business Intelligence Asset Base components. The metrics will be applied in much the same manner and at the same time during the audit.

Business Goals are definitions of specific management plans and objectives which have been communicated to and are used by the organization in running the business. These should include both strategic objectives and tactical goals. Strategic objectives are long term and these identify organization direction and planning strategies, i.e. up to five years or more. Tactical goals are short term, usually a year or less, and include goals which are designed to support the satisfaction of the long term strategic plans. For example, there may be short term goals which call for an addition of three new products for a specific product line or a 10% sales increase in identified products for the central regions.

Those organizations with the *best* Business Intelligence will gain the business advantage. However, defining what is the *best* Business Intelligence is not so clear. *'Best'* depends on what the organization needs. Clear targets and understandings about the business must be defined by management and communicated throughout the organization. They should become an integral part of the strategies and tactics for the Business Intelligence and Enterprise Data Warehouse communities. Setting the goals for the organization also sets the direction and contents for the Enterprise Data Warehouse and the corresponding Analytics Platform. The measurement factor to be identified and assessed here is - *are there clearly defined Business Goals which have been documented and communicated to those responsible for creating and managing business intelligence.* (The next KPI, Alignment of those goals, will be the metric for use in assessing how well those goals have been integrated into the business intelligence component.)

The ***Business Requirements*** are defined at a different level than the business goals. These are directly tied to tactical business plans for the organization and should impact directly on the make up of individual subsets of the Business Intelligence Asset Base, i.e. the individual business application. When a Business Intelligence application is conceived and developed, there are specific requirements which must be documented and included in the resulting business intelligence. The creators and users of the Business Intelligence data need to understand each of the business requirements. Each should be clearly written in actionable phrasing - *e.g. provide the telephone customer service support representative with the name, address, & other key facts about the customer who is on the phone - in less than 3 seconds.* Each new Business Intelligence application or enhancement should incorporate definite and specific business requirements and these requirements should match or be a subset of those necessary to meet the strategic and tactical plans for the organization.

Standard Metrics:

We will measure these characteristics:

1. Documented and communicated. Have the Business Goals been documented? Have the Business Requirements been documented?

2. For the Business Requirements, we will measure the *incorporation into Business Intelligence construct* as assessed through

a. the perceptions of both the class 1/business user customer and the class 2/organization customers.

b. metrics, such as number of modifications required after initial pilot.

Rating Scale:

We will use the following scale to assess the success of each component within the Business Intelligence Asset Base for the

Business Goals and Business Requirements KPI.

Business Goals & Requirements	
5	Excellent. Well developed; Well communicated
4	Useful and Incorprated into Business Intelligence
3	Clear Documentation. Communicated and Used
2	Sketchy Documentation. Limited Communication
1	No Documentation or Communication of Goals
0	

1. There is no documentation and/or communication of Goals/Requirements.
2. The goals/requirements have been documented. The documentation may be sketchy and there is only a limited congruence of the goals/requirements documentation to the business intelligence construct.
3. The goals/requirements are clearly documented. The requirements incorporation into the business intelligence construct is at a useful level.
4. Both the documentation and the incorporation into the business intelligence construct have been accomplished and the results provide for a fair to good level of business intelligence.
5. Goals and Requirements clearly established; excellent communication and utility

KPI: Business Alignment

<u>KPI Definition:</u>

Business Intelligence plans and goals should reflect and match the business goals and plans for the organization. The organization needs the 'right' information at the 'right' time. Most organizations are now spending large amounts of their resources on creating and managing business intelligence. The returns on those resources, and the success of the organization, are dependent, in large part, on how well the goals have been defined, communicated and translated into relevant and actionable business intelligence. The previous key performance indicator is used to rate the business goals - creation, documentation and communication. The Business Alignment key performance indicator is used to measure just how well those defined goals are translated into actionable terms and incorporated into the business intelligence for the organization.

KPI Assessment and Measurement

This Key Performance Indicator should be applied to essentially every one of the X factors, i.e. business intelligence asset base component. Everything from the infrastructures to the information library should be aligned to the organization goals.

The metric should include the following:

1. Communication of Goals. The successful incorporation of goals into the business intelligence requirements and ultimately the business intelligence for the organization depends, in large part, on communication of the business goals. How will the people who are creating and managing the business intelligence know what to include?
2. Translation into actionable terms. Have the organization goals been translated into actionable terms for business in-

telligence creation and management? For example, exactly what categories and groups of data must be added to the data warehouse and when must the data be available?

3. Integration of Goals. Have the goals been integrated into the available business intelligence and business intelligence constructs?
4. Repeatable alignment process. Has a process for alignment with organization goals been incorporated into the Business Intelligence planning, design and development strategies and methodologies?
5. Management knowledge base. Does management understand exactly what can and cannot be accomplished through the creation and use of business intelligence given all the organization and industry capabilities, constraints, and available data?
6. Review process. Is there a review, feedback and correction process in place?

Note: Quality Business Intelligence does not just mean utilization within the current operations. An aggressive program for the integration of business intelligence should provide for changes in the operations as appropriate to take advantage of business intelligence in new ways for better business.

<u>Rating Scale</u>

Communication of Goals

Translation into actionable terminology

Integration into business intelligence

Repeatable alignment process

Management knowledge base

Review process

Using the above factors, assess how well organization business goals have been aligned to and incorporated into Business Intelligence.

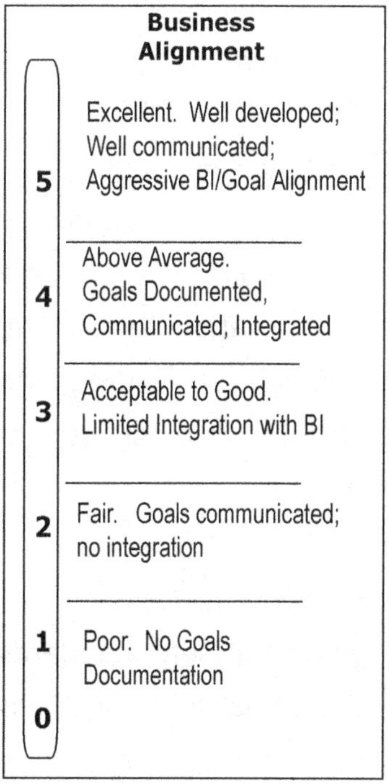

1. Poor. Goals not communicated or integrated.
2. Fair. Goals may be documented, but little communication, little integration.
3. Acceptable to good. Goals may be communicated and/or integrated at some level.
4. Above average. Well Communicated. Some Alignment and integration into BI.
5. Excellent. All factors are present and well established.

KPI: Business-IT Partnership

KPI Definition:

This KPI is used to measure the extent to which business intelligence applications are designed and developed with the involvement of both the information technology as well as the business specialists. The creation of successful business intelligence requires the participation of both groups. Historically, when one or the other has worked in isolation, the results are much less successful. If the business people try to develop their own business information, the results frequently include isolated data marts and a proliferation of desktop data bases and spread sheets, which just add to the information quality issues for the organization. The reverse path also causes problems. When the Information Technology resources have built enterprise data warehouses - without the partnership with key business people - the result most often is failure because no one comes to their party.

KPI Assessment and Measurement

1. Joint team make up - documented in development standards and methods. Documented methods and standards for business intelligence applications development which include both IT and Business specialist on every team during every part of the design and development.
2. Observed joint team efforts. Clear evidence of joint teams working together.
3. Defined roles and responsibilities.
4. Process training and support.
5. Reviews and follow-up.

Rating Scale

Assess each of the Measurement Factors and determine to what extent the business intelligence for the organization is designed and developed with the participation of both business and information technology specialists.

Factors:

Documentation of joint team membership in development process.

Definition of roles and responsibilities.

Training and support for team membership.

Joint reviews and follow-ups.

1. Limited to no partnership. Most of the BI applications are either IT or business defined and led.
2. Some BI applications with IT-BI partnership.
3. Most to all BI applications with IT-BI partnership. Participation may not be well documented.
4. IT-Business partnership is documented. Some Factors may not be present.
5. IT-Business partnership mandated and very successful.

KPI: Integration

<u>KPI Definition:</u>

This Key Performance Indicator is a measure of the level to which a construct is unified and works together as a single unit. The construct could be, for example, an infrastructure, data, application, system, or the whole of six sigma business intelligence. In assessing an X Factor using this metric, we will concentrate on the following characteristics:

- Unification of the parts; and
- A combined use of those unified parts, i.e. working together toward a single set of goals.

Data is a good example of a construct which should be integrated. We measure the level to which data is collated, translated and stored as single uniform entities. There must be a common business language across the organization. Quality of information requires that data is single source with no replication and distortion of information. Integration of the disparate data from across the organization is one of the most important considerations in rating the maturity of the organization in the creation and management of Business Intelligence.

Thus, a basic construct of Business Intelligence is the collection of source data and the cleansing, transformation and ***integration*** into a data warehouse. This data integration is key to the availability of a single source of data which is uniformly formatted, has the same values and means the same thing, or is essentially, a *single source of truth* across the organization. These data from multiple, disparate application and operational data stores are brought together and turned into high quality, business information.

The Technical and nonTechnical infrastructures are other examples of constructs which should be measured using the Integration metric. Has the Data Warehouse technical infrastructure been built to work together in all the functions necessary for data sourcing and acting as information library for the organization?

In the remaining chapters, we will discuss each of the Business Intelligence Asset Base components. Each component is described and some audit guidelines are given. For each of these components, you should carefully research the relevance and application of the Integration metric. In most cases, integration plays a part in the success of each of these components.

KPI Assessment and Measurement

The questions an auditor should resolve are:

- How is the integration accomplished;
- How well is it accomplished, i.e. are the parts unified in some manner; and
- Does the unified construct work together toward a common set of goals?

Much of the research and analysis involved in answering these questions requires some reliance on subjective and intuitive reasoning. However, that is not to say that the final decisions related to successful integration should be based on a best guess approach. Dig out the specifics. For example, data integration may be assessed based on number of artifacts across the organization like stand alone 'silos' of data which are definitely not communicating with the rest of the organization as well as the design and operability of the data warehouse ETL functions, if present. The technical infrastructure may have been pasted together over a decade and there may be little evidence of the meshing of the hardware and software parts. What does that mean in your organization? This kind of audit research is necessary and may only take finding the right technical specialists to guide you through the process.

Rating Scale:

	Integration
5	Outstanding. Parts work together to achieve goals
4	Good to Excellent
3	Fair to Good
2	Limited integration
1	Little/no Integration
0	

The scale for rating the integration within the component/construct being assessed is:

1. Construct should be integrated, but there is little or integration.
2. The integration is limited and does not provide the necessary level required for the constructs and tasks being assessed.
3. Integration is fair to good and provides a workable solution/construct.
4. Good to excellent integration. Construct works together in a successful

manner.

5. All factors are present to provide an outstanding unified construct. Goals are known and all parts work together toward that goal.

KPI: Scalability

KPI Definition:

Large scale Business Intelligence systems must support thousands of users who interactively access the same reports and data, and ever growing volumes of data and queries. Scalability refers to the ability to meet the changing requirements of the organization in terms of number of users, type and number of reports, applications, and data volumes. *Scalability* refers to the ability to support these increases in data, queries, users (i.e. all the load and access transactions) quickly, effectively, efficiently and with no downtime to the system. Choosing vendors and products which will allow for both inherent scalability, as well as, where necessary, rapid and easy to accomplish upgrades, enlargements and enhancements is difficult. Integrating all into a set of architectures and an infrastructure which will not be broken by rapid increases in users and volumes of data is especially difficult. Sometimes a lot of money, time, sweat and tears can be expended in the process. Having a scalable system takes continuous planning, monitoring, adjusting and reinvention on the part of the unsung information technology specialists - as well as the industry dreamers and suppliers of technology.

Scalability is very difficult to design into Business Intelligence platforms and components. Consideration has to be given to internal requirements which may not be well understood at the time of vendor selection. How many internal users? What kind of response times? How complex are the queries? What percentage are simple canned report viewers vs interactive drill-down reports and ad hoc users who may have increasingly complex needs. In addition, of course, requirements may change dramatically as users begin to appreciate and want more Business Intelligence. Rising use and rapidly increasing volumes can create performance nightmares and actually bring systems to a halt if the infrastructures are not carefully planned and architected.

Metrics:

1. Can the component, the product, and/or the software being assessed accommodate increased users, data, communications?
2. Speed of accommodation to increased volumes? Can the needs be met within the defined requirements?
3. Has there been clearly documented planning for changes in volumes in data, users, queries? Have all known and planned volume requirements been identified and incorporated into the component being assessed?
4. Are there monitors in place to ensure volumes are as expected? Monitors to identify potential problems and required adjustments?

Rating Scale:

Level 1. Little to no planning for volume requirements; no monitoring; component being assessed includes limitations based on current loading.

Level 2. There is some leeway in the component/parts which

Scalability

5	Level 4 + balancing of size, risks & costs + resource allocation
4	Documented plans & monitoring of system; Over 15% scalable
3	Documented plans. Current loading + 10% scalable
2	Current Loading + 5-10% scalable Minimal planning
1	No Planning, Supports current only
0	

would provide for volume increases of 5% to 10%. Time for providing the larger scale may be unknown.

Level 3. Documented plans for meeting estimated volumes - based on organization statistics. Component(s) being assessed are capable of current loading plus at least 10% adjustments. Timing requirements on adjustments adequate to fair.

Level 4. Documented plans for meeting estimated volumes - based on organization statistics. Component(s) being assessed are capable of current loading plus at least 15% adjustments. Timing requirements on adjustments good. Monitoring of components as required to anticipate and avoid volume issues.

5. Documented plans for meeting estimated volumes - based on organization statistics. Component(s) being assessed are capable of current loading plus at least 25% adjustments. Timing requirements on adjustments good. Monitoring of components as required to anticipate and avoid volume issues. Management has allocated resources on an as needed basis to ensure continued good to excellent responsiveness.

KPI: Adaptability

KPI Definition:

Adaptability refers to the capability for rapid response to the changing needs for Business Intelligence. All the BI asset components must be designed to be flexible. They must have the ability to grow and evolve along with the organization understanding and requirements for Business Intelligence, as well as, for changing technologies. This means, for example, that a data warehouse staging library should be able to accommodate new files and categories of files as technology changes. It means that, not only should we be able to quickly react to changes in volumes of users and data (i.e., scalability), all the BI asset structures should be designed for rapid changes due to new and evolving technologies and product requirements. We should be factoring in such possibilities as new acquisitions and other changing business requirements. New paradigms for creating and managing Business Intelligence are difficult to plan into a current system architecture. However, much of the standard growth and change can and should be anticipated in the design and development of the business intelligence assets. In assessing the X Factor (i.e. Business Intelligence Asset Base component) using this KPI, we need to review specifics of the infrastructures as well as how the business intelligence applications are designed and developed. Are requirements focused only on specific current requirements? Are broader business goals and forecasted requirements also included?

<u>Standard Metrics:</u>

Flexibility. What flexibility is built into the initial system? What can it accommodate in terms of new or changing requirements.

Planning. Has there been an attempt to foresee changes and/or additions to original requirements?

The organization model for Business Intelligence application development. Is it based on an iterative design and development or waterfall methodology? Are prototypes and pilots built into the development process. This can mean the difference between treating evolving requirements as part of a single development process or having to obtain new project signoffs for every change. The differences in the amount of overhead work, resources, and time can be substantial.

In assessing the flexibility and adaptability of the X Factor (component/construct) being audited, the following questions should be evaluated:

1. Can the component/construct be expanded in terms of related functionality?
2. Can new, related business requirements be accommodated easily?
3. How well are evolving business requirements handled?
4. Can the component/construct be applied to other areas of the organization which need similar functionality?
5. Data/information. Can additional requirements for data, files, classes be added easily?
6. Can we accommodate new and/or changing technologies?

7. Organization acquisitions and major changes. How much additional work is involved in adding large new sets of users and variances due to acquisitions or major organization changes?

Ratings:

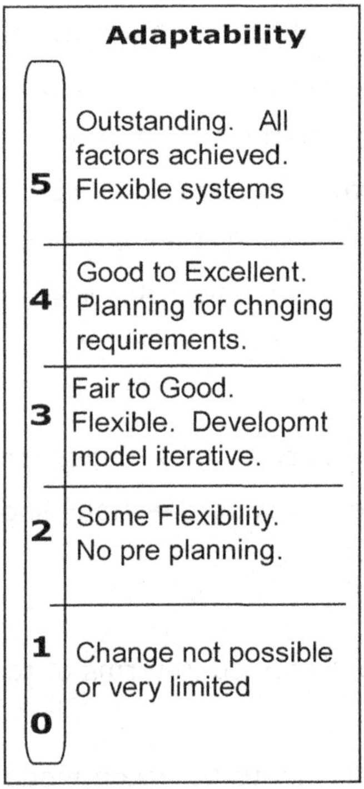

Level 1.

Flexibility: Change within the component/construct not possible or very limited. New application development would be required for anything except relatively minor expansion. Planning: No documented plans for expansion. Development model: Waterfall - not iterative.

Level 2.

Flexibility: Some flexibility but no pre planning recognized. System could be expanded with some difficulty. New development might be preferred and cost justified. Planning: No documented plans for expansion. Development Model: May be iterative or other.

Level 3.

Flexibility: Component/construct flexibility and demonstrated capability for meeting expanded or changing requirements fair to good. Some expansion capability without additional development work possible. Any substantial new related expansion would be integrated into current construct/system. Resource utilization would likely be in 40% - 70% of a new application. Planning: May or may not have documented plans for evolving requirements/changes. Development Model: Iterative.

Level 4.

Flexibility: Documented planning for specific adaptations. Flexibility and demonstrated capability for meeting expanded or evolving requirements good to excellent. Substantial expansion possibilities within current framework without major rework.

Level 5.

Flexibility: Organization models for design and development of business intelligence include recognition of the evolving nature of the components, the infrastructures, and the constructs. There is excellent flexibility and a high capability for meeting expanded or evolving requirements. There is strong management support for integration of the necessary qualities. Planning: documented planning for evolving/changing requirements. Development Model: Iterative, with organization mandates for limited administrative interference in processes.

KPI: Performance

KPI Definition:

The definition for Performance, as used here, as a metric for the X factors, does not correlate exactly to the Critical to Quality Factor, performance. The CTQ factor is used to monitor the quality of the product for the customer, and most often refers to response times. We use this KPI, Performance, as a metric to understand and rate the components of the Business Intelligence Asset Base. Performance may very well apply to a query response time. However, performance should also be applied to each of the characteristics and Key Assessment Features of the Business Intelligence Asset Base component. This may mean assessing the Technical Infrastructure and rating the ETL software based on certain performance characteristics which are specific to that software.

Performance	
5	Outstanding and consistent.
4	Good to Excellent
3	Good
2	Fair to good. Inconsistent
1	Poor to fair. Inconsistent
0	

Standard Metrics:

There should be specific characteristics defined for each Business Intelligence Asset Base component and key assessment feature. These should designed to capture the idiosyncrasies of the specific feature/component. We should identify these characteristics just as we defined *response time* as an indicator for what is important to the customer in rating performance.

Then we will use these identified performance characteristics to assess the level of capability and success for each component and key assessment feature being rated.

Ratings:

Level 1: Current performance inconsistent and may be poor to good.

Level 2: Current performance may be inconsistent; probable rating of poor to good.

Level 3: Current performance has some inconsistency but is usually good.

Level 4: Current performance is consistent; good to excellent.

Level 5. Current performance is consistent and excellent.

KPI: Ease of Use

KPI Definition:

In most cases, this KPI is used as a metric for those components which incorporate some form of interface with the user, i.e. analytics and reporting. However, we may also wish to apply this metric to other aspects of the Business Intelligence Asset Base. Wherever there are human - computer interfaces of any kind inherent in the component, then we will want to rate how efficient and how well designed is the interface. For example, we might consider the ETL software or any of the modeling tools. Each is a part of the Business Intelligence Asset Base and has a definite influence on the business intelligence for the organization. The business intelligence end user most often interfaces with the analytics and reporting characteristics of the system. It is important to rate these, as well as, all the other human - computer interfaces.

Standard Metrics:

Level and flexibility of interface. Can any level of user immediately interface and understand the objectives and use the software or information.

Intuitive presentation. How easy is it to understand what is being presented - in terms of format and navigation.

User level of comprehension. Are there levels of user capabilities? Elementary to well experienced or 'power' user. How smooth is the transition between levels of learning?

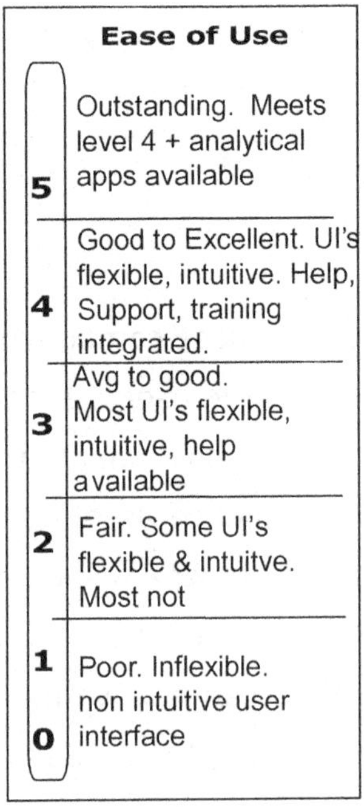

Integrated help and support. Is it easy to find and use the help facilities?

Integrated training. Are there embedded links to tutorials? Well placed?

Ratings:

Level 1. Poor. Inflexible, non intuitive user interfaces.

Level 2. Fair. Some UI's flexible and intuitive. Most not.

Level 3. Average to Good. UI's mostly

flexible and intuitive. Help and support available.

Level 4. Good to Excellent. UI's flexible and intuitive. Help, support and training integrated and easily accessible.

Level 5. Outstanding. Level 4 plus analytical, evolutionary step through applications.

KPI: Comprehension

KPI Definition:

Do we have all the parts of the component and all the functionality which is needed for success? During the audit, for every part of the Business Intelligence Asset Base, this is a key question for assessment. This can apply to a review of the analytical platform and reporting – referring to the answering of a single question, a BI application or a complex analytical process. This assessment should be made, as well, for the Data Integration Platform and that *single source of truth*, the information presentation library, as well as, information requirements for specific business information applications. Have we anticipated the data needs for the organization to meet all the business objectives for some planned period of time? We may also apply this KPI to any of the Business Intelligence Asset Base components for which the auditor may see some application requirements. The relevant question: Is everything included which should be included?

Standard Metrics:

Current needs. Do we have everything? For example, for information: Has the full range of organization data been reviewed to include and integrate all necessary data elements? If we left something out, do we know why?

Current function needs. What and where are the required functions - documented and integrated?

Goals and future needs. Do we have not only what is necessary currently, but are there, also, planned and documented goals for the future. Are we designing and developing to provide for future needs.

Ratings:

Level 1. Poor. Current needs not completely covered. Development design does not have reviews and follow up to ensure comprehension.

Level 2. Fair. Current needs usually met. Future goals and needs not included.

Level 3. Average to Good. Current needs almost always met - both information and functionality.

Level 4. Good to Excellent. Current needs almost always met - both information and functionality. Some goals for future are documented.

Level 5. Outstanding. Current and future needs and goals documented and included in the applications and systems development efforts.

Comprehension

5	Outstanding. Meets level 4 + all documented, broad comprehension
4	Good to excellent. Data sourcing & functions documented & relatively complete.
3	Avg to good. Current needs met. Data sourcing & level functionality good
2	Fair. Current needs usually met.
1	Poor. Current Needs frequently not included.
0	

KPI: Product Quality

KPI Definition:

What is product quality? The Business Intelligence product is essentially information plus the interface of that information with the human or system user. However, in using this KPI to measure each of the components of the Business Intelligence Asset Base, we will use the term 'product quality' to refer to the effectiveness and utility of any of the constructs and objects within the Business Intelligence Asset Base. For example, we may find that product quality is of critical importance for some of the software or hardware parts which make up the technical infrastructure. We should use this KPI metric to help in the assessment wherever it enables the audit process.

As for the end product for business intelligence, some of the following notes and guidelines should apply. Product quality may certainly refer to information quality. Product quality of information may be judged on characteristics such as, the inherent data, the interface, and the intellect or system which integrates the information. In a business intelligence audit, it is probably most relevant to focus on information and the information to integrator interface. How accurate is the information? Is it accepted as truth across the organization? How many replications of the same data element exist in how many separate locations across the organization? How do we keep them in synchronization? Or, do we even try? Some of the source data systems for the data warehouse may be using the same data fields in multiple ways? Do we check that out before we collect and dump it into the data warehouse final library? Is there a gold or certified copy of the data somewhere in the organization which we know can be accepted as accurate? Are there stewards for the data who are responsible for maintaining the quality of the data? Is the information accurate, timely, up to date and is it consistent across the organization? Does anyone or everyone trust it? Product quality is information quality and at the heart is data quality. Defining data quality is relatively easy. Ensuring data quality is extremely difficult.

How do we audit for product quality in a BI audit? We ask all the relevant questions which identify what quality is? and how well does the product under consideration meet those qualifications? For information or the business intelligence product, this may mean searching out a data quality initiative that may have been started three years ago and then disappeared. It will most often mean asking the users for anecdotal evidence of problems or good experiences. Problems that have occurred should be easy to find and relatively easy to track. The audit specifics depend on the organization, the business asset base component being assessed and what the research uncovers within the organization.

<u>Standard Metrics:</u>

We identify specific characteristics of the product being assessed which indicate quality. Those success characteristics depend on the Business Intelligence Asset Base construct being assessed. Just as we determine who the customers are for business intelligence and identify product quality based on their needs and perceptions, we must do that for the product under consideration. After those characteristics have been identified, then we assess the product based on the level of incorporation of those characteristics.

Standard Metrics:

What makes product quality? We will use the characteristics which have been identified based on the specific product within the Business Intelligence Asset Base. Then we use those characteristics for measurement. In the case of the product, business information, we might use the following characteristics:

- Information quality - including accuracy, timeliness, completeness.
- Information availability - including comprehension, meeting of goals of organization and end users.
- Use of technology - how well is it used to match organization constraints and goals
- Training and expertise of the people - they make up the 'other' half of the business intelligence product

These are just a few of the characteristics which we should use and attempt to quantify in assessing product quality for business intelligence.

Rating Scale (this applies to the information/business intelligence product, specifically). You would use some of the identified characteristics specific to the product under consideration:

1. Poor. Quality is poor, haphazard, at best. For business intelligence - i.e. information - no major initiatives or special efforts to get rid of silos of data and improve information quality.

2. Fair. Quality issues have been recognized as deserving of attention and some efforts have been made, especially in the ETL processing within the data warehouse. Any improvement efforts are local.

3. Average to Good. Sill some silos of data. Data Quality issues. Improvement efforts local.

4. Good to Excellent. Initiative for improvement of information is in place. Still not effective across the organization.

5. Outstanding. Business Intelligence and Information quality is recognized as an organization issue. There are initiatives in place which include integration and quality of data; training of users; master data management and Six Sigma Initiatives for improvement of the business intelligence product.

KPI: Velocity

KPI Definition:

The term, velocity, in this context describes how fast data moves from entry into the system through the interim processing and becomes information available for use. The business requirements are changing and we are moving quite rapidly, as an industry, into the realm of real time or near real time expectations for information availability. This KPI becomes more critical as the requirements and expectations within the organization evolve. There are some limited best practice assumptions that can be made for how long the data should take from point of entry into a data warehouse and through to the end user.

Another question refers to how fast we pick up the data from the source systems. Do we need to have a federated, or similar, technology to map and access directly from the operational, real time systems with a later entry into some data integration platform, such as the data warehouse? Or, can we wait until that data can be processed and integrated into a data warehouse, which may be from a few hours to overnight? The organization must decide how fast they need the data, based business requirements. The business intelligence audit must include some identification of velocity goals. A BI audit needs to assess what is happening now within the organization. Do goals exist and are they being met? The audit team also needs to be aware that vendors are offering federated systems directly to business users. These systems can then extract the data and place it into a convenient database for that specific business user. This is a new avenue for the proliferation of silos of data. One of the most useful results of a BI audit is to provide an understanding of exactly what is happening related to the data across the organization. In most cases, IT cannot stop the process. However, with recognition comes, at least, the ability to face the issues and try to resolve them.

Standard Metrics:

How do we assess velocity?

We can realistically expect to be able to measure the time the data is extracted from multiple transactional data bases to the time of availability in the data warehouse library of information. With the logging and transfer information from the operational, data base and data warehouse software, this should be relatively easy to gather the statistics.

There are two characteristics which should be assessed:

- What are the organization goals and how well do we meet those goals?
- How well is the organization using the available industry technology to increase the velocity of the business information?

Rating Scale:

1. Poor. Velocity is not a recognized statistic for data collection. Goals are either not set or not met.
2. Fair. Some level of expectations from transaction time to

Velocity

Level	Description
5	Outstanding. Level 4 plus leading edge architecture & streaming data, where needed.
4	Good to excellent. Level 3 plus well documented statistics for velocity. .
3	Avg to good. Goals set, velocity measured, some exploration of near real time
2	Fair. Goals & some level of satisfaction of goals.
1	Poor. No goals. No level of interest.
0	

time required for retrieval. Goals may or may not be met.

3. Average to good. Goals are set and velocity is measured.

4. Good to Excellent. Level 3 plus some higher level of technology being used to increase the velocity of data.

5. Outstanding. Organization has moved to an integrated, streaming data architecture, or a mixed architecture platform which meets well defined organization goals.

KPI: Value

KPI Definition:

How much did the business intelligence cost in time, money, and human resources? What are the benefits and what is the level of return? We use this KPI in the overall ranking factor for the organization. We also use this KPI, to a somewhat lesser extent, to assess each of the Business Intelligence Asset Base components. You may find, however, that researching and assessing the value of each particular component and key assessment feature may, in fact, help in assessing whether the right tools, processes, standards, etc. are being used. You should judge whether assessing the component using this KPI will add anything to your assessment results for each of the X factors.

This is probably the most difficult of our audit measurements. A reasonable figure can usually be calculated for costs for the overall organization using total resources expended and other costs. Estimates of Value returned are always more difficult and less easily accepted. On another level, we expect (or hope) that any IT project which makes changes or adds to the BI Assets will include some value (cost/benefit) estimates. These are measurements which can be important to management in prioritizing and planning Business Intelligence efforts for the organization. The crucial requirements here for a BI audit include the following:

1. Obtain and get some management agreement for benefits to cost estimates for the organization. This will assist in the ranking of the BI capabilities of the organization.
2. Identify and assess any practices being used for BI projects.
3. Determine how the organization is using the application and infrastructure enhancement project estimates.

<u>Standard Metrics:</u>
How do we assess value?

- Identify and agree on benefits and assign some dollar estimates.
- Costs. For example, there should be accounting figures, as well as numbers like resource utilization which will be available.

This Key Performance Indicator is really the culmination of the efforts to assign cost and benefit numbers to business intelligence. Since so much of the value is in intangibles, the usual caveats apply. There are whole libraries which cover this subject. If you need to make this assessment, then you will most likely need to explore the other references and expand your efforts, depending on who the sponsors are of the effort.

	Value
5	Outstanding. General recognition of excellent BI values.
4	Good to excellent. Perceptions and figures show good value received.
3	Avg to good. Estimates and cost to benefit reasonable.
2	Fair. Barely worth the costs incurred or no estimates.
1	Poor. Low value estimated for return on BI
0	

Rating Scale:

1. Poor. Return is not considered worth the expenditures.
2. Fair. Some value to the business intelligence product.
3. Average to good.
4. Good to Excellent. Perception and cost:benefit figures show high rate of return.
5. Good to Excellent. General appreciation and high value.

$$Y = f(X) + E$$

The Six Sigma *Breakthrough* **Formula**

Figure 12-A

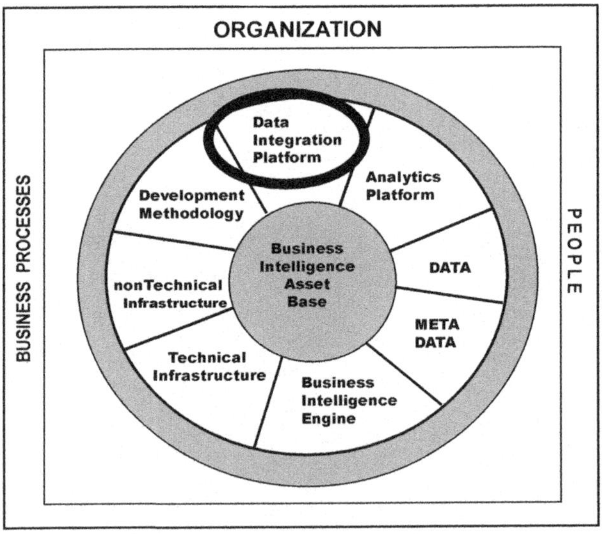

Business Intelligence
Product, Causal and Impacting Factors

CHAPTER 12

BI Continuing Improvement Model 60

Defining the Causal (X) Factors

Business Intelligence Asset Base:

Data Integration Platform

This chapter describes the Data Integration Platform and the key factors which may cause or impact the quality of the Business Intelligence product.

Chapter Contents and goals:

- Describe the Data Integration Platform,
- Identify and describe the Key Assessment Features for the Data Integration Platform; i.e. decompose and describe each of the subsidiary elements of the Data Integration Platform;
- Provide guidelines for auditing the Data Integration Platform;
- Discuss the relationship between the Data Integration Platform, its sub components (i.e. the Key Assessment Features)

and the quality of the Business Intelligence product.

- identify the relevant metrics for each of the subsidiary components.

Note: *The information provided here should help in assessing this X component. However, the audit team should include business and information technical specialists who have a clear understanding of the organization and accepted business practices. The team should also include a Six Sigma knowledgeable resource.*

The goal is not to make the reader a Business Intelligence expert. The goal is to Identify and introduce the X Factors which are the components which comprise the Business Intelligence Asset Base. The intent, also, is to provide some helpful information and guidelines for those who are not experts.

The primary objectives for this chapter are:

- *to identify the specific relevant constructs and features and assist in the process of analyzing those X factors which cause or impact the quality of the Business Intelligence product; and*
- *to enable and guide the use of those X factors and metrics in a process for improvement of the Business Intelligence product.*

The Organization, the People and the Business Processes of the organization are of critical importance to the quality of the business intelligence product. Those are described in Chapter 11. However, it is the Business Intelligence Asset Base which includes all the constructs and components which are directly related to the creation and management of the business intelligence product(s). Defining and clearly describing all the X Factors provides the foundation for determining the causes for product quality - i.e. excellence, variations, limitations and problems. There is no way to study and analyze the business intelligence assets if they cannot be defined.

Key Performance Indicators

Management Support
Business Goals/Requirements
Business Alignment
Business - IT Partnership
Integration
Scalability
Adaptability
Performance
Ease of Use
Comprehension
Product Quality
Velocity
Value

Figure 12-C

These Key Performance Indicators are the metrics which will be used in assessing and rating how well the organization is succeeding in creation and management the specific components and key assessment features of the Business Intelligence Asset Base. Each of the Key Performance Indicators are described in Chapter 11. That chapter also includes a discussion of the assessment and rating scales for each.

Key Assessment Features. Each of the primary factors, i.e. components, of the Business Intelligence Base may be further subdivided. These secondary level factors are identified as Key Assessment Features and the audit process will focus on them. This is the level which will give us the most information about how well each base component is performing. During the audit process, we will assess each Key Assessment Feature using the relevant Key Performance Indicators and develop numeric results. These results will assist in the determination of how well each of these subcomponents is performing and how it is impacting the quality of the Business Intelligence product. The results of the assessment of each Key Assessment Feature will be combined and rolled up to provide a better understanding of the effectiveness of the Business Intelligence Base component. We will use the ratings for each of these Key Assessment Features to more precisely pinpoint the causes of any variances, issues, or excellence found in the Business Intelligence product.

What is the Data Integration Platform?

The Data Integration Platform is the component of the Business Intelligence Asset Base which includes all the necessary elements to collect the data and translate it into a unified library of information for the organization. In order to understand and analyze just how the Data Integration Platform impacts the quality of the Business Intelligence product, we will define and describe each of the parts. We will also identify the relevant Key Performance Indicators, i.e. the measurement factors, which should be used in the assessment of the subsidiary components. The figure

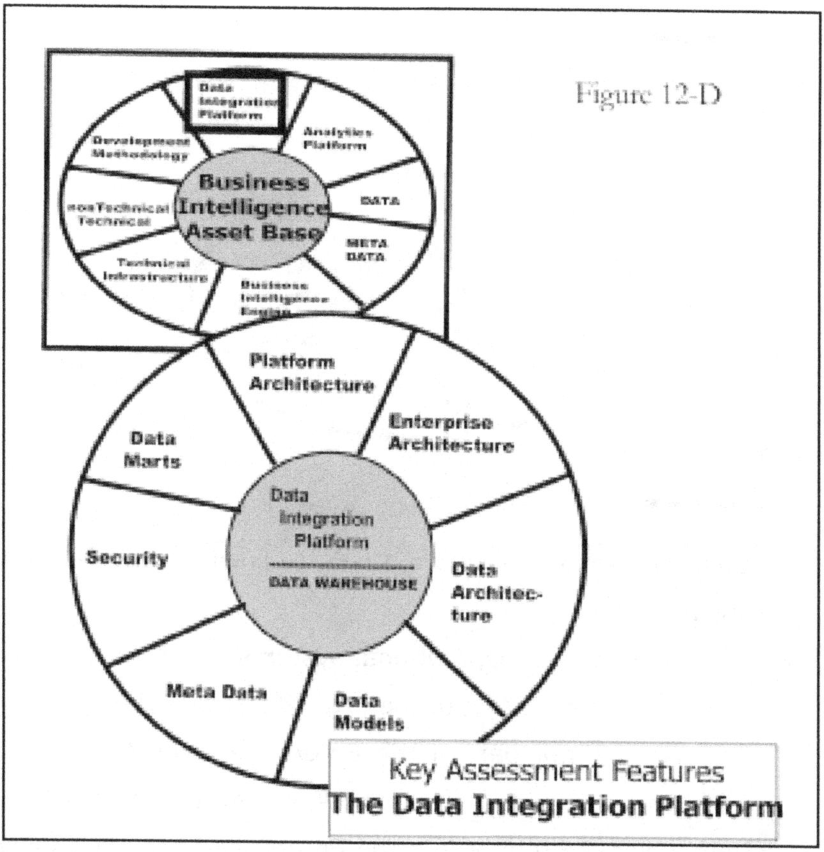

Figure 12-D

here depicts an 'audit wheel', from the BI-CIM, which includes each of these Key Assessment Features.

The Key Assessment Features

Key Assessment Feature: Platform Architecture

The Platform Architecture defines the elements and the basic structure of the Data Integration Platform. What are the parts of the Data Warehouse (or alternative Data Integration Platform) and how do they work? The elements which compose the Data

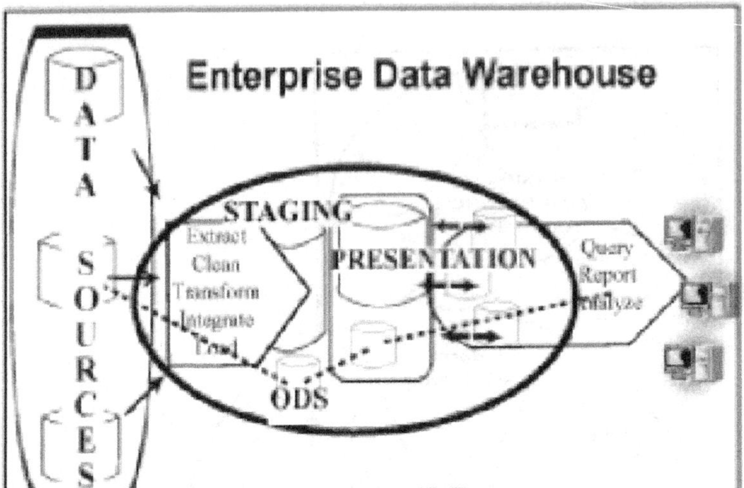

Figure 12-E

Warehouse are shown in Figure 12-E. Following are short descriptions for each.

- Source Systems - Operational systems which capture the transactions/activities of the organization. These source systems are not part of the Enterprise Data Warehouse. They are included in the discussion because most of the data which is brought into the Enterprise Data Warehouse comes from these source systems. This is one of the points of intersection of the Business Intelligence Asset Base and the regular business processes of the organization. The importance of quality of the data in these systems cannot be over emphasized.
- Data Staging Area. This is a storage and 'work in process' area which includes all the data files, databases, tools, and processes which clean, transform, integrate, archive (support, replication and management of aging data) and other support & maintenance activities - plus any other

intermediate processing requirements. This area may be considered logically as a single unit. However, in reality, there may be numerous flat files, databases, servers, etc. This is a working environment, where data is cleaned, re-formatted, and integrated into the overall architecture and structures to meet the requirements of the presentation library.

- Presentation Area. This is the environment which houses the data which is used for direct querying, report writers, and other business intelligence analytical applications (i.e. for interface to the Analytical Platform). This area may be explicitly termed the Data Warehouse in much of the industry documentation, which actually makes a lot of sense, i.e. this is the 'warehouse' of information which is available to end users.
- Operational Data Store. There is some ambiguity in the use of this term in the industry. One of the prevailing definitions is that the Operational Data Store is an information library which is used as an interim area and houses data which is more up to date, i.e. provides faster access to the latest available information. This interim area may be updated directly by business operations (rather than by the standard ETL software and processing). It is commonly used to allow quick access to smaller amounts of 'real time' data, i.e. the most recent data available.

(ODS systems were originally developed as administrative reporting systems, usually updated daily. Organizations vary in their use and definitions.)

- Data Mart. A data mart is a logical subset of the data warehouse library. A data mart may include summarized and/or aggregated data. Usually the data mart objectives are focused on meeting the specialized needs of a particular group of users.

There are two primary philosophies for designing an Enterprise Data Warehouse. These are reflected in differences in data models; the data integration techniques; and the development methods. (see the discussion on data model differences in the next section.) You should understand the design your organization has elected to use. If used effectively, a quality Business Intelligence product can result from either approach. However, there are some specific idiosyncrasies which need to be addressed, depending on which method is used.

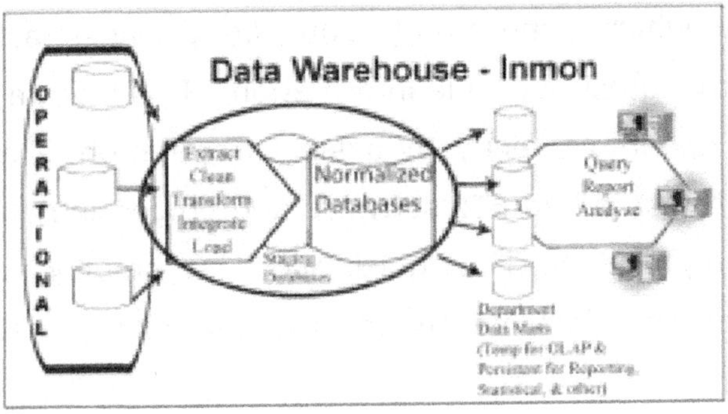

- Inmon method: There are central libraries, designed using

normalized data models, which contain the data at a detail level. Associated data marts are dimensional and have summarized and/or aggregated level data. The data marts are not considered as part of the Enterprise Data Warehouse. Integration relies on the normalized data structures.

- Kimball method: Central library, designed using dimensional

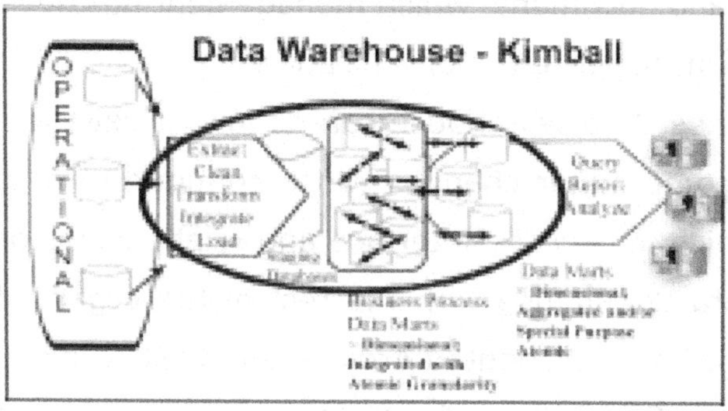

data models, which contain the data at a detail level. Associated data marts are based on dimensional models and have summarized and/or aggregated level data. All are considered to be part of the Enterprise Data Warehouse. Integration is through a Data Warehouse BUS, which consists of individual data marts (sets of dimensional tables and associated analytics) which are part of a single system with integration through the use of identical data structures, i.e. conformed tables. (note - conformed means that exactly the same definitions and formats are mandated.)

Key Assessment Feature: Enterprise Architecture

Enterprise Architecture is defined and used here in two different ways

1. Enterprise Architecture refers to the physical structures and constructs of the organization.
2. Enterprise Architecture can also refer to a set of models, constructs and documents which management has developed as a blueprint to guide the organization.

The Enterprise Data Warehouse can no longer exist in isolation. There are some major changes which continue to occur in the industry which impact the interface and relationships of the Enterprise Data Warehouse with the rest of the organization. In many cases, Service Oriented Architectures (SOA) have become integral to the foundation infrastructures of an organization.

> *SOA is an architectural style which allows for easy interoperability and communications among applications, whatever the platform. SOA divides, i.e. segments, applications and components into simpler, functionally complete pieces. An application, which was formerly a single program may be comprised of many generic parts or services, which may be, in turn, used by multiple applications. (i.e. 'off the shelf' programming and interoperability constructs) Architectural services, which provide for transmission of data among various platforms and applications may be comprised of multiple smaller functionally complete pieces. Each of the functional pieces are distinct and independent. They are called services. These services may be grouped together, depending on the*

needed functionality, to perform tasks. The independence of the functional pieces allow for sharing of the business or technical 'services' for multiple applications.

Where enterprise architectures have changed, the interfaces of the Enterprise Data Warehouse must reflect the changes. Instead of a standard, platform to platform, extraction of data from application data stores, the collection and distribution process may be changed to include such features as 'web services'.

Streaming data. The organization may have moved to 'real time' or near real time data collection. This most likely will mean that the organization is using 'streaming data' from the operational data sources rather than regularly scheduled data extractions. Since this is an entirely new paradigm for the industry, auditing this process will require a comprehensive research of the organization practices.

Architecture Blueprints

Look for documentation related to an organization Enterprise architecture. There are at least three different parts of an Enterprise Architecture blueprint which will impact the Enterprise Data Warehouse.

A. Strategic Objectives and Tactical Goals
B. Master Data Management Map
C. Applications Inventory and Planning Guide

If an Enterprise Architecture is available and includes these features, then the organization may be rated highly in this area. The fact that these topics are documented is evidence that management has spent some time on conceptualizing and planning. There must be an understanding about the requirements for Business Intelligence and other Information Technology needs. Although the rest of the Enterprise Architecture may be of interest for Business Intelligence needs, the following three topics and any associated information from this Enterprise Architecture documentation will be most useful.

A. Strategic Objectives and Tactical Goals

The most ideal documentation would include clearly stated and defined Objectives and Goals. There should also be an inventory of applications, both for transactional and business intelligence. This inventory should reflect a direct association with a list of Business Intelligence requirements. The planned data additions for the Enterprise Data Warehouse should be relatively easy to decipher from such a set of goals and requirements. This would also mean that there is some clear evidence of management support and Business Alignment with Business Intelligence Goals - two of the Key Performance Indicators which are to be rated during the audit process.

B. Master Data Management Map

There may be program initiatives underway within an organization to provide clear identification, descriptions and integration of commonly used (e.g. information about such things as customers, products, vendors, etc.) reference data or subject data which is used or can be readily adopted across the organization. These programs are usually attempts at providing uniformity of format and use starting at the detailed data level. However, the optimum situation would be to have clear maps of all the organization data which are tied back into master data - i.e. data which is used across the organization and which is uniformly defined and formatted. Anyone or any application which has need of the data would be constrained by the definitions, formats and other information about data which is included in the formal Enterprise Architecture. (The Conformed tables which provide the integration for the Kimball methodology essentially fulfill a large part of these requirements.) This could make a very real difference in the creation of an integrated set of data and make the whole process of creation and integration much easier. Rate your organization and the component higher if a master data management map/ program is in place.

C. Applications Inventory and Planning Guide

This is the Inventory discussed in A above. Such an inventory would indicate a great deal about management involvement and support of the Business Intelligence creation and management across the organization. There is a lot of work and planning which is involved in developing such an inventory. Much of the work includes the identification of business objectives and goals and the creation of targets which will allow the Business Intelligence area to meet the requirements of the business.

Key Assessment Feature: Data Architecture

Key Assessment Feature: Data Models

How the data is designed and structured is of crucial importance to the accessibility and usability of the Enterprise Data Warehouse. Two of the major characteristics to be considered are:

a. the design of the data base storage structures
b. the methods used to integrate the data.

The physical data stores are designed and structured using *Logical Data Models,* which are maps detailing the layout and potential access paths of data within the physical data structures.

The two principal design possibilities for the data base models and resulting storage structures are *normalized* and *dimensional*.

Normalized Data Models.

A normalized data model is a logical database design which separates data into discrete, unique entities, i.e. relational tables. The structure of the data in the normalized data model closely resembles the data as used in the business. With this structure, there can be only one table for each data object. Each of these data objects, i.e. relational database tables, are connected to all the other data objects through known associations within the data.

This very simple sounding concept has several complex and unique results.

1. First, it is very difficult and cumbersome to create a truly normalized data model. The process demands that information technology specialists do the work. The result is that business people are frequently not closely involved with the process.
2. This normalized data model removes data redundancy by the separation of the data into the discrete entities.
3. Normalization of the data also provides the basis for integration of the data. The data is present only once in the model and all the data relationships are built directly into the physical structure of the data.

This normalized data model has been chosen for the Inmon approach to Enterprise Data Warehouse architecture as the basic structure for data within the warehouse. This structure does provide for integration and unified presentation of the data. The structure has some deficiencies for the data warehouse requirements, however. It is ideal for transaction based systems which are focused on performance issues for the transaction applications which create and update the initial data stores. Creation, update, deletion activities are optimized with this structure. However, this data structure does not optimize the activities required for identification, selection, access and use of the data -- which are the primary requirements for the Enterprise Data Warehouse information presentation library. Therefore, the Inmon architecture recognizes this limitation and advocates this normalized data structure for only a centralized storage of data at the lowest *granularity.* (*Granularity* refers to the level of detail which is captured. The level of granularity is important to the warehouse because the lowest level of detail acts as a constraint on the capabilities and flexibility, of the data. It forever limits the information access to the data granularity initially collected.) They include a second tier of data stores designed for easy, more flexible user access, i.e. Data Marts. These Data Marts are built using dimensional data structures.

Dimensional Data Models.

A dimensional data model is a logical database design which optimizes the data structure to make it easy to use in access and use of the data for management decision support, i.e. easy to access, fast responsive query performance. There are fact tables, which hold the measurements and dimension tables which describe exactly what is known about those measurements, e.g. products and times, related to the measurement of the transaction in question, say the sale of a grocery item. Because of the structure of the single *measurement table* to many surrounding *dimension tables,* this model is often called a *star schema.* There may be multiple copies of the data attributes (data units), i.e. lots of redundant data. Therefore, dimensional data models are unlike the normalized data model, where there are strict mandates against redundancy of the data.

Kimball has defined and advocates dimensional data models using conformed dimensions (see previous note in this chapter on Kimball BUS.) for use in integrating the data within the Enterprise Data Warehouse. Dimensions, i.e. the tables which contain the describing data, are conformed when they are exactly the same, or one is a subset of the other. Data units (attributes) and formats must be identical. Therefore, the descriptions and format of any data which is entered into the Enterprise Data Warehouse and which uses the same name as a previously accepted data table must be exactly the same. For example, the PRODUCT table is defined and everyone must use the same PRODUCT table when formatting and loading data into the Enterprise Data Warehouse.

The Kimball approach to the construction and integration of data within the Enterprise Data Warehouse mandates that all the data be designed and stored using Dimensional Models. There are data dimensional tables built for data at a very detailed granularity. There are separate dimensional tables built for data at summarized and aggregated levels, also called data marts. These are closely tied to the related detailed tables and are considered as part of the Enterprise Data Warehouse.

More about Logical Data Models

Logical Data Models are the front end to the physical data stores. They are the easy to understand and use pictures which can be automatically translated by the software into the physical data stores. One of the most important aspects of the use of these models is operational. How are the logical data models created and used? And, subsequently, when a change is made, is the change made to the logical data model and fed through to the physical data model and data? The audit process should include some analysis and review of the operational and physical aspects of the logical data models and physical data stores.

Audit Guidelines.

There are several considerations to be made in audit of these Key Asset Features. The auditor should check on how the organization is designing and structuring the data and, in parallel, what are the data models which are being used. This usually just means asking several people who do the job. They should be able to guide you through the process and provide some documentation and data results. Look for documentation related to the methodology and architecture.

Both the Inmon or the Kimball approaches for the design and architecture of the data have been proven to be successful. However, the auditor needs to ensure that the following questions are answered and considered:

1. *Is there a clear understanding and application of the selected method.* The auditor should ensure that those who design and manage the Business Intelligence assets have a clear understanding of the selected approach. Look for data modeling speciality groups for the normalized data bases. Check with those who are designing. Find out exactly what the goals are for the data stores. Do they understand how the

data is being integrated?

2. *Is the selected method used uniformly.* Make sure that there is no ambiguity about the application and use of the design and construction methods and processes. For example, if all the data structures are dimensional, then there must be an integrating BUS structure, i.e. conforming data tables. Find out how it is defined and applied. There may be disagreement within the organization among the designers and managers of the process about which approach. One or the other of the methodologies and architectures should be used consistently. This is important. If some Business Intelligence applications are designed using one and some another, then the results can be chaotic, at best. Integration of the data can suffer if there is no uniform application of a method to make it happen.

Key Assessment Feature: Meta Data

Meta Data is described in a separate chapter, as a separate component of the Business Intelligence Asset Base. However, there should be some review of meta data in the context of the Enterprise Data Warehouse. The auditor should review the meta data within the Enterprise Data Warehouse. This review should include comprehension, formats, and accessibility. The three types of meta data are listed below. The Administrative meta data may, (and usually is) categorized with the technical meta data category:

a. technical meta data which is created and follows the movement of data across the Enterprise Data Warehouse;

b. administrative meta data, which provides all the audit information about the data, e.g. who created, data created, date archived, etc.
c. business meta data, which provides all the associated business definitions and other necessary business information about the data.

The auditor needs to follow-up on the meta data while walking through the platform audit for the Enterprise Data Warehouse: Is the meta data created, and is everything captured which is needed? This includes ensuring that information statistics are captured for any movement within the Enterprise Data Warehouse.

Key Assessment Feature: Security

The Enterprise Data Warehouse contains a comprehensive information library for the organization. This means there can be some very sensitive data included. The data security requirements will range from 'data available to anyone in the organization' to highly confidential. In fact, the information library could contain governmentally regulated data, like patient health records, which are protected by law, or proprietary product information which are subject to industrial espionage. The highly confidential information may be isolated into entirely separate data bases which are accessible only to those with the proper credentials. However, these data may also be included in the common information library and protected using views or stored procedures for access restriction. The organization may also have decided to encrypt the most highly sensitive information. In most cases, the data is accessible through the standard 'role based' identifications and passwords of the remainder of the organization information technology system.

For the audit, become familiar with the security needs and protection methods employed within the organization. To do this, find the right specialists and also do some more in-depth research on up to date security methods, as required. This field changes rapidly. This means if the organization has some particular security needs, make sure the audit team has the background and the knowledge of current industry standards and practices.

Key Assessment Feature: Data Marts

Data Marts are considered as a separate Key Assessment Feature for several reasons. For a mature Enterprise Data Warehouse, the data within the data marts are integral parts of the whole library and are integrated into the enterprise library. However, for initial Business Intelligence environments, this might not be true. The data marts may be silos of data. Any audit needs to research and review the existing data marts and determine how the data is integrated into a organization library of information. If there is no integration then this should have a major influence on the rating for the organization.

Audit Assessment

Each of the Key Assessment Features for the Data Integration Platform is described in this chapter. When reviewing the type of architectures, data models, and other Key Assessment Features, note and rate the warehouse on the audit research and results obtained, not on any bias towards one or another of the principal architectures. Be sure, however, to clarify the results related to how the particular design method in use meets the requirements of each Key Performance Indicator. These Key Performance Indicators are described and audit details are provided in Chapter 11.

Note: Rating the organization - You may wish to take advantage of the results obtained from a full audit to rate the overall organization capability and maturity in the creation and use of business intelligence. This will give you a better idea of how the organization compares to the rest of the industry. This may be useful in setting goals and general action plans for improvement. Organization ratings and how to measure and use these ratings are discussed in the book - Measuring Business Intelligence Success.

If you decide to rate the organization, as a whole:
All ratings should be on a scale of 1 to 5, with 5 as the highest rating, i.e. the organization shows the highest level of maturity based on their requirements, industry technology and the impressions of the auditor.

Give an overall rating to the Enterprise Data Warehouse based on the following:

- Assess and rate each of the Key Assessment Features. Give the Enterprise Data Warehouse - overall - a rating using a summation/average of these individual ratings.

- Assess and rate the Enterprise Data Warehouse - overall - using the Key Performance Indicators.

Overall - Levels of Competency:

- Level 1 - if there are independent data marts, with no established integrating architecture, rate the organization no higher than a Level 1.
- Rate the organization Business Intelligence as Level 5 only if the following are in place and operating successfully:
    1. Both structured and unstructured data - integrated
    2. User self service - for the Presentation Library,
    3. A comprehensive web based Enterprise Meta Data Library.
    4. Search features similar to best of the online capabilities.
    5. Operational Business Intelligence - 'streaming data' for real time or near real time functions.

If 1 through 4 are in place and successful, the auditor may assign a rating of 5. There should be some consideration here regarding the requirements of the organization for the real time data. Assign the '5' rating, if there is no real time capability but there are no obvious requirements for real time.

$$Y = f(X) + E$$

The Six Sigma *Breakthrough* **Formula**

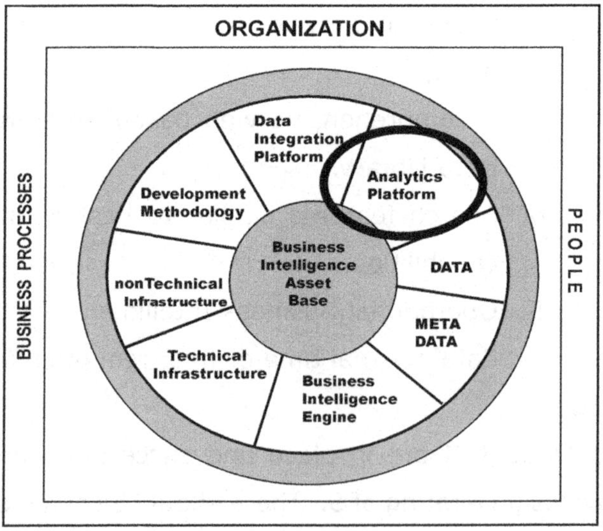

Business Intelligence
Product, Causal and Impacting Factors

CHAPTER 13

BI Continuing Improvement Model 68

Defining the Causal (X) Factors

Business Intelligence Asset Base:

The Analytics Platform

This chapter describes the Analytics Platform and the key features which may cause or impact the quality of the Business Intelligence product.

The chapter contents and goals are:

- Describe the Analytics Platform,
- Identify and describe the Key Assessment Features for the Analytics Platform, i.e. decompose and describe each of the subsidiary elements of the Analytics Platform;
- Provide guidelines for auditing the Analytics Platform;
- Discuss the relationship between the Analytics Platform, its

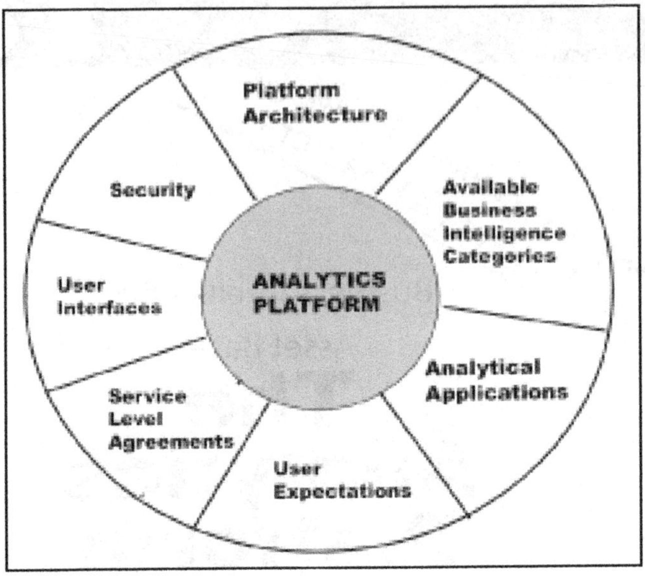

Key Assessment Features - Analytics Platform

sub components (i.e. the Key Assessment Features) and the quality of the Business Intelligence product.

- identify the relevant metrics for each of the subsidiary components.

Note: *The information provided here should help in assessing this X component. However, the audit team should include business and information technical specialists who have a clear understanding of the organization and accepted business practices. The team should also include a Six Sigma knowledgeable resource.*

The goal is not to make the reader a Business Intelligence expert. The goal is to Identify and introduce the X Factors which are the components which comprise the Business Intelligence Asset Base. The intent, also, is to provide some helpful information and guidelines for those who are not experts.

The primary objectives for this chapter are:

- *to identify the specific relevant constructs and features and assist in the process of analyzing those X factors which cause or impact the quality of the Business Intelligence product; and*

- *to enable and guide the use of those X factors and metrics in a process for improvement of the Business Intelligence product.*

Platform Architecture

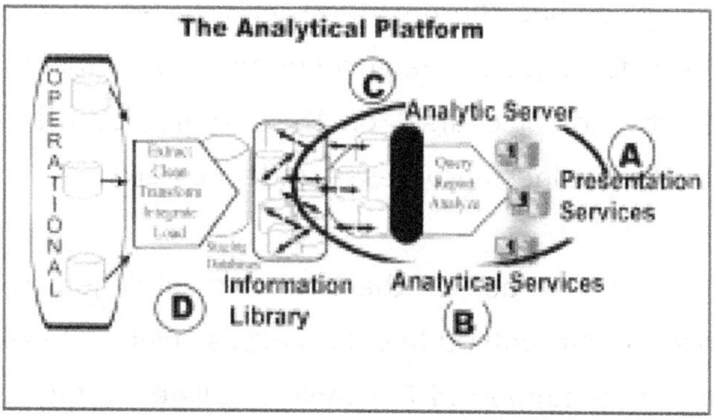

The Analytical Platform includes the following:

A. *Presentation Services* - This includes:

- the direct interface with the user, i.e. how the user sees and interacts with the information. The interface should be easy to use and intuitive for the business user. This most often means a graphical user interface (GUI) and common business terminology. Both should be simple and intuitive. The underlying layers of the architecture should be transparent to the user. For example, users should not be required to know or use SQL statements and there should be no hunting for data.
- delivery mechanisms. The user may access a spe-

cial web portal for all standard reporting needs or the reports may be delivered via e-mail. Also, users may have access to specialty Business Intelligence software which allow for direct query and analysis by the user.

B. *Analytical Services.* This includes the underlying functionality behind the presentation services. There should be a wide range of analytical services available to an end user, based, of course, on the requirements associated with the business processes under review.

The user may access the Business Intelligence analysis functions through ad hoc data access using one of the organization supported Business Intelligence toolsets, e.g. like Cognos, Hyperion, or Business Objects. Look for a wide variety of standard reports.

C. *Analytical Server.* This is where the end-user requests are processed (i.e. obtaining the reports and data). This server is also where security, administration, monitoring and other support activities take place. (The term, *server,* here should be interpreted as whatever hardware and software is necessary. See further notes on the servers in the later chapter on The Technical Infrastructure.)

D. *Information Library.* The Information Library which is accessed may be any one of several data stores. There are stand-alone data marts, the presentation library of the Enterprise Data Warehouse or data marts which are associated with or part of the data warehouse. The data models and databases which are directly accessed for use in the Analytical Platform should be structured to provide for simplicity and performance in getting the data out of the database. This means that the library must be in a form which provides the necessary dimensional structures for speed and ease of access.

Styles and Categories of Business Intelligence.

The organization needs to be able to deliver at least the following functions and styles of Business Intelligence:

A. Query

Anyone should be able to access the data warehouse presentation library using standard SQL or query tools. These queries can access any data within the data base and the questions may be in any format which is acceptable SQL, i.e. in a format which can be understood by the data base.

B. Standardized Reports

The standard, persistent reports are created and made available to satisfy specific business requirements. These are Business Intelligence reports which are produced and delivered on a regular basis, or as requested, to those users who need them. These reports should not be confused with the older versions of two dimensional printed reports. These are three dimensional and the user can *drill down* for information at more detailed levels. There is also *drill across* functionality which, in effect, will provide a broader view (i.e. more data). The report package should be complete with all the relevant data, report formats, and the mechanisms for analysis. The data necessary for the report is extracted from the data warehouse and is included with the report. The report package may be presented via a portal or sent via e-mail. Since this is a report package, the report could include sales for a product line for all regions by week, month and year. The report might be published each week with the latest data. Each user could see the overall USA sales by product for the week, for the month to date, and for the year (or whatever time frames might be required.) With the drill down features, the user could then see any or all products for any region or sales territory. With the drill across features, the user might add and view two or more separate sales territories.

The reports may be formatted as spread sheets, i.e. matrix, layouts or they may be custom, specially formatted reports. In most cases, there is a built-in *refresh* feature which will allow the update of the report by extracting the latest data from the data warehouse and reformatting the 'report'.

C. *Ad-Hoc Analysis*

Ad hoc refers to the direct access of the primary data warehouse presentation libraries (including data marts) for Business Intelligence analysis.

D. Online Analytical Processing (OLAP)

This term was derived from the previous OLTP, i.e. online transaction processing. This approach can provide quick answers for queries which require a multidimensional answer. In fact, speed of response is a primary factor in deciding to use this type of analysis. The data model is multidimensional, similar, in fact, to the dimensional models already described. The query output is usually displayed as a matrix, with the dimensions displayed as the rows and columns. The data values are the measures. This includes a presentation which is similar to the standardized reports in B.

The data for the OLAP query and analysis is built in the form of a cube. This cube of data has essentially the same characteristics and content structure as the dimensional data model of a data mart, i.e. includes dimensions, measures, and a star structure to hold the data values.

MOLAP - Multidimensional Online Analytical Processing. This is essentially the cube technology of certain vendors like Cognos. MOLAP allows high speed analysis of data through the use of a multidimensional data model, MOLAP uses pre-computation and storage of information in the cube, i.e. snapshot data from the main data warehouse presentation library. Probably the most crucial factor in providing the speed of analysis is that these cubes are of aggregated and summarized data, i.e. the granularity is changed and in some cases, the dimensions may be grouped.

ROLAP - Relational On Line Analytical Processing. Both ROLAP and MOLAP analytic tools are designed to allow analysis of data through the use of a multidimensional data model. ROLAP does not use a pre-computation and storage of information. Instead, ROLAP tools directly access the primary, relational data warehouse library.

E. **Dashboards and Scorecards**

These are charts and other graphics which report a short hand, 'picture' version of what is happening across the organization - based on predefined requirements. Dashboards report what is happening. Scorecards are usually different in that the reporting is compared to some predefined measures and filters to identify how well the organization is doing in the specific areas being reported. These scorecards may be part of a 'balanced scorecard' approach to monitoring and managing business.

F. **Forecasting and statistical analysis**

These are usually complex and specialized Business Intelligence applications and data stores. The results require in depth search and analysis of the specialized data bases. At some level, most of the search, analysis and filtering of the data will be by specialty software and/or specialists. The goal is to extract useful information from large sets of data which have been collected and integrated into a single library. The users of these types of applications are also, most often, trained specialists. The specialty data bases may have entirely different formats and may even be in separate libraries.

G. **Event or threshold triggers and alerts**

These are predefined events or data values which are defined and set up to act like alarm clocks to set off some notification or event. These may be checks for tolerance or event levels and trigger events like special reports, scorecards, events or special e-mail notifications. Creation and distribution of Dashboards or Scorecards may be triggered in this manner. However, the usual practice is for Dashboards and Scorecards to be distributed on a regular basis. There may even be special triggers which will activate automatic updates or changes to the data in the library.

H. Analytical Applications

These are guided analytics, which are rule based, predesigned and developed set of processes, tasks, screens and data analysis. This is a function based application where the required user tasks and objectives have been carefully studied and incorporated. The standard operating practices and procedures involved in managing some part of the business have been defined and incorporated into a computer based, guided application. See the following section for a more complete definition.

End User Interfaces

Who are the Users? These are the customers whom we have identified in earlier chapters. There are several different types of users and they can be grouped by how they interface with the analytical applications and interfaces. First is the end user who needs and uses the predesigned and developed analytical reports. This user rarely does more than report viewing and simple drill down or across activities. Another category of user is the *power* user who is most often a business analyst or specialist who analyzes the information in greater depth and on a regular basis. This power user frequently may also create new reports and make them available to the other users in the system. The developers of the reports and the analytical applications are most often Information Technology staff, in combination with these business specialists.

End User Expectations

The primary objective of the Analytical Platform is to deliver information for decision support to the 'client' - i.e. end users, directly or through specialized tools. These clients require fast, easily accessible, quality information. A great deal, i.e. most of the information, will be delivered in pre-defined formats and packaged for easy analysis. The analysis for these clients, in most cases, will be in the form of drilling down or across the information, based on focused measures and dimensions.

The end user expectations make several features mandatory for interface and reporting. It should be

- Easy to use, i.e. easy and intuitive for the business user
- Web based, i.e. universal access
- Enterprise supported toolsets, which provide useful built-in functionality and are simple, flexible and easy to use, i.e. OLAP based
- High performance access (response based on user requirements). i.e. requiring, among other things, data which is stored in a dimensional format which is designed and optimized specifically for user interface performance

In the near future, we should also see the incorporation of several additional features:

- both structured and unstructured data,
- good search engines which should match the capabilities of the best of the web engines
- easy, universal & quick access and design which does not require any special training.

Although, this would necessarily be transparent to the users, there should also be automated update of the volumes of reports in the organization decision support library. Actually, something many organizations do not have today is an inventory of those analytical documents, reports and applications. Also, to be truly effective, a comprehensive Enterprise Meta Data Repository should also be online.

Service Level Agreements

Service Level Agreements are key to providing consistent and quality Business Intelligence to business users. These are contracts between those who are responsible for creating and delivering Business Intelligence, usually the Information Technology groups, and the end users. These Service Level Agreements incorporate such topics as levels of performance which will be delivered, i.e. timing, formats, and quality and comprehension of data.

Security

Security issues for the Analytical Platform are primarily handled within the infrastructures and data stores. The delivery mechanisms and user access to secure data within the libraries should be audited to ensure that there are no lapses. This should require some random validation of security passwords and report access procedures.

Audit Guidelines

In assessing the Presentation Services and the Analytical Services areas of the Analytical Platform, the auditor should review such questions as: How long does it take to learn the application or tool? How fast is the work done? Do the users like using the application or tool? How complete is the application, in terms of required functionality and extension to tools like spreadsheets? For toolsets, e.g. OLAP, there should be a full range of services, like simple and complex queries and full analytical capabilities, including What? and Why? which are presented in easy to understand formats.

User Expectations should be assessed in terms of the nature and level of demand for services. There should be Service Level Agreements for every set of Business Intelligence reporting and data. Business Intelligence applications are usually created for small groups of users at a time. The auditor should be able to identify these groups, identify what the goals for the Business

Intelligence Application were and determine how well those goals were met. This is in addition to auditing the overall effectiveness and satisfaction with the analytical services.

There are several topics to be addressed:

- How well do the platform, the software, and the services work technically? Are the performance statistics collected and documented? Are the Business Intelligence toolsets working as planned and what are the issues or problems with them?
- What are the expectations of the various categories of users? Have these expectations been managed and are they realistic? Interview users from all the categories of users, including the *power* users. Are the Service Level Agreements for performance being created, addressed and consistently met.
- What is the satisfaction level of the users?

There are many things which can be measured within the technical aspects of the Business Intelligence Asset Base. One of the most crucial aspects, however, is how well the Business Intelligence being used to manage the business and to make things easier for the business resources. Ask them. And listen to the answers.

Audit Rating

Each of the Key Assessment Features has been described in this chapter. Review each of these features as they relate to and are employed by the organization. Assess each for the relevant Key Performance Indicators. These Key Performance Indicators are described and audit details are provided in Chapter 8.

All ratings should be on a scale of 1 to 5, with 5 as the highest rating, i.e. the organization shows the highest level of maturity based on their requirements, industry technology best practices and the impressions of the auditor. Details for rating the Key Assessment Features as a 0, 1, or 5 are included in this section.

Levels of Competency:

- Level 1 - Rate the Analytical Platform as 0 or 1, if there is not an Enterprise Data Warehouse or other integrating constructs.
- Level 5 - Rate the Analytical Platform as 5 only if there are some special leadership topics which have been addressed and incorporated. This might include such things as Analytical Applications; integration of unstructured data; comprehensive meta data including an Enterprise Meta Data Repository; web based, general user access, with a global search engine; and generally high ratings on all Key Assessment Features.

> *Note: Rating the organization - You may wish to take advantage of the results obtained from a full audit to rate the overall organization capability and maturity in the creation and use of business intelligence. This will give you a better idea of how the organization compares to the rest of the industry. This may be useful in setting goals and general action plans for improvement. Organization ratings and how to measure and use these ratings are discussed in the book - Measuring Business Intelligence Success.*

If you decide to rate the organization, as a whole:

All ratings should be on a scale of 1 to 5, with 5 as the highest rating, i.e. the organization shows the highest level of maturity based on their requirements, industry technology and the impressions of the auditor.

Key Assessment Features	KEY PERFORMANCE INDICATORS											
Rate each Key Assessment Feature for each of the KPI's. Rating should be 1 to 5, with 5 as highest rating. See the appropriate chapter for audit and rating guidelines.	Mangment Support	BUSINESS ALIGNMENT	PARTNERSHIP	Business Goals	Scalability	INTEGRATION	ADAPTABILITY	PERFORMANCE	USER FRIENDLY	COMPREHENSION	QUALITY	VALUE
Platform Architecture												
Analytical Categories												
Analytical Applications												
User Expectations												
Service Level Agreements												
User Interface												
Security												
The Analytics Platform												

$$Y = f(X) + E$$

The Six Sigma *Breakthrough* **Formula**

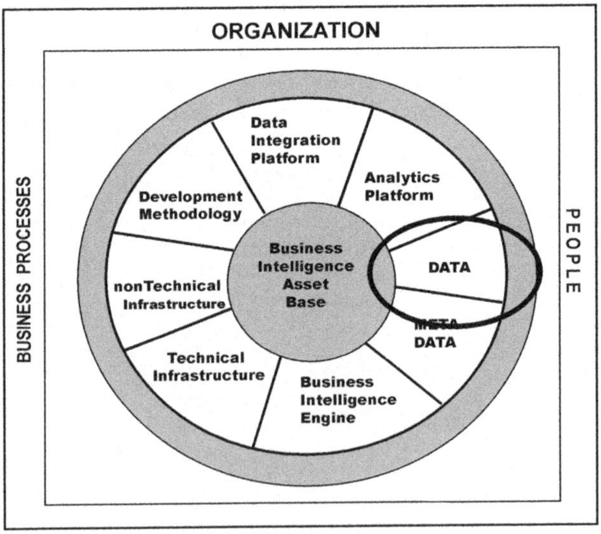

Business Intelligence
Product, Causal and Impacting Factors

CHAPTER 14

BI Continuing Improvement Model 6σ

Defining the Causal (X) Factors

Business Intelligence Asset Base:

Data

Quality data is the first, second, third and final ingredient of most importance in Business Intelligence. Accuracy and consistency can only be achieved with the commitment of everyone in the organization. Each person in the organization, at some point, is responsible for entering and/or using data. Accuracy and other quality factors can only be maintained when entry and use is monitored and everyone is constantly and automatically vigilant. Each person has a part to play in creating and maintaining quality data. In this chapter, we discuss what is involved in creating and managing quality data, with results that are successful and consistent. We will discuss how to assess the results.

Note: *The information provided here should help in assessing this X component. However, the audit team should include business and information technical specialists who have a clear understanding of the organization and accepted business practices. The team should also include a Six Sigma knowledgeable resource.*

The goal is not to make the reader a Business Intelligence expert. The goal is to Identify and introduce the X Factors which are the components which comprise the Business Intelligence Asset Base and provide some helpful information and guidelines for those who are not experts.

The primary objectives for this chapter are:

- *to identify the specific relevant constructs and features and assist in the process of analyzing those X factors which cause or impact the quality of the Business Intelligence product; and*
- *to enable and guide the use of those X factors and metrics in a process for improvement of the Business Intelligence product.*

Definition. The term, Data, unless otherwise noted, refers to the product of Business Intelligence systems. The *raw* product of the Business Intelligence systems and infrastructures is data. Data is collected and goes through a comprehensive set of transformations and integration to become the final product - ***business information*** and then ***business intelligence.*** There are a number of concepts, methods, initiatives, and inherent features of data and business information which are reviewed here.

The Audit Wheel

The Key Assessment Features for the DATA component of the Business Intelligence Asset Base have been identified and are included in the Audit Wheel (Figure 14-A). Auditing the DATA component of the Business Intelligence Asset Base should include an assessment of each one of these Key Assessment Features and an overall assessment of DATA within the organization. The materials in this chapter should provide an understanding of the features and the basic descriptions.

Key Assessment Features

Figure 14-A

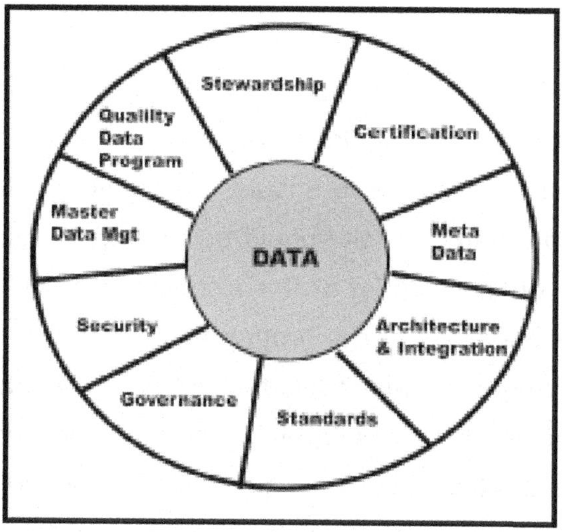

Quality Data

What is quality data? Quality Data refers to data that is accurate, that can be easily located and identified, with a single version of the data, and all the information needed to use the data is readily available.

How does the organization ensure that their data is of the highest quality? Actually, the conditions which have been prevalent in most organizations over the last decades have instead insured that the available data was anything but 'quality'. Because separate departments and groups of developers created 'silos' of information for 'silos' of people using that information. There was no reason that was perceived as important enough for integrating and reconciling the data with the rest of the organization. That has changed. Now, the payment for that parochial style of information technology is due -- and paying the bill is proving very costly. For example, the whole of the Extract, Transform and Load (ETL) can be 60% - 80% of the total Data Warehouse operations.

Assessing the data quality of an organization. Any audit of the data for an organization will depend to a great extent on determining what has been done to ensure the quality of their data. What are the programs which should be in place? How do we judge the data quality? A lot of this also has to do with the answers to the question: Are the programs in place to ensure the data quality? Another major topic for audit and review is: How successful have the Business Intelligence development projects been? A Data Quality Program should be in place and it should be a well recognized effort across the organization.

Monitor and Governance

Data monitoring requires a consistent policy of review of data to verify that all standards are being met. There should be a zero tolerance acceptance for data errors. This means that, even though there will be errors, each one must be followed up, corrected and any changes to procedures made, if necessary.

Look for documented and embedded activities in development and implementation of Business Intelligence applications for the review of data for compliance with master or common data mandates and all other standards.

Enforcement of Data Quality. Data Quality must be carefully monitored and there should be programs, standards and governance in place to ensure a continuing stream of quality data for the organization. A Data Quality program or initiative within the organization will include some team or group which has responsibility for ensuring operations and governance for at least the programs and internal operations which follow. Before a Business Intelligence application can go into production, there should be reviews of all of the quality standards and guidelines. For example, this will include data certification, data stewardship, and, of course, the validation of incoming source data, as well as the transformation and integration methods for each piece of data.

Management Support. There should be strong management support for any data quality programs, groups and governance activities. Look for adequate funding and allocation of the necessary resources. Look for recognition, documentation, and communication to the organization by management of the critical nature for the organization of a 'single source of truth'. In other words, recognition that data be cleaned, reformatted to meet a common view, and reconciled so that there is a single piece of data to meet the common understanding with a common meaning.

Data Stewardship.

Each group, category and unit of data should be assigned a business owner, who is directly responsible for the quality of that data. The assignments may be for specific categories and groups. Most often this stewardship will be the responsibility of the associated business departments or business area. This means that the data stewardship is usually assigned to those who have the responsibility for the transactions or operational activities which are associated with collecting the data. Stewardship requires that the data, as well as all, the meta data which should be connected to that data, is validated by those who understand the data best, for organization use. If there is a problem with the accuracy or any aspect of the data, then that data steward is the person to whom questions and repair assignments are directed. There should be a single person, i.e. specific role, not necessarily by name (with backup) with the primary responsibility for specific data. That person, i.e. the role, should also be responsible for input, update and general documentation and communication of the meta data or information about that data. This should include all the related meta data for the data, including the Enterprise Meta Data Repository, if there is one.

Data Certification.

This is a program and tagging operation which allows for identifying data which is original, validated and reconciled - the recognized 'single source of truth'. The certification is essentially a mark of approval for the data which is branded somehow (perhaps a unique attribute) - so that everyone will know that they are not getting an unauthorized replication.

Data Profiling. More Data Warehouse and Business Intelligence implementations have failed due to inaccuracies and general *junkiness* of the source data than can be counted. The system is architected, designed, fully developed and the first streams of data are no good. Weeks and months are usually spent trying to clean up and reconcile the source data. In many cases, it just cannot be done. The data is hopelessly unusable. The source data may not even contain values which correlate to the field definitions which are described in the application documentation. In this case, the integrity and accuracy of the expected data for the Data Warehouse can be completely destroyed. The only answer to this is to include a special set of activities in every Business Intelligence development which is designed to test and profile the source data before any major money and time is spent. If this is a part of the development methodology, there should be full documentation as well as anecdotal evidence of its use and effectiveness. Look for this data profiling pre-development work.

Master Data Management.

Any organization has a set number of business processes and associated data sets. The master data are the core elements, along with their dimensions, hierarchies, properties, attributes. which are used across the organization. Product and Customer data are just two examples of master or common data for the organization. The master data might consist of the common tables (dimensions) of the Kimball Data Warehouse BUS architecture. Master Data should be part of a data architecture plan in the Enterprise Architecture. Master Data is *not* transaction or operational data. (These are activity related and describe the operations of the business.) The Master Data are what the transactions are 'about'. For example, two of Product *abc* were sold across the counter at Joe's grocery store on May 9. What exactly is product *abc*? Ensuring that these master data are kept standardized, completely the same in format and in common use, with exactly the same data elements and descriptors, is of crucial importance. There should be a cross organization team of both business and information technology specialists who select and govern these master data. This team should be responsible for setting up Change Control mechanisms and enforcing data uniformity and integrity for any new Business Intelligence applications. This might be the same team which is responsible for data stewardship and data certification programs.

Architecture and Integration

The internal operations of the Data Warehouse includes sourcing, reformatting, cleansing, and integration of the data. Any audit of the data quality for an organization needs to include a review of the data integration platform and the Business Intelligence Engine.

Meta Data.

In Chapter 15, there are descriptions of the meta data; and the important part meta data plays in the nonTechnical infrastructure for Business Intelligence is highlighted. In data quality, meta data is the prime player. Without information about the data, there is no data to information to intelligence translation. The meta data requirements should be specifically documented and the entry and tag of that meta data should be subject to review and governance. Meta data includes anything which describes the data, e.g. the history of the data, location, and business descriptions. For example, some of the meta data are: table names and allowed values; column names and allowed values; data steward; definitions, business rules, transformation rules, dates and 'who did it' audit information for all changes or movement of the data, including ETL and archival activities. Meta data is not just tied to single data tables and columns, however. There should be meta data which describes the data models and the physical databases. There also should be meta data which describes business processes and activities - essentially any parts of the enterprise architecture and associated models. If there is no formal enterprise architecture, then there should still be meta data which describes the processes. Where is the meta data kept? There should be clear documentation on exactly where the meta data is stored, how it is associated with the data and who maintains it. In other words, which is system derived and which is manually or otherwise, entered.

Common Business Language. An Enterprise Meta Data Repository is an excellent source of integration activities and interface for users. Queries can be expedited when there is a place for users to look up and identify common business identifiers. If the Enterprise Meta Data Repository is interactive, this allows an evolution of the business language. This would mean that, not only can the users search for and use the contents of the repository, but they can also create and update the contents. These updates should then be fed back into the systems - e.g. logical data models - and used to update the applications. This kind of interactive Enterprise Meta Data Repository is not common. See what the organization has, anyway. This would be a major plus in their rating. (Also, call me - I want to see it.)

Standards

There should be well documented standards for every aspect of data which will impact quality and consistency. This includes everything from naming standards and conventions, abbreviations, formats, meta data requirements, to mapping and input profiling.

A Data Quality Cross Organization team should be in place with responsibility for all those standards and policies and procedures necessary to ensure data quality.

Monitor and Governance

Data monitoring requires a consistent policy of review of data to verify that all standards are being met. There should be a zero tolerance for data errors. This means that, even though there will be errors, each one must be followed up, corrected and any necessary changes to data, as well as, to procedures should also be made, as necessary.

Look for documented and embedded activities in development and implementation of Business Intelligence applications. Look for the regular data reviews for compliance with master or common data mandates and all other standards.

Audit Guidelines

Use the information in this chapter. Review Chapter 11 for the Key Performance Indicators. If there is little evidence of the target Key Assessment Feature, rate it as 0 or 1. Highest level should be 4, with a level 5 rating given only in outstanding circumstances. A rating of 5 for the whole of the Data component requires a rating 5 for each of the Key Assessment Features. The Overall rating should include all the features and may be an average or some features may be given more weight, depending on auditor judgment.

Business Intelligence Product

KEY PERFORMANCE INDICATORS

KEY ASSESSMENT FEATURES — Rate each Key Assessment Feature of the Analytics Platform for each of the Key Performance Indicators. Use the Key Assessment Feature Ratings to derive the Overall Rating for the Asset Base. Ratings should be 1 - 5, with 5 as highest rating.	Mangment Support	BUSINESS ALGNMNT	PARTNERSHIP	Business Goals	Scalability	INTEGRATION	ADAPTABILITY	PERFORMANCE	USER FRIENDLY	COMPREHENSION
DATA Quality Program										
Data Stewardship										
Data Certification										
Meta Data										
Data Architecture & Integration										
Standards										
Governance										
Security										
Master Data Management										
DATA										

$$Y = f(X) + E$$

The Six Sigma *Breakthrough* Formula

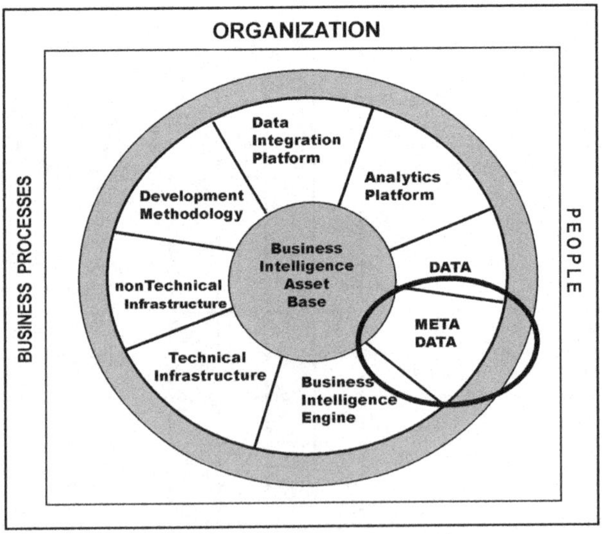

Business Intelligence
Product, Causal and Impacting Factors

CHAPTER 15

BI Continuing Improvement Model 6σ

Defining the Causal (X) Factors

Business Intelligence
Asset Base:

Meta Data

This chapter describes the Meta Data and the relevant features which may cause and/or impact the quality of the Business Intelligence product.

Chapter Contents and goals:

- Describe the Meta Data of the organization;
- Identify and describe the Key Assessment Features for the Meta data, i.e. decompose and describe each of the subsidiary elements of the Business Intelligence Asset Base;
- Provide guidelines for auditing the Meta Data of the organization;
- Discuss the relationship between the Meta data, its sub com-

ponents (i.e. the Key Assessment Features) and the quality of the Business Intelligence product.

- identify the relevant metrics for each of the Key Assessment Features

> ***Note:*** *The information provided here should help in assessing this X component. However, the audit team should include business and information technical specialists who have a clear understanding of the organization and accepted business practices. The team should also include a Six Sigma knowledgeable resource.*
>
> *The goal is not to make the reader a Business Intelligence expert. The goal is to Identify and introduce the X Factors which are the components which comprise the Business Intelligence Asset Base. The intent, also, is to provide some helpful information and guidelines for those who are not experts.*
>
> *The primary objectives for this chapter are:*
>
> - *to identify the specific relevant constructs and features and assist in the process of analyzing those X factors which cause or impact the quality of the Business Intelligence product; and*
> - *to enable and guide the use of those X factors and metrics in a process for improvement of the Business Intelligence product.*

Introduction

Meta data is information about data. Meta data may be combined with raw data to transform it into information. We need to be able to see it, access it, use it and change it, at any time, in a fast, easy manner. The current state of meta data architecture and technology does not make it easy for an organization to provide for visibility, communications and accessibility across the Business Intelligence Asset Base. Meta data points of collection are usually the toolsets within the Business Intelligence Asset Base, e.g. ETL and data modeling. There is no unified, central architecture. Any unification comes from customized applications. There are several vendor developed Enterprise Meta Data Repositories which provide some functionality for accessibility and a meta data map.

The Audit Wheel

The Key Assessment Features for Meta data are identified in the audit wheel. These Key Assessment Features will drive the audit and review of the meta data creation and use within the organization. The remainder of this chapter describes the features in more detail.

Key Assessment Features

Quality

Meta data quality refers to the following aspects of the meta

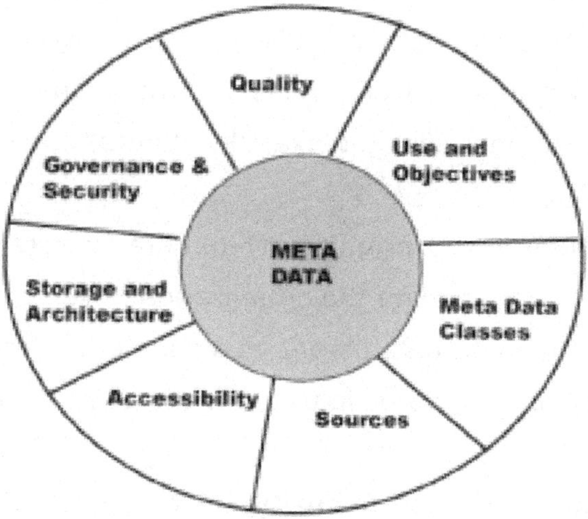

Audit Wheel
Meta Data

data:

- Complete, i.e. comprehension. Have all the meta data which are required to understand and use the data been collected and made accessible and available.
- Accuracy -- is it accurate and up to date.
- Timeliness - is it available when needed
- Format - is the format usable?
- Accessible - can anyone with the need and proper security get to the meta data.
- Uniform and integrated -- is the meta data consistent across the enterprise data stores.

Use and Objectives

Data Description. Meta data describes the data. What is it? What are the exact meanings? Where did it come from? Meta data traces the exact path of DATA across the organization infrastructures and stores. It describes and traces the business history. Meta data identifies the exact location(s) of the data.

Common Business Language. Meta data also creates a common business language for the organization. Everyone should be able to use the meta data library as a source for definitions and data descriptions for words in use in the organization.

Audit, Administration, Security. Meta data provides the audit and administration information for the data, e.g. who is the data steward? who created the data? how do we know that the data is *certified,* i.e. approved for use?

Impact Analysis The meta data should be an excellent map and guide to the data in the data bases. Where is all the data which will be impacted by any change? However, meta data also needs to be changed, at times. A major requirement for impact analysis is that each and every piece of data and meta data should be quickly identifiable, locatable, and accessible, across the whole of the Business Intelligence Asset Base. All relationships must be equally identifiable and accessible.

Meta Data Categories

Meta data may be described more fully by defining the type and uses. A major classification method which is useful in understanding more about meta data are the categories of Business and Technical Meta Data.

Business Meta Data

Business meta data is developed in cooperation with and used most extensively by organization members outside information technology. Much of this business meta data has a similar content as technical meta data, since there is a need for names, descriptions and locations of data for both. However, there is additional information required by the business community. Data derivations, timing and various alias and other descriptive and associated information, including graphics, might be important to the business user. This meta data also includes all those components which are required for query, research and reporting against the data warehouse data. The structure and presentation of this business meta data is designed to meet the business requirements and includes at least subject and function hierarchies. Some of the types of uses are for:

1. Query and Analysis
2. Standard Reporting
3. Common Business Language
4. Management special needs.

Technical Meta Data

Technical Meta Data is used by the applications and by information technology professionals and business power users in extracting and processing data. Technical meta data describes the physical properties and locations of the data elements, i.e. databases, formats, names of rows, tables, descriptions, formats. Technical meta data also includes information about how the data is sourced and moved about the organization structures, stores and systems. It is important to be able to trace the origins and movements of the data across the Business Intelligence Asset Base and history.

Meta Data Sources

Meta data comes into the Business Intelligence Asset Base from various entry points. Some of the sources are:

- Applications, including reports and source data stores and data maps and models

- Business Intelligence Tools
- Design and development of new Business Intelligence Applications, i.e. data models, data collection and design services
- Data Base Management Systems, which collect and distribute technical meta data
- Data Dictionaries
- Audit, scheduling and operations tools and processes
- ETL tools and processes
- Data Mining tools
- Data Profiling
- Enterprise Meta Data Repositories
- Direct entry into Enterprise Data Repositories

Meta Data Accessibility

There are several key points to make about Meta Data accessibility. Accessibility means locating data and meta data wherever it is in the Business Intelligence Asset Base. Accessibility means locating each and every related piece of data and meta data and providing relevant relationships among them. Accessibility requirements are dictated by the requirements and objectives for the data and the meta data.

1. Cross organization access and use. Impact Analysis requires the capability of identifying and locating each piece of data, whatever the toolset or location. If we make changes to data or meta data, there is a need to access all related data and meta data across the sys-

tem. We need to be able to identify and locate every piece of associated data and meta data.

2. Common Business Language - Everyone in the organization must have the same understanding of business terms and must be using the same business terms in reference to specific data. All should have access and should be able to update and create new meta data. This allows for the growth and evolution of the meta data into a quality foundation for a common business language.
3. Audit and history of data and meta data - There is a need to know who created the data and meta data, and statistics about the movement and change. If something is wrong (or right) or needs follow-up, then this meta data becomes a crucial factor. Sometimes even the success of the organization may rest on tracing specific data and meta data. For example, regulatory bodies may request information which can only be found with an excellent meta data system and repository.
4. Understand the data. Complete descriptions and definitions of data. We need complete information about names, definitions, and how the data is used in order to understand the data.

Storage and Architecture

Meta data architecture may be one of the most important leading indicators of how well an organization is handling the creation and management of Business Intelligence Assets. There are, for practical purposes, several different architectures which may apply to the organization meta data storage. Customization by the organization is the primary way that any upgrades to meta data architecture can be made at the current state of the technology base.

A basic architecture is the one which naturally occurs by the collection and use of various tools which collect meta data. The meta data is collected and retained in various tools used across the organization - i.e. ETL, CASE, DBMS.

This elementary level of meta data architecture may be all that the organization has in place. The organization has essentially no real meta data plan. There is no communication or bridges across the tools except what has been included in the original toolsets. There is no way to provide for impact analysis or sharing of common language and movement of technical and audit data through the Business Intelligence Asset Base. This type of meta data architecture should be considered as a Level 1 maturity level.

There are a number of other levels and types of meta data libraries which satisfy to a certain extent the primary objectives. At a high level of maturity, one of the possible architectures would be a Data Warehouse for meta data. There might also be some form of centralized meta data repository and a full set of bridges, channels, and access and search methods which tie all the meta data together across the Business Intelligence Asset Base.

The objectives for a mature architecture for meta data for the Business Intelligence Asset Base include the following:

- Full integration of the meta data with full warehouse-like capabilities for identification, location, access and use.
- Full accessibility to all the meta data across the Business Intelligence Asset Base, with bridges or a centralized integrated storage library.
- Research, search, and manipulation of meta data, as data values.
- Use of a standard meta model and mapping process for design and development.
- Support of existing meta data in existing tools and allows for creation and update through the tools sets or through the Meta Data warehouse toolsets.
- Portals and universal access from across the enterprise, with creation and update capabilities and reverse direction update into the toolsets as well as the meta data central repository (or meta data warehouse).
- Automated processes for maintaining meta data from collection points and streaming data or other methods for updating meta data central data repository or meta data warehouse.

Governance and Security

How are security for meta data and for data different? The fields and values for the meta data may be sensitive and, depending on the organization, may be proprietary. In all cases, the meta data will give any competitor a good approximation of what the company data is and where it is located. Therefore, it is most sensible to treat the meta data as a special form of data values. The security demanded by the organization for their data may apply to meta data. The organization must make this determination. For auditing purposes, review each of the toolsets or points of collection for the meta data and find out exactly what security precautions are taken. The accessibility through user interfaces, e.g. portals, and meta data repositories should be explored.

Audit Guidelines

The list of objectives and highest level potential for capabilities for a meta data system and architecture which has been described in this chapter, is simply a wish list for what might happen in the future. Because of the current state of technology, most organizations are closer to Level 1 than Level 5. However, the auditor should look for some visible sign that organization management has recognized the needs for access to meta data across the Business Intelligence Asset Base. Designers and management should be exploring a next step in the technological evolution of meta data architectures. Auditors should carefully review comprehension and quality of the meta data being collected. How much is collected, what kinds, how is it accessed, how is it used? Can the meta data be accessed quickly? How much is visible? and is it possible to use the meta data for impact analysis? This means, if there is a need to change something, do we know everywhere the change needs to be made? The auditor should find that meta data is being collected from all the major sources and that there is meta data to satisfy all the major functions required for meta data - e.g. audit, administration, history and tracking, business definitions and descriptions, technical meta data, including locations, formats, and stewards and certification information.

Audit of Architecture and Meta Data Systems

Industry environment and practices today have not evolved to the point of a common industry recognition, as well as, a technology base which supports the need for a centralized meta data management system. Meta data is embedded in multiple tools sets, from ETL drivers to CASE tools. Meta data is incorporated and plays a major role in the *services* objects in Service Oriented Architectures. In fact, the use of meta data is common in vendor tools and software.

In assessing the organization meta data resources, the audit team should research and evaluate based on the following criteria:

- Level 1: The organization meta data is limited to that which is embedded in the toolsets and various services and applications requirements.
- Level 2: There is some mechanism for interfacing the meta data among some of the various tools and applications.
- Level 3: There is a mechanism for making the meta data *visible*, and accessing and using any of the meta data in the Business Intelligence Asset Base.
- Level 4: There is a strong connectivity among all the points, or nodes, which contain meta data. All the meta data in the system is 'visible' and can be accessed. The access is

universal and users can see and use the meta data through search engines or similar toolsets.

- Level 5: A strong, centralized meta data library exists which allows for interconnectivity and visibility of all meta data in the system. This library includes a creation, update and management system which allows users and developers to access and update the meta data. There is universal access the meta data. In addition, there is a strong, monitored and well managed system for creation and governance of technical and business meta data. This includes the development and support for a business language repository.

	KEY PERFORMANCE INDICATORS											
Rate each Key Assessment Feature of the Analytics Platform for each of the Key Performance Indicators. Use the Key Assessment Feature Ratings to derive the Overall Rating for the Asset Base. Ratings should be 1 - 5, with 5 as highest rating.	Mangment Support	BUSINESS ALIGNMENT	PARTNERSHIP	Business Goals	Scalability	INTEGRATION	ADAPTABILITY	PERFORMANCE	USER FRIENDLY	COMPREHENSION	QUALITY	VALUE
KEY ASSESSMENT FEATURES												
Quality												
Use & Objectives												
Classes												
Sources												
Accessibility												
Architecture												
Governance & Security												
META DATA												

Meta Data Audit Scorecard

$$Y = f(X) + E$$

The Six Sigma *Breakthrough* **Formula**

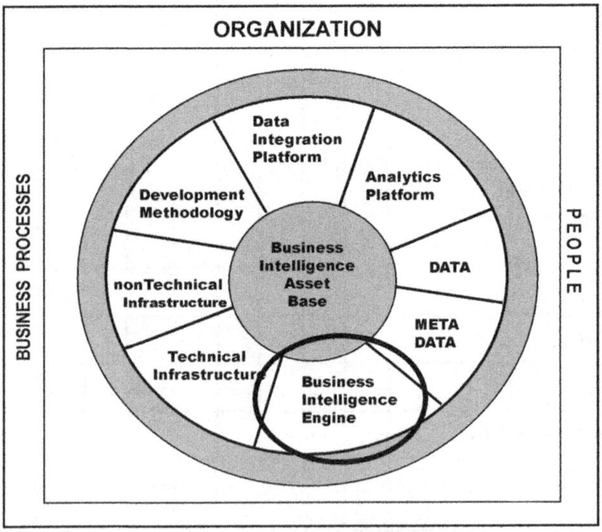

Business Intelligence
Product, Causal and Impacting Factors

CHAPTER 16

Defining the Causal (X) Factors

BI Continuing Improvement Model 68

Business Intelligence

Asset Base:

Business Intelligence Engine

This chapter describes the Business Intelligence Engine and the relevant features which may cause or impact the quality of the Business Intelligence product. The Business Intelligence Engine is the term which has been coined to identify the Extract, Transform and Load (ETL) processes, along with the expanded features which have come to be associated with that process.

Chapter Contents and goals:

- Describe the Business Intelligence Engine (Extract, Transform, Load) of the organization,
- Identify and describe the Key Assessment Features for the Business Intelligence Engine, i.e. decompose and describe

each of the subsidiary elements of the Business Intelligence Engine;

- Provide guidelines for auditing the organization Business Intelligence Engine;
- Discuss the relationship between the Business Intelligence Engine, its sub components (i.e. the Key Assessment Features) and the quality of the Business Intelligence product.
- identify the relevant metrics for each of the Key Assessment Features

Note: *The information provided here should help in assessing this X component. However, the audit team should include business and information technical specialists who have a clear understanding of the organization and accepted business practices. The team should also include a Six Sigma knowledgeable resource.*

The goal is not to make the reader a Business Intelligence expert. The goal is to Identify and introduce the X Factors which are the components which comprise the Business Intelligence Asset Base. The intent, also, is to provide some helpful information and guidelines for those who are not experts.

The primary objectives for this chapter are:

- *to identify the specific relevant constructs and features and assist in the process of analyzing those X factors which cause or impact the quality of the Business Intelligence product; and*
- *to enable and guide the use of those X factors and metrics in a process for improvement of the Business Intelligence product.*

This Business Intelligence Engine is the powerhouse and driver for Business Intelligence. It collects data from multiple source systems, transforms and melds that data into a single, integrated library of information which is accurate integrated, cleaned, reconciled and easily accessible. The resulting presentation library of information is the 'single source of truth' which can be used by the organization with faith in the underlying quality. The value of a well designed, effective and efficient Business Intelligence Engine cannot be overstated.

History and Rationale

The Toughest Job For decades, transaction applications have been built in relative isolation from the remainder of the organization. The result was multiple silos of transaction data. Now, a new plateau has been reached in the industry. Much of the transaction application work has been through several cycles of development. There is a recognized need to see and use the information in these silos of transaction data from across the organization. There has been a large price to be paid to do this. From the many versions of the transaction data, we need to build one unified and integrated whole. How do we take those 3-4-5 or even 15 versions of individual data elements and fold them into a central information library which is integrated, unified, accurate and can provide the information needed by the organization to manage the business.

Actually, in some cases, it just cannot be accomplished. This situation is one of the major reasons for failure for a Business Intelligence application. Understanding that the impossible can be encountered, recognizing it and building all the relevant implications into the Business Intelligence development methodology is important. In most cases, however, if the data is present in the source data stores, there are ways to clean, reformat and integrate that data.

Each set of transaction data now must be reintegrated into a unified set of data for the use of the whole organization. Extract, Transform and Load systems are the answer to that dilemma. It is truly amazing what can be done with this technology, hard work, and careful analysis. The software in this arena has become increasingly automated, complex and capable.

Definition and Objectives

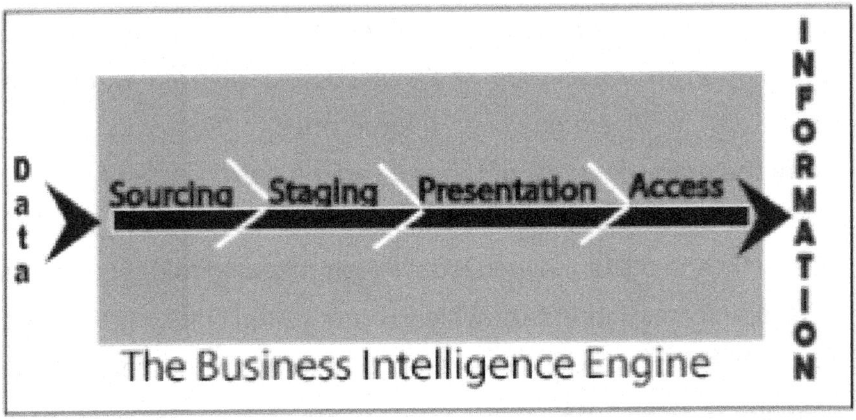

ETL is like the 'little engine that could'. *ETL* stands for Extract, Transform and Load. It is much more than data collection, transformation and transfer, however. Although those are the basics. This Business Intelligence Engine fixes mistakes in the original data, captures that transaction data for the organization and unifies and integrates it into a high quality, secure, common access library. It creates all the documentation necessary to meet government regulations and organization requirements for data tracking and follow-up. It provides all the meta data and documentation necessary for use of the data as business information to leverage performance and operations improvements for the organization.

The Business Intelligence Engine and its various process stages are described in this chapter. This includes movement across the organization of the Business Intelligence *product* through the various stages of transformation from the *raw data* to *information* to *business Intelligence.*

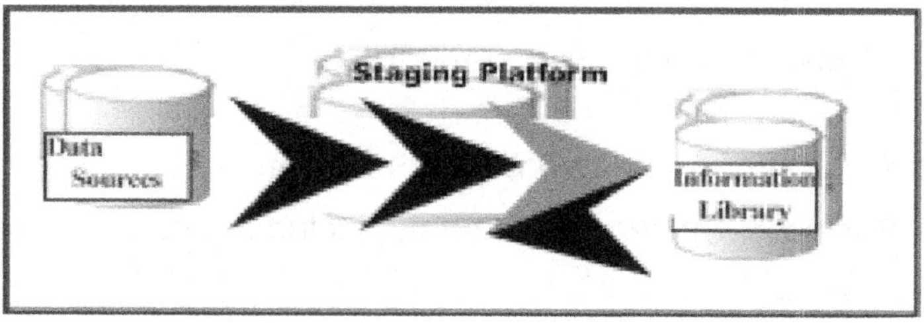

Platforms and Data Movement

As the data is moved across the organization infrastructures, there are certain stages and transitions which should be noted:

> Sourcing - how and where is the data coming from; how effective is the collection; how comprehensive?

> Staging - The data staging area of the data warehouse is both a storage area and a set of processes commonly referred to as extract-transformation-load (ETL). The data

staging area is for the work in process and includes everything between the operational source systems and the data presentation area. This is also referred to as the *back room* of the data warehouse.

Presentation - This is where the data is organized, stored, and made available for direct querying by users, report writers, and other analytical applications.

Access - This is the arena which includes the interface with the users, i.e. access tools, like ad hoc reporting; query; and data mining. All the data access tools available within the organization along with the other user interface components are part of this stage.

Extract, Transform and Load Functions

The Business Intelligence Engine includes the following functions:

- Design
- Document
- Operations
    1. Extract
    2. Transform
    3. Load

These functions may be provided by one of the many excellent ETL toolsets on the market today. They may also be created by developers in house, or there may be a combination of ETL vendor software and internal development software.

The Evolving Marketplace.

Several things have been happening in the industry.

- The Data Warehouse has, in most cases, reached a level of demand which forces 24 x 7 operations. There is no longer a 'batch window' for update of the data.
- We are moving toward real time or near real time collection of source data. Streaming data architectures for real time operational data capture and change data capture methods are a reality. (Change data capture does not require extraction of the whole of the source data base, and extraction is based on logs or other event triggers to collect only the data which has been changed since the last pass.)
- The Extract, Transform, Load (ETL) architectures are changing. In many cases, there is a lot of competition from other types of software for the ETL functionality. For example, database management systems are building in more and more of the required ETL capabilities.
- The platform itself, i.e. the physical location for the transformation processing, has changed. The processing may occur on source or target system platforms, or even on a separate platform, entirely. For higher volume operations, a separate platform is most often adopted.
- There is a growing recognition of the crucial need for

meta data at all stages and in all its forms, This includes describing in detail the source conditions, the transformation logic, and other details of the processing history. This meta data is seen to be an integral part of every ETL stage, from the initial collection to the final movement into archival storage. The meta data processing and storage must be an integrated part of the Business Intelligence Engine.

The Audit Wheel

The basic power within the Business Intelligence Engine is the

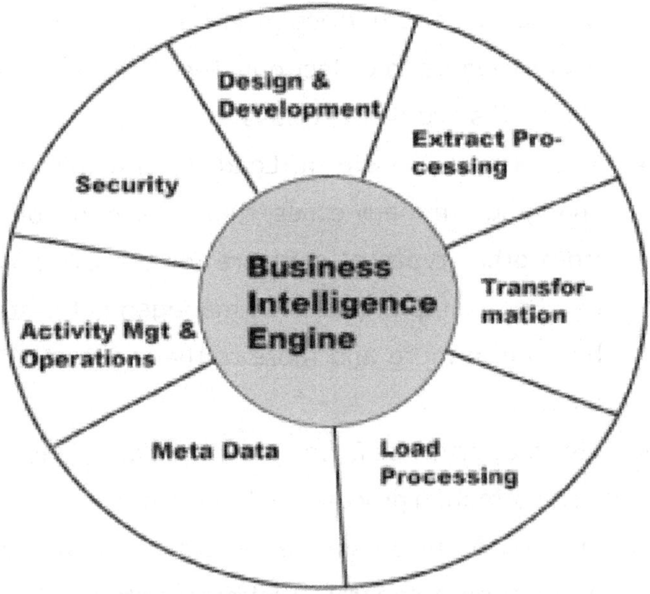

Extract, Transform, Load software and processes. We include both the core functions, as well as some expanded integration capabilities and requirements. This whole technology arena is

changing rapidly. Vendors are moving quickly to respond to client requirements and to meet competitor initiatives. Performance management and integration vendor entries are further complicating and enhancing the overall potential here.

The Audit Wheel for the Business Intelligence Engine has been developed to guide the analysis and review of this arena of Business Intelligence. The Key Assessment Features are shown in the Audit Wheel. These Key Assessment Features will be described in this chapter. Audit guidelines and comments will be made where relevant to the subject.

Key Assessment Features

Design and Development

Defining the Requirements

The primary steps in the design and development of the ETL processing:

1. Business Requirements. We gather the business requirements and the information needs of the users for a specific business intelligence application or application subset. These are business requirements for the Business Intelligence application - i.e. how is the business information to be used.
2. From these business requirements, the details of the target databases within the Enterprise Data Warehouse are designed. The information requirements dictate the exact data to be added to the Enterprise Data Warehouse and identify the sources for that data.

Business Needs.

A detailed list of all the known requirements for the business applications is compiled, checked, recompiled, and checked again. The target database which represents the requirements for Business Intelligence (the integrated data warehouse) is designed, developed and a test data base is used for testing of the basic assumptions and realities.

ETL Tools and Description

The design arena for the Business Intelligence Engine most often provides a 'user friendly' interface for the developer and it includes easy to use graphics and pictorial tools. Using this graphical environment, the developer can:

- Map source data to target data;
- Define any necessary transformations in the data;
- Detail the process flows;
- Define and set up the operations activities.

Considerations

Some of the considerations and background information which is relevant to the design and development arena are:

- The raw data will be collected, transformed and loaded into target data stores.
- These target data stores will most likely have been designed as a part of a Business Intelligence application project. A map, i.e data model, is created.

- The mapping process includes the selection of each data item from a graphical representation of the source data set and then identification of the matched data item within a map of the target data set.
- Any necessary transformations to the data and intermediate processing steps will be identified and documented using the ETL Design tools.
- This design process also allows the definition of all jobs, operations activities and documentation requirements.

Extract Processing

Runtime processing. The data is extracted from the source data bases which have been identified and mapped during the design process. *The data extraction may be relatively straightforward and problem free. However, in most cases this is not the case. A careful analysis of the source data and the source data bases well before the actual production sourcing of the Business Intelligence data is required. (Be sure to check for this in the audit.) There can be numerous issues with the data as well as the data base structures. This could include, for example, data values which are not consistent with the definitions plus undocumented changes to the data base structures.*

The data may be extracted from the source data stores using any of the tools and platforms available within the organization. This will most likely include SQL scripting tools and adapters like ODBC (Open Data Base Connectivity.)

Extraction includes - contacting and connecting with the data source; scheduling and capturing the source data; and writing the data to temporary storage (i.e. data staging). Depending on the structure of the source, the data is usually written to flat files (for legacy data in structures like IMS and XML type data) or relational databases. Other than extraction and writing to temporary storage, the only transformation issues to be handled in this stage concern some of the low level data structures, like repeating groups and data formats. This step of the runtime processing must be as fast and efficient as possible. Otherwise, application processing may be impacted or the data may not be extracted completely and efficiently.

Throughout the process, the stored data mappings from the design process are used as the guide for the extraction.

Audit Notes

The auditors should follow the trail of the developers and of the extract processing. Identify and understand the whole of the design process, the source data structures and data, and find out what kinds of problems have been encountered in the past. Some specifics and questions to be asked during the Audit Process are:

- How comprehensive is the design process and the resulting designs?
- Exactly what ETL tools are being used and how effective are

they?

- Exactly what extract methods are being used and how effective are they?
- What kind of meta data is collected? Where is it stored? How is it accessed?
- How effective is the design? i.e. what kinds of problems occur and how persistent are they? Are the problems persistent or recurring?
- Is there always a preliminary study of the data -- well before anticipated production is required?
- How and where is the data coming from; how effective is the collection; how comprehensive?

Transformation

The Business Intelligence Engine profiles the data, looking for errors, inconsistencies and generally providing the necessary base for ensuring accuracy. It integrates the data from multiple sources and ensures that each piece of that data is checked for consistency (For example, are the names and addresses the same in every case?) This ETL Engine incorporates all the multiple data points into a single piece of data in the integrated library and ensures that it is formatted 'correctly' and labeled correctly.

Any unit of data in the Enterprise Data Warehouse has a specific name and a specific definition. Wherever the name and/or the definition of any source data point is the same as the target data point in the Enterprise Data Warehouse, then the source data must be somehow translated into a form which will match the target. The definition and layout of the necessary transformation activities and steps are primary objectives of the design process. The goal of the transformation process is to take each of the multiple sources of that matching data unit and translate it 'on the fly' to a data value which can be stored in the data warehouse.

The data to be transformed, at this stage of processing, will have been extracted from the source data stores and is now available in the Staging area of the Enterprise Data Warehouse. Most likely the first step in this process will start with data in a flat file format. The final data base storage will be a relational database in either a normalized or dimensional data base format. There may be some transformations which are requisite to making the data suitable for these data base structures. This will have been part of the ETL design process.

Cleaning of the data includes - ensuring unified structures and properties; enforcing rules for the data and values, as well as the business rules; building the detailed meta data to describe the data and the transformations. Data cleaning steps can be complex and may be automated with double checks by computer/human combinations. Some of examples of data cleaning are:

- values - presence, validity, consistency - i.e. addresses
- duplicate data -- does a customer exist more than once - with, for example, slightly different attributes
- business rule compliance

Data Integration. The data mapping for the ETL processes occurs after the design process and provides an integrated database design, or model, which describes how the data will be stored. The data is mapped to the proper location within the integrated database, as defined in that design process. Data integration means ensuring that a single version and only a single version for the same piece of data exists. If there are differences which cannot be reconciled, then that data is considered separate and named as a separate piece of data.

This means that, since the data is coming from multiple data sources, there are some required housekeeping and conforming steps. Queries cannot be made unless there is an integration of the data. The textual labels must be identical and the measures must be rationalized. This data conformation is the result of a lot of up front work in terms of agreements by the users related to the definitions and design of the data. Any special indexing and other query features will be structured in the database and any checks for operability should be done in preliminary design phases.

Audit Notes

The primary guidelines are as noted above for the Extract process. Follow the requirements. See how the design is accomplished and how it ties in to the runtime processing. Make sure that all the necessary meta data is captured (see the Meta Data Key Assessment Feature in later section.) Identify any specific issues or problems.

Load

The transformed data is stored as the final form in the Staging, i.e. working, arena, of the Enterprise Data Warehouse. It is ready to be loaded into the target data stores of the Presentation Library. The formats of the target data stores are relational data bases with a normalized data base or dimensional data base structure. The target data models have been described in the design model and the appropriate data has been mapped. The data may be loaded using SQL scripts or bulk loaders - which will insert or modify the data values in the target data stores.

Delivering

The last step is to structure the data and load it into the final database for presentation, i.e. the library of information which can be used by the business intelligence analytical applications and end users. For the Kimball data warehouse, the final database structure is dimensional, i.e. based on star schema models with facts and dimension tables. Although there is some dispute over whether some of these steps are 'back room' processing or 'front room', this question is more related to the type of data warehouse and the data model rather than the nature of the processing. In every case, the data must go through each of the primary steps. In the case of the Inmon style data warehouse, with its first level normalized data base with follow-on aggregates, two sets of ETL processing may be required.

Audit Guidelines

Note the forms of the data which are sources and targets for the load process. Check the comprehension of the documentation within the ETL Toolset(s). There should be some additional documentation, which describes the flow and movement of the data and formats of the intermediate data stores.

Meta Data

There should be a meta data repository associated with the ETL software. This repository should parallel all the activities within ETL design, development and production. Comprehensive meta data must be collected at every stage - from design through archiving through runtime activities. That means that all target mapping through the actual collection, transformation and load of the data values must be captured in the meta data library. All the audit information needs to be collected, including such meta data as, relevant times of extraction and movement, any identification of data stewards, and complete information about where the data is stored and what are the intermediate and final forms.

This meta data should be accessible to the Business Intelligence Engine throughout the process. All the meta data must also be available to rest of the system, both Business Intelligence and other information technology systems through easy to access interfaces.

Audit Guidelines

The meta data of the Business Intelligence Engine is critical to all the other parts of the Business Intelligence Asset Base. The importance of collecting, storing and sharing of this information cannot be overstated.

Identify what meta data is being collected. How is it being stored? Is it updated in parallel with the data design and processing? Is it in a form which can be easily understood and accessed by other systems, programs and users? Is the meta data used? How and in what other areas of the Business Intelligence Asset Base is it most critical?

Activity Management and Operations

This is a combined subject area which includes all the infrastructure and operational activities associated with the Business Intelligence Engine. The software of the engine, i.e. the ETL software and in some cases combined with additional operational infrastructures of the organization, includes the necessary components to accomplish the following.

- Utilities and Job Structuring and Processing - technical administrators schedule the ETL jobs, run and monitor them. The standard protocols and processes apply. The jobs are monitored, events are logged, and if there are any problems, then there are recovery and restart and data reconciliation procedures. The major operational functions are:

- job scheduling
- job execution
- exception handling
- recovery and restart
- quality checking
- release
- support

(It has been noted in another chapter that the streaming data requirement for real time data capture is most often considered an entirely different paradigm. For one thing, even the collection of source data is different, in that the data may actually be 'pushed' into the data information collection area, based on events or value changes.)

- Meta data management - There is a meta data repository which stores and manages all the information about the design and runtime process. This meta data is accessed and used throughout the design and runtime stages of the ETL processing. This meta data is crucial. See the notes in the previous section.
- The extraction process, as noted above, consults the meta data repository management system to identify the data to be extracted. The extraction is handled using available organization system infrastructure tools, e.g. ODBC or SQL or other adapters.
- Loading of the data is managed using SQL scripts, data adapters, or bulk loaders - to insert and update the target data in the Enterprise Data Warehouse - i.e. the presentation library data stores

- Movement of the data - tools and software use the common file protocols and networks in use within the organization to move data into and out of the data stores and memory caches.

Some Notes about the Processing

A few points about the process should be made here:

- Query activity should not be allowed in any of the staging databases or processing areas. There are a number of reasons for this, including the fact that the data is not fully prepared and the *back room processing* should not be burdened with the additional work of ensuring that the data is prepared to be queried, security issues, etc.
- There is not necessarily a single flow of data within the back room processing. There can be parallel and embedded operations.
- Data may be collected which is not required in the current Business Intelligence Presentation library. In some cases, e.g. for compliance or archival reasons, this extraneous data may be saved in auxiliary databases.

Data Latency. This term refers to the timing requirements for delivery of the data to the end user. The industry continues to move to 'near real time to real time' presentation of the business information. Most often the organization will be using batch processing for collection of the data for the data warehouse. This processing can be speeded up and made very acceptable for even 24 x 7 operations of the data warehouses and for most needs for historical data. However, when an organization develops a real time or near real time business intelligence application, then the whole of the Business Intelligence Engine structure and processing changes. This would be an entirely separate set of processes, either replacing the batch collection system or in addition to it. Most likely, there would be a separate arena for the organization and the drivers and inherent requirements might be altogether different. This 'real time' arena should be audited as a separate entity and clear definitions sought for requirements and objectives. Any audit should be based on those definitions and requirements.

Security & Compliance

Compliance Requirements. Government requirements for tracking and auditing of data are more strict now than ever. ETL processing is one of the Business Intelligence Asset Base components which should have logical points to ensure that all the data has the associated meta data and tracking mechanisms to be able to provide for these requirements. Depending on the organization, the industry and the specific requirements, any audit of ETL will have to include a detailed review of these requirements and how they are being met.

Security Requirements. Data security is of crucial importance to an organization for many reasons, including proprietary information and customer safety reasons. Data security is also a government mandated requirement for many industries, like health care. However, everything about the data warehouse is focused on providing readily available, easy to access information. So security may be low in priority for ETL data processing. That should not be the case. (Check this carefully during the audit. This is not so much a factor of what the customer perceives in the final product, but more to the point, how to make the organization safer.)

Within the ETL arena, the primary audit for security should be an identification of the exact security needs and a review of any security activities in the design and processing. There should be a check to ensure that the organization is using role based security systems, which means that access to the data is defined by what role the person plays within the organization. If there is a different security method, then there should be further analysis of that method. However, the other major concerns for audit of the security aspects of the ETL processing go more to the vetting of the people involved and the lock down and tracking of the physical data materials, like tapes and files. A major item for the auditor to check is the availability of a documented data security program. Where is it? What is in it?

Meta data is equally important. The meta data for the Business Intelligence applications must include all the information about the data. That includes any security notes, audit information, as well as data stewards and certification meta data. Because the data may be rolled off the active data stores within the Enterprise Data Warehouse, there must be some method of tracking, auditing, and securing the data.

Audit Notes

Find out how the data security is handled. How is the tracking and auditing of the data handled? If the data is archived or channeled off the active production stores during the processing - identify the method for securing the data in the alternate data paths.

Audit Guidelines

A primary reason for auditing the Business Intelligence Engine is to get an overall picture of the movement of data across the organization. We should be auditing each of the components and the infrastructures, as part of other audit segments. With the Business Intelligence Engine, we want to get a good picture of the overall design and management of the data movement. Is it seamless? Are there major arterial clogs where data seems always to have translation or movement issues? For this audit, we should follow some data clusters and try to identify where they are coming from and how they are getting from point to point.

Some of the points which should be identified and rated are:

- Data
    1. Extract - speed, efficiency, low level data format and other translations
    2. Clean - speed, effectiveness, product results, manual intervention requirements
    3. Integrate - data model/database categories, integration results, one from many processing

4. Load - much of the complexity related to data load processing may be in the modeling of the database.

- Operations - execution, performance, capabilities for restart/recovery, speed, effectiveness, efficiency.
- Associated
    - Documentation - Full documentation of processes, infrastructures and toolsets; full documentation of all processes, like near-line and archiving operations (which may be considered as completely separate functions)
    - Meta data - full technical meta data for all extraction sources, transformations, and associated issues encountered. Full audit flow information.
    - Front Room/Back Room delineations - No query operations should be allowed in the back room staging areas - if so -- then the 'back room processing' area becomes essentially a secondary presentation library with all the requirements for security, query formatting, apply.
    - Security - check administration and lock down of disks, tapes, paper documents. Government and proprietary requirements for data security mandate physical security of areas for processing. Data security for disk internals is most often covered with rule based security systems. Check what these are and how effective.
    - Streaming vs Batch - Has the organization moved to a whole new paradigm of streaming data and if so, check on success of operations

flow and which data impacted.

- Pre operations - data profiling and tested data and procedures - Although not actually a part of the operational aspects of data integration, the success and efficiency is impacted by the preliminary design, data profiling and testing to ensure that the data being extracted is accurate. Was the data profiled for accuracy and proof of concept testing accomplished pre operations?

Rate the Data Flow Processing and the Operations separately.

Business Intelligence Engine

KEY PERFORMANCE INDICATORS

KEY ASSESSMENT FEATURES

Rate each Key Assessment Feature for each of the KPI's. Rating should be 1 to 5, with 5 as highest rating. See the appropriate chapter for audit and rating guidelines.	Mangment Support	BUSINESS ALIGNMNT	PARTNERSHIP	Business Goals	Scalability	INTEGRATION	ADAPTABILITY	PERFORMANCE	USER FRIENDLY	COMPREHENSION	QUALITY	VALUE
Design & Development												
Extract Processing												
Transformation												
Load Processing												
Meta Data												
Operations												
Security												
Business Intelligence Engine												

$$Y = f(X) + E$$

The Six Sigma *Breakthrough* Formula

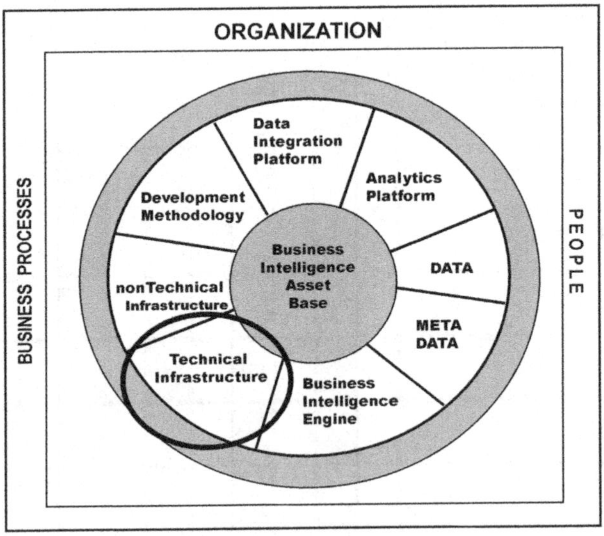

Business Intelligence
Product, Causal and Impacting Factors

CHAPTER 17

BI Continuing Improvement Model 68

Defining the Causal (X) Factors

Business Intelligence Asset Base:

Technical Infrastructure

The Technical Infrastructure provides the framework, the foundation and transportation systems for Business Intelligence Data. These components must be in place or nothing works. This technical infrastructure is the first layer of the Business Intelligence architecture. It is the underlying technical environment on which the remainder of Business Intelligence is built. The technical infrastructure includes: hardware, middleware, operating systems, networks, database and meta data management systems (including product software). The vendor software includes everything from the middleware or messaging infrastructure to the

Extract, Transform and Load (ETL) engine as well as the database, meta data engine, data cleansing engines, schedulers, and so on. All the components of this technical infrastructure should be well selected and adapted to match the business intelligence requirements of the organization. However, too often, the infrastructure has been constructed over time and the parts and architecture have not been focused on meeting the specific needs for Business Intelligence.

> ***Note:*** *The information provided here should help in assessing this X component. However, the audit team should include business and information technical specialists who have a clear understanding of the organization and accepted business practices. The team should also include a Six Sigma knowledgeable resource.*
>
> *The goal is not to make the reader a Business Intelligence expert. The goal is to introduce the X Components and provide some helpful information and guidelines for those who are not experts.*
>
> *The primary objectives for this chapter are:*
>
> 1. *to identify the specific relevant constructs and features and assist in the process of analyzing those X factors which cause and/or impact the quality of the Business Intelligence product; and*
> 2. *to enable and guide the use of those X factors and metrics in a process for improvement of the Business Intelligence product.*

The Audit Wheel

The Key Assessment Features have been identified and can be seen in the Audit Wheel. Each of the Key Assessment Features is defined and described in the remainder of the chapter. Audit notes and assessment guidelines are included both in the section related to each feature and in the summary section, Audit

Guidelines.

Key Assessment Features

The Key Assessment Features of the Technical Infrastructure are identified in the Audit Wheel. Data and Meta data are the work products and are considered separately from either the technical or non technical infrastructures.

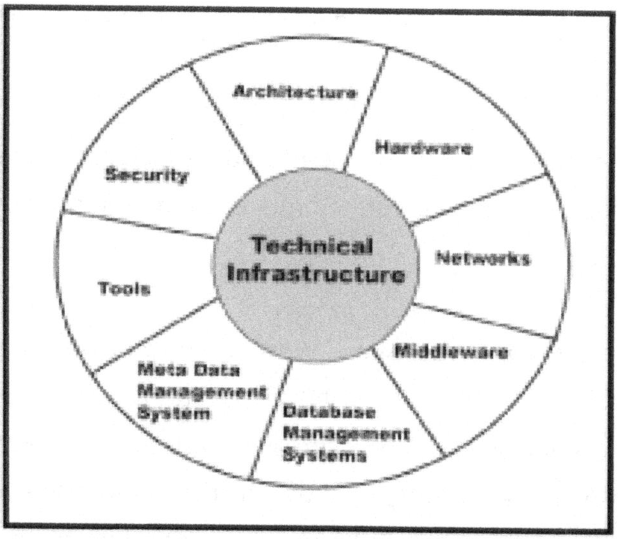

Architectures

(I would like to thank **Carnegie Mellon** *and the contributors to their web site for much of the information in this section. The web site is www.sei.cmu.edu Any mistakes are my own.)*

Computer and system architectures have changed consistently

and sometimes dramatically over the last few decades. The Service Oriented Architecture which is in an initial stage of introduction and change today is derived from and represents a form of the client server architectures in place since before 1990. In this section, we will describe some of the various architectures which have been used and are in use today. This discussion should provide a foundation for understanding the parts of the technical infrastructure, e.g. the hardware, middleware, networks, Where possible, some of the advantages to specific systems are identified.

The predominant architecture in middle to large scale organizations today is client-server. Some of the recent architectures are described below:

Mainframe Architecture. With mainframe architectures, all intelligence is in the central host computer. The user interacts with the central computer through terminals. Terminals may be PC's or workstations. In the current industry environment, mainframes have come to be used more and more as large scale file servers in distributed - client/server environments. Mainframes with terminals could not accommodate the upsurge in graphical user interfaces.

File sharing architecture. (PC/LAN) In this architecture, the file is downloaded from the server to the user work environment. Then the job is run - with both data and logic - in the local, desk top, environment. This works only for very small amounts of data, and a small number of users.

In the 1990's the PC LAN environment changed, pushed by ever larger numbers of users and the popularity of graphical user interfaces.

Client Server architecture is a versatile, message based, modular infrastructure that is intended to improve usability, flexibility, scalability, and interoperability as compared with the older centralized, mainframe, timesharing computer systems. A client is defined as a requestor of services. A Server is defined as the provider of services. A single machine can be both a client and a server, depending on the software configuration.

Client server architecture. The limitations in the file server architecture pushed the introduction and use of the client server architecture. A database server replaced the file server. With a Data Base Management System, queries for data can be answered directly - rather than sending the whole file to the application. This reduces network traffic and also allows for multi-user update and access through a GUI front end. The language for communication between the client and server uses either remote procedure calls (RPC) or standard query language (SQL)

There may be two tier systems with a user system in local desktop machines and database management services in a server which is more powerful and handles many clients. This two tier configuration is most suitable for a smaller number of clients.

The three tier architecture for client servers emerged to solve the restrictions imposed by the two tier model. A middle tier is added between the user and the server. This middle tier can perform queuing, application processing, and database staging. This allows the client and server to be able to deliver messages to the middle tier, then disengage. The middle tier handles scheduling and prioritization. This three tier approach provides the flexibility and capacities needed for large scale systems.

Types of middle layer:

Transaction Processing Monitor technology -- this is a type of message queuing, transaction, scheduling and prioritization. The client connects to the TP monitor (in the middle layer) and the TP monitor takes over scheduling and managing the request. To be most effective this middle layer is usually handled by third party vendor software and can manage large numbers of users. In some smaller cases, the middle layer could be handled by the data base management systems - but this is not as effective and service is rapidly degraded with number of users and volumes.
This middle layer - or TP monitor also provides for

- the ability to update multiple different databases in a single transaction
- transaction prioritizing
- capability for connection to a variety of different data sources - e.g. flat files, non relational dbms and the mainframe

This architecture is scalable and cost effective for large systems.

Three Tier Client Server Architecture with messaging - Messaging is another way to implement three tier architectures. The messages are

- prioritized
- processed asynchronously
- consist of headers and the message. The header contains address and id numbers and any priority info.

The *three tier architecture with messaging* places intelligence in the messages. The TP monitor technology has the intelligence in the monitor and just transports 'dumb' messages.

Three tier client server - with application server. The application is run mainly on a shared host. The application server does not drive the GUI - but it shares logic, computations and a data retrieval engine. With this approach there is less logic on the client machine. There is also less security on the client to worry about. The application is more scalable, and support and maintenance costs are much lower. Essentially there is only the single server to maintain rather than many desk top, local, clients. Cost, scalability and security are best served with this architecture.

Three tier with an ORB architecture. This is an evolving technology which supports distributed objects. The architecture allows for independence from language, Operating Systems, and technology based implementation requirements. This extends the distributed object technologies. The distributed objects support interoperability across languages and platforms and enhance maintainability and adaptability of the system. Two current examples are CORBA - Common Object Request Broker and COM/ DCOM - component object model. The industry association, Object Mapping Group (OMG), has supplied the mapping necessary to relate the two.

Distributed/Collaborative enterprise architecture. This architecture is based on the ORB architecture, but extends it by using shared, reusable components consisting of business models (not just objects) across the enterprise. This combines the standardized business object with distributed object computing. Instead of the limited messages of prior architectures, the intermediate products are full objects, which are essentially contained 'systems', or business models. These contained reusable business models provides much more flexibility. The potential of the concepts is tremendous. This is the foundation for Service Oriented Architectures.

Service Oriented Architectures. This architecture is a major step forward involving the concepts and technologies for distributed processing and modular programming. The unit for distribution is called a *service.* These services are larger, self contained units which are to be distributed across the network, i.e. between client and server. These services are very small function groups, usually of some larger set of functions, (i.e.

what might have been coded into an application program in pre-services technology). Such a service might be to place an order, or pay a bill. Services are relatively large objects or units for specific functions which are self contained. These services are sent, then mapped together, or orchestrated, by a receiver. This architecture should allow for much more flexibility, and for costs to go down, since an organization only needs to develop or purchase exactly those services which meets their requirements. This is a major jump forward over the initial data object which was the initial basketball for the client server technology.

Hardware

Definition. The Hardware Key Assessment Feature of the Business Intelligence Technical Infrastructure includes all the basic computer machinery, from work stations to servers and any other boxes which are part of the platform. Computer hardware is the physical part of a computer.

Hardware Characteristics.

Consistent and stable environment. The hardware of a computer system is relatively consistent and stable. This may be contrasted with the software tools which are usually more easily migrated in and out of the infrastructure base. It is fairly common for the hardware platform to have been built slowly, over time. The requirements for each selection have, most likely, been dictated by the environment at the time of purchase. This sometimes makes for a disparate collection, which is not necessarily the best overall infrastructure for Business Intelligence.

Power. The hardware must have sufficient power to handle complex access and analysis requirements against large volumes of data. It has to support not only predefined, simple queries on summary data, but also ad hoc complex queries on detailed data.

The term 'power' refers essentially to speed and size requirements.

At the 'front-end', the technical infrastructure which supports the Data Warehouse Presentation Library, including associated data marts, it is critical to provide for plenty of power to ensure satisfactory performance. Query and report performance and other similar user interface activities demand rapid response and delivery of data.

The 'back room' processing of the Data Warehouse refers to the parts of the platform where the data is extracted, transformed and integrated and loaded into the Presentation Library. Computing strength is also important here. However, the performance issues (for a Data Warehouse which contains only historical data) may not be so time critical. However, as the organization moves toward more real time data availability, this 'back room' power and responsiveness moves up on the priority scale.

Scalable. The hardware must be scalable, i.e. easily upgraded to meet new requirements. The hardware platform must be flexible and easily upgraded to handle changes in data volumes, data updates, access patterns. The hardware platform must also be able to accommodate changes and fast growth in interface and access of the Business Intelligence data - e.g. number of people, reports & analytical activity, tools, and the systems interfaces. If new hardware is added 'on the fly', then the system must be able to use it to improve performance.

Audit notes. Identifying the hardware within the Business Intelligence environment is a first step in the audit process. Everything which is part of the infrastructure which supports and/or impacts the Data Integration Platform and the Analytics Platform should be identified and reviewed. This can be accomplished by listing the expected functions and requirements for Business Intelligence and correlating these with the available hardware. There should be extensive documentation for the systems and run time operational statistics.

During any audit of the technical infrastructure, the following questions should be addressed:

- What hardware are we using for Business Intelligence?
- Is there enough staff to maintain and support all of it?
- Do we have enough hardware for our data and user requirements?
- How scalable it the hardware and how rapidly can it

be upgraded?
- Does the hardware perform as an integrated whole?

Capacity and Growth Capabilities

What are we looking at? Servers, workstations, operating systems, and associated technologies. What are we looking for? Assessing the hardware requires reviewing the planning, capacity and other documentation and it means talking with the technical architecture engineers, capacity planners and the Business Intelligence planners and managers. How much growth in data and user volumes have been planned for? Have the Business Intelligence planners kept the engineers informed? Have the engineers been an integral part of all required meetings, etc? Is there a team of business and technology staff with the responsibility for planning and managing the technology, including the hardware?

In many cases, the growth within the Business Intelligence arena may have been piecemeal and chaotic. There should be some responsible group or individual or even just a set of documentation which shows an enterprise understanding and the directives for management of the overall Business Intelligence Asset Base. The assessment of hardware for the Business Intelligence Asset Base should identify whether there is such an understanding and also how effective it is. Are there staff members whose job it is to assess and plan for growth - to monitor performance? In many cases, hardware assessment takes place after the fact, when it is self-evident that there is 'not enough'; when performance has already eroded and the system has turned to molasses. Look for evidence and anecdotal experiences. There should be management software, logs and other systems documentation. Find out what is available, ask for it and review it carefully.

Key Performance Indicators. Review the organization hardware using each of the relevant Key Performance Indicators.

Networks

Networks include all the communications, interface and sharing resources involved in the organization's computer systems. (A network is usually defined as *two or more computers connected together using a telecommunication system for the purpose of communicating and sharing resources. The devices can be separated by a few feet through Local Area Networks, or thousands of miles through Wide Area Networks. A wide area network (WAN) is a computer network that covers a broad geographical area. This is usually a network that uses routers and public communications links. The internet is essentially a large WAN. A computer network is any set of computers or devices connected to each other. (NOTE; Thank you to WIKIPEDIA - a great website. We love you - the site and everyone who contributes, whoever and wherever you are.)*

The major relevance to an assessment project or to the Business Intelligence Asset Base becomes evident only when the network structure does NOT work. Does the system provide the basic functions required? Also, and this is the principal question for analysis of the infrastructure ---

> *Is there enough bandwidth to provide for current requirements and for rapid, high volume growth?*

For assessment purposes, we ask similar questions to the same specialists as noted under the hardware components. The network architecture should be essentially transparent to developers and users. However, those charged with making sure that the system is scalable and flexible will need to know who to talk with and who will decide how much band width and what kinds of communications infrastructure are required. The communication engineers will be able to ascertain how much and what is needed. They also know if the organization has what it needs.

Some specific questions for these engineers, during the audit, are: what kinds of data, what volumes of data, how many users and what categories of users are they planning for in their projections for their systems and platforms? If there is no documentation and they don't know or do not have the information readily available - there may be a problem. This area may need further evaluation, at any rate. Advice to the auditor: *Seek until they know.*

Middleware

Middleware is a term which describes a piece of software that connects two or more software applications so that they can exchange data. Middleware is the runtime software layer which lies between the operating system and the applications *Middleware* acts a bridge for integration of the application programs and other software in the arena of client/server architectures and complex networked architectures in a distributed computing environment.

The Middleware should support:

- ...directory services,
- ...message-passing mechanisms;
- ...and specifically - database gateways.

A directory service is software which stores and organizes information about a computer network's users and network resources. It allows network administrators to manage users' access to the resources.

Most Middleware falls into one of the following categories:

- ...Data Management Middleware - this connects an application or DBMS on one platform with a DBMS running on another platform;
- ...Distributed logic middleware - this middleware supports program to program communication between two pieces of custom written code.

Large organizations will often have a middleware or messaging infrastructures such as IBM Websphere MQ, Microsoft BizTalk, Tibco or Oracle Fusion Middleware.

Data Management middleware includes database gateways. Database gateways give end users a way to access information stored in disparate databases. To house the mountains of information they generate, large corporations today rely on a wide range of database management systems (DBMSs). These databases most often use proprietary technology. This means that in order to provide access to the data in these databases, organizations add in a layer of software that identifies and translates DBMS differences.

These database management gateways are required to connect the various network architectures of desktops, other clients and servers to the enterprise main servers. There are four major categories:

- ...point to point - which provide access to a single type of data base management system
- ...universal - which provide general access across a set of platforms
- ...SQL - provides access to relational databases - the gateway translates the request into native SQL used by the server's relational database.
- ...ODBC type gateways - (open database connectivity) - these are based on vendor specifications.

Database drivers (DLL) link applications to the database management system.

For the assessment and rating of the organization capability in this area, the analyst should ensure that the middleware being used is at least industry standard and provides for performance and efficiency for data movement through the system. Essentially, the issue is: Do we have the middleware necessary to retrieve the operational data from multiple different platforms; transfer it into our Business Intelligence environment then to provide the necessary movement through that environment?

Database Management Systems

A database management system (DBMS) is computer software designed for the purpose of managing databases. Typical examples of DBMSs include Oracle, Microsoft SQL Server, MySQL, DB2.

The database management infrastructure includes not only the Database Management System, but also the software and hardware which move the data between the application and the data storage.

Perhaps the single most critical set of components in providing for performance of Business Intelligence systems are the underlying database management systems. Database management platforms may range from local file servers in isolation to workgroup/ server structures to full blown enterprise wide and/or mainframe type platforms. Size and requirements for the DBMS infrastructure are dictated by the requirements of the Business Intelligence organization, including short and long term projections. A single data mart application might be satisfied with a local file server - e.g. with a desktop database. An organization with this type of basic DBMS platform, exclusively, should be rated no higher than a Maturity Level of 1. Larger applications may require a workgroup type of structure with a relational database management system for a small group of users and applications. An enterprise wide system of a complex, encompassing Business Intelligence Asset Base will require heavy duty, high volume relational data base hardware and software.

Database management systems have been available for a long time in the industry. The Very Large Scale Database Management Systems are complex and amazing to contemplate in their sheer responsiveness and capabilities.

There are other features of a database management system which are specific to the requirements for Business Intelligence. Some of these are: Aggregation and summary data; dimensional data marts - star schemas; recognition of the types of data structures and automated, integrated processing of these particular structures; partitioning and bitmap indexing and other specialized indexing schemes; materialized views and advanced query optimization and processing; transparent performance enhancements for sort, aggregation and other important Business Intelligence Operations.

In fact, what we need to look for from the Business Intelligence perspective are mostly well thought out capabilities which will do the jobs necessary and provide high speed performance. Understanding and integrating these capabilities is critical to a successful Business Intelligence Asset Base. In most cases the vendors of these data base management systems have anticipated and built in tremendous numbers of services and capabilities which address all the Business Intelligence requirements. In fact, many are moving into areas which compete with other vendor arenas, like ETL. Keep in mind that your organization is probably suffering if some of these specific Business Intelligence related features are missing. Those features should be available to give you the performance boost needed for your applications performance or allow your particular set of Business Intelligence tools to function well. Also, if your organization has succumbed to the newer hardware additions to the marketplace of the Business Intelligence appliances, (i.e. 'boxes' which include the Data Base Management system - hardwired) the auditor should carefully review the list of specific expectations for the Data Base Management System. Since, at this time, appliances are newer on the market, there may be 'bugs' to be fixed and enhancements which need to be made. Look for bugs or missing features which the organization needs. As usual, the best way to find out is to ask those within the organization who are using the appliance.

Audit and Assessment: When do we need more DBMS power and storage. The assessments we should be making for our Business Intelligence Capability Model are: Does the organization have the expertise to make the proper decisions? Is there a documented and in-place process and team of experts reviewing performance statistics and continually determining whether more power and storage are needed? The auditor should review the statistics with the organization experts and assess their process and resources for ensuring that there is enough power for peak loads, for 24 hour production/online operations, and for handling, offline, all the back up and restore.

The Key Performance Indicators are discussed in more detail in Chapter 11. Some of the Key Performance Indicators which are of particular interest in the DBMS for Business Intelligence requirements are discussed below.

Assessing features for the Database Management System and whether the organization has the 'best' of the marketplace is a question for the experts. The organization needs to determine what their Business Intelligence requirements are and select a solution which is cost effective and meets those requirements.

Following are many of the features and Key Performance Indicators which the database management system should address.

- Scalability -- Planning should provide for rapid changes in: data volumes; data update frequencies; data access patterns; # reports/queries; BI users; Toolset Access volumes; operational data feeds. DBMS capabilities should be planned for and accommodated with all these factors in mind.
- Dimensional Support - focused support for star schema models, data loading and use

- Aggregation Support - fast, easy load and use of pre-compiled summaries and aggregations of data. (Summaries are added numerics; aggregates differ slightly, in that several different fields may be grouped and made additive.)
- Archiving Support - There should be a comprehensive system of support for the 'roll-off' of data from the active information library, based on age and use. This should include an automated process, including predefined triggers and transfer of data to inactive storage.
- Support for dating and other audit information - automatic collection and marking of data with dates, times and other information for data movement and changes.
- Support and Administration - All the standard and not so standard features - unattended operations; audit and tracking; workload tracking and tuning mechanisms; monitoring of resources, users, data volumes; preset triggers for user warnings for things like resource overloads.
- Triggers and stored procedures - Event driven, automatic (by the DBMS) running of prestored code - by data element and event.
- Resource limits and alerts - There should be user communications related to timing of queries, etc. if over preset limits of resources and times.
- Workload tracking and load balancing and manage-

ment - close monitoring, reporting, for integration of performance and automated realignment of resources, as necessary.

- Location Transparency - Wherever the data is located in the system, users should not have to be involved in any way.
- Performance - How well and how fast are queries and analytical applications handled - i.e. this may depend on degree of parallelism and other factors.
- Normalized as well as Dimensional Data Structures
- Advanced indexing - special index schemes for performance enhancement
- Internet support - Many of the analytical toolsets are internet based. How well does the DBMS interact?
- Multiple Platforms - Should be able to house the DBMS on multiple heterogeneous platforms, i.e. Business Intelligence systems may include various sized data stores (usually data marts) on multiple platforms.
- Coordination with other hardware - software, e.g. other DBMS.
- Operations. 24 hour production/operations - with some sort of double back up and fault tolerance features; Checkpoint, restart, recovery internals;
- Scaling --- Effective cacheing and sharing of data to minimize bottlenecks; multiple parallel tasking; multiple processor compatibility
- Security system - comprehensive - with fully restricted access to views, table, and data elements.

- Meta data - interfaces and collection and communications with meta data repositories.

Any audit should include a review of the database management system, the staff and the support and maintenance processes to determine how well the organization handles the issues. Although there should be some assessment of the architecture and the specific trade-offs made with the organization DBMS - still the ultimate test is 'how well does it work'? Has it handled the work load changes and what is the prognosis for tomorrow? Have there been degradations in performance?

Performance - How fast and how responsive for both the loading of the source data and the retrieval for user, i.e. timing of sending of query and return of the business information to the user. There are a number of features which are key here ---

- the degree of parallelism in handling queries and data loads. The DBMS manufacturers have performed miracles in the area
- advanced indexing schemas
- use of parallel processing in handling queries and for data loading
- clustering servers and databases

Scalability. In order to be considered scalable, a database must be able to take advantage of additional resources (memory and processors). The computer may be a small single processor system or at the other end of the spectrum. If more memory or processors are thrown at it, the DBMS should be able to recognize and use the extras to improve performance and throughput. Scalability is the capability of handling growing amounts of work automatically and transparently, i.e. the system can be readily enlarged. If performance improves after adding hardware, (keeping everything else, like services, steady) then the organization has a scalable system. Of course, it is not quite that simple. But, on the whole, that is what defines scalable for the database management system. For example, a scalable database management system is one that can be upgraded to process more transactions by adding new processors, devices and storage. It should allow for easy, transparent upgrades without shutting down the system. Some methods being used by DBMS vendors to optimize scalability include powerful data compression features, grids or clusters of servers; Oracle states that their extensive parallel processing is at the heart of its scalability. Not only is parallelism central to query processing, it plays a key role in ETL tasks.

Database scalability is a long thought over and debated topic, and there are no easy answers. There are several ways to achieve greater scalability out of the organization's database, however the chosen architecture should fit the needs of the organization. When it comes to scalability, there seem to be two ways to achieve it -- scaling up or scaling out. Scaling up is to handle volume on a single high performance server, while scaling out is to distribute load among many lower cost servers. When scaling up you add processors to your server, when scaling out, you add servers to your cluster.

Scalability also refers to capabilities for

- expanding the capability of the data base and database management system to process and store records - i.e. storage space and processing performance.
- 24X7 availability. With continuing globalization, most large organizations require that their Business Intelligence systems be available on a continuous basis. So modification should not require 'bringing down' the system.

Meta Data Management Systems

Meta data is embedded in multiple tools sets, from ETL drivers to CASE tools. We have noted the assessment guidelines for meta data in Chapter 15, the Meta Data Business Intelligence Asset Base component. For this Technical Infrastructure review, you may wish to limit the assessment to identifying where the meta data is collected and how well the various tools and any management systems are working.

Business Intelligence Tools

As the organization matures in the Business Intelligence arena, the selection and use of the Business Intelligence tools should become more standardized and the responsibility for selection and support should be at the enterprise level.

In this chapter, the most prevalent types of tools which should be considered as part of the Business Intelligence arena are identified.

These tools are described. Some considerations are discussed related to why the organization needs them; standardization issues; and assessment points.

The primary sets of tools required for Business Intelligence can be described by the requirements to be met:

Business Intelligence Tools
Development CASE Data Integration (e.g. ETL) Analytical Query & Reporting OLAP Dashboard & Scorecard Planning - Modeling Statistics & Data Mining Production Reporting

Development. These are tools used by the developers and creators of the Business Intelligence data structures and analytical applications.

This includes toolsets for:

- creating the logical and physical models, (like ERwin) and those to extract and
- create the information libraries (ETL).

The data modeling tools are used during the development phases of the application most heavily - to create the normalized and the dimensional models which are necessary to the Business Intelligence analytical tools.

The Extract, Transform, Load activities in building and supporting Business Intelligence systems takes more time than any other. There are a number of tools which are necessary for these tasks - including the basic ETL, plus special data cleansing software, and others.

Analytical. The Analytical toolsets are used by both the developers and the end users to access the data warehouse presentation library and data marts. These vary tremendously in their nature and capabilities. In some, if not most, organizations, many sets of tools are in use by various groups. This is especially true for the query and reporting tools. The desktop versions of spreadsheets and probably desktop database tools are major players in the initial stages for data mart development. In many cases, use proliferates to the point of chaos. Assessment should include identifying all the analytical tools and where they are being used, as well as the users of the tools.

What are the costs associated with the unrestrained proliferation of these tools? At any rate, there may be a need for more than a single toolset across the organization for such functions as query, reporting and OLAP. Of course, some of the other tools are very specific to the type of analytical processing to be accomplished. Review the chapter on the analytics platform for more information.

- Query and Reporting - Extract, format and present the

information.

- Production Reporting - Reports are developed (frequently by Information Technology developers) and made available to the general user population on a regular basis - either through 'push' via e-mail or user access via the web or enterprise portal.
- Dashboard and Scorecard - Some of these may be incorporated into the primary toolsets in use. There may also be some specialized tools. This is particularly true for process oriented manufacturing cultures, which have been more accustomed to the dashboard capabilities in their manufacturing facilities.
- Planning - Modeling tools - These simulation and forecasting tools allow management to ask questions, like 'what if'.
- Statistics and Data Mining - These are the toolsets which are most likely to be missing from the available tools for an organization. They are complex and usually require an entirely different data structure for optimal performance.

More Audit Notes

Review the tools in terms of how many of each category are available, how well the functions are being performed and user satisfaction. Use the Key Performance Indicators, where applicable. There should be one or two standardized, enterprise supported tools for general use across the organization for such functions as query, reporting and OLAP. There may be a need for more than a single standardized, enterprise supported toolset for these functions, since the tools may vary in performance capabilities. Some, like Cognos, use a proprietary MOLAP (or cube) technology which many users have grown used to and find faster for their summarized and aggregated data. Although, these vendors will claim that all the 'necessary' functions are covered, many users may have special reasons for another toolset. However, if there are more than two in use, analyze the who, what, why factors carefully. Cost and integration factors are especially important to assess. There are, of course, some excellent reasons for the standardization at the enterprise level, including the support and maintenance of the software, as well as the potential for centralized help for the users.

Audit Guidelines

The Key Assessment Features have been identified and described in this chapter. As with the rest of the Business Intelligence audit areas, use the relevant Key Performance Indicators. We have already identified particular Key Performance Indicators which should be most closely assessed, along with some pointers on particular impact issues. In addition, general audit notes have been included for each of these features. Many of the areas, in fact, most, are specialized and require the assistance and input from the organization information technology specialists. However, the assessment should be based, also, on identifying how these specialists do their jobs and what are their tools for monitoring, review and correction, as much as on the actual functions of the hardware, middleware, DBMS, and other Technical Infrastructure Key Assessment Features.

The audit and assessment notes are included in the sections on the Key Assessment Features and these should be carefully reviewed and followed during the audit process. This should include an analysis of each Key Assessment Feature, as well as, how well all the features of the Technical Infrastructure work together. This should include a review of the requirements for a sound, integrated and comprehensive Data Integration Platform and Analytics Platform.

Each of the Key Assessment Features of the Business Intelligence Asset Base should be assessed by how well it matches the Business Intelligence and specific platform requirements for the organization. The Key Performance Indicators from Chapter 8 should guide the auditor in the review.

Some of these Key Performance Indicators which are of particular importance in the assessment of the Technical Infrastructure, are:

- Performance - do the Business Intelligence users get their information as rapidly and in the formats, as needed
- Scalability - can we add data and users to the system easily and quickly
- Integration - Is there a common, unified, integrated view of the data and the resulting information, i.e. 'sin-

gle source of truth'?

- Efficiency - economy - Is there a common set of resources and infrastructure which reduces the costs and maintainability of the Business Intelligence Technical Infrastructure

A few other audit considerations: Are the software components chosen to provide for the general Business Intelligence requirements and also to meet the specific needs of the organization --- e.g. data modeling tools which will enable normalized and dimensional modeling; extract, transform and load (ETL) tools; user access tools, like Business Intelligence reporting and data mining, forecasting.

We cannot emphasize enough the importance of scalability and adaptability for the Technical Infrastructure. The rapid and frequently unplanned growth and changes in number of users and volumes of data can rupture the fabric of the platforms, if they are not built with flexibility and scalability in mind.

For the *over all rating of the Technical Infrastructure* -

- Level 1 or 0 - Rate the organization at Level 0 or 1, if there is no Data Integration Platform and associated enterprise supported infrastructure. This would mean usually that there are Data Marts scattered around the organization - in use by specific groups.
- Level 5 - Rate the organization at Level 5 only if all the Features can be rated comfortably at a Level 5. Level 4 is a good, competent, mature rating for an or-

ganization for infrastructures. If there is also support and infrastructure capabilities for unstructured data, for an enterprise portal (essentially not usually just for Business Intelligence) and specialized web and portal based search facilities - then consider the Level 5 rating

Business Intelligence Technical Infrastructure

KEY PERFORMANCE INDICATORS

Rate each Key Assessment Feature for each of the KPI's. Rating should be 1 to 5, with 5 as highest rating. See the appropriate chapter for audit and rating guidelines.	Mangement Support	BUSINESS ALIGNMENT	PARTNERSHIP	Business Goals	Scalability	INTEGRATION	ADAPTABILITY	PERFORMANCE	USER FRIENDLY	COMPREHENSION	QUALITY
Architecture											
Hardware											
Networks											
Middleware											
Database Management Systems											
Meta Data Management Systems											
Tools											
Security											
Technical Infrastructure											

KEY ASSESSMENT FEATURES

$$Y = f(X) + E$$

The Six Sigma *Breakthrough* Formula

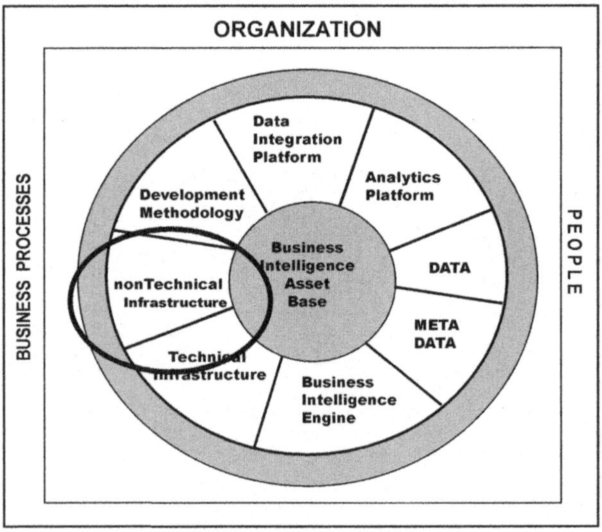

Business Intelligence
Product, Causal and Impacting Factors

CHAPTER 18

BI Continuing Improvement Model 68
Defining the Causal (X) Factors

Business Intelligence
Asset Base:

nonTechnical Infrastructure

The nonTechnical infrastructure is made up of all those constructs and features which are not tangible (unlike hardware), but which provide a framework for consistency, integration and seamless, efficient operations within the Business Intelligence Asset Base. This framework must cover all the Business Intelligence assets and ensure a comprehensive cross organization infrastructure.

Because of the cross organization nature of the nonTechnical infrastructure, auditors should expect to find management and support teams, which are composed of both business and information technology groups. These groups will also, most likely, have membership from various functional arenas, depending on the topic for management.

Note: *The information provided here should help in assessing this X component. However, the audit team should include business and information technical specialists who have a clear understanding of the organization and accepted business practices. The team should also include a Six Sigma knowledgeable resource.*

The goal is not to make the reader a Business Intelligence expert. The goal is to introduce the X Components and provide some helpful information and guidelines for those who are not experts.

The primary objectives for this chapter are:

1. *to identify the specific relevant constructs and features and assist in the process of analyzing those X factors which cause and/or impact the quality of the Business Intelligence product; and*
2. *to enable and guide the use of those X factors and metrics in a process for improvement of the Business Intelligence product.*

The Audit Wheel

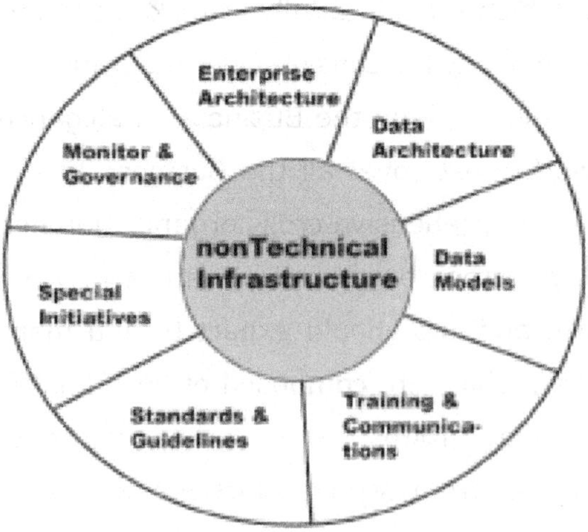

The Key Assessment Features for the nonTechnical Infrastructure have been identified and are included in the Audit Wheel. Auditing the nonTechnical Infrastructure component of the Business Intelligence Asset Base should include an assessment of each one of these Key Assessment Features and an overall assessment of the nonTechnical Infrastructure component of the Business Intelligence Asset Base. The materials in this chapter should provide an understanding of the features and the basic descriptions.

Key Assessment Features

Enterprise Architecture

The organization should have a well planned and documented Enterprise Architecture. The architecture of the Business Intelligence Asset Base should be closely integrated with this Enterprise Architecture. The Enterprise Architecture is described in Chapter 12, The Data Integration Platform. Parts of that discussion will be summarized here for the purposes of describing the relationship and relevance to the nonTechnical Infrastructure. The term 'Enterprise Architecture' may have two distinct definitions:

A. *Enterprise Architecture* may refer to the physical structures and constructs of the organization. This refers to the whole of the organization information technology infrastructure. For example, the organization may have adopted concepts and structures which are Service Oriented Architecture in nature.

B. *Enterprise Architecture* can also refer to a set of models, constructs and documents which management has developed as a blueprint to guide the organization.

The definition of most relevance for the nonTechnical Infrastructure is the second. Thus, the Enterprise Architecture is defined as a set of documents and plans which have been created by business and information technology members, jointly, to define, map and describe the structures, data and applications - both transactional and business information management - for the organization.

There should be a set of current *maps*, as well as planning documents. This *Enterprise Architecture* should be widely available, e.g. on an easily accessible Enterprise Portal. There should be well documented and recognized ownership, stewardship and designation of accepted responsibility for the models, application and data inventories, documentation and communication of contents. This should not be an Information Technology responsibility. The business community should be at least jointly responsible and should retain 'ownership'. The development and existence of this *Enterprise Architecture* is an important base for Business Intelligence creation and management. The presence of such an Enterprise Architecture is itself an indication of management support. The Enterprise Architecture indicates that there has been some planning, groundwork and growth in forging necessary ties between the information technology groups and the business arena.

The value of joint efforts in the creation and maintenance of such an Enterprise Architecture to the organization is important. However, the content of the Enterprise Architecture is equally crucial. Just one example of the critical nature of this work is to provide a base for data integration for Business Intelligence. Data Integration efforts and success can be tied directly to the Enterprise and Data Architecture and the associated data models.

An *Enterprise Architecture*, among other things, is a blueprint of the operations and business information management systems for the organization. It should include:

- organization plans and structures
- applications inventory and models (logical data models should be linked to the applications)
- prioritized list of applications, based on business requirements
- business functions inventory and model
- business processes inventory and model
- enterprise data architecture, including master data and other common data artifacts, e.g. reference data

Each of these components of the *Enterprise Architecture* should include full descriptions and any necessary accompanying documentation. Review and update should be periodic and frequent - since these are the basis for all planning for the information technology of the organization. The Enterprise Architecture is designed, developed and kept updated on a regular basis. Any Business plans for the organization should reference this architecture and any changes to strategic or tactical plans and goals should be integrated into the Enterprise Architecture. For example, there should be a priority list for development of new systems and enhancement of others. This priority list should be modified regularly based on business direction and requirements.

Data Architecture

Data Models

The most important aspects of the data architecture and the data models for the nonTechnical Infrastructure perspective can be summarized quickly.

- The Data Architecture should be clearly documented and well planned. There needs to be a unifying overall design. Whatever the form, i.e. tools and documentation, it should be easy to understand and readily available to everyone.
- There should be no ambiguity about how the Data Integration Platform is to be structured. The data integration methods should be clear and well documented. If there is to be a normalized central data storage arena for detailed data with dimensional data marts for summarized and aggregated data, everyone needs to understand and follow that design. If, instead, all

the data stores are to be designed as dimensional structures, with an integration which uses a BUS architecture of conformed tables, then that should be a recognized design which is universally followed by all Business Intelligence application developers.

- There should be a clear, well designed set of structures for the data. These designs should reflect the requirements associated with the data. The data warehouse presentation data should be easy to access, and allow for fast data retrieval and user response. The design for the relational data stores should reflect the need to find the information and get it out to the users and software interfaces in the required time frames.
- There should be software and methods which are easy to understand and easy to use which will allow for the design of the data. This means that business users need to be able to understand and be involved in the development process.

Database structures. Two of the primary objectives of the database architecture are:

1. The data needs to be designed and structured to allow for integration of the data.
2. The data in the Presentation Library of the Data Integration Platform needs to be easily identified, located and quickly accessible.

What is a Logical Data Model. The logical data models define:

- the data objects in the business activities,
- the business relationships among these data objects,
- data structures, elements, and
- the business rules which govern the data objects.

These data models are used to create the physical databases. The structure of the logical data models, as well as, how they are constructed directly impacts:

- success of data integration,
- database performance - both in the back room and front room activities, and
- joint design efforts - i.e. the normalized models are not business intuitive and easy to understand.

There should be maps and models of both the source data stores as well as the Presentation Library of the Data Integration Platform. Source system data models are essential to the identification and location of source data.

Data models are discussed in more detail in Chapter 12, The Data Integration Platform. There are two primary types of logical data models for relational data within an Enterprise Data Warehouse - normalized and dimensional. The database structures reflect these logical data models, i.e. pictorial design maps.

Normalized Data Model. A normalized data model is a logical database design for relational tables which separates data into discrete, unique entities. The structure of the data in the normalized data model closely resembles the data as used in the business. With this structure, there is a single table for each data object. Each of these data objects, i.e. relational database tables, are connected to all the other data objects through known associations within the data. Normalization of the data also provides the basis for integration of the data. Normalization involves the rules used for laying out the tables for data. The data is present only once in the model and all the data relationships are built directly into the physical structure of the data. This data structure was developed as an efficient way to collect and update transaction data.

Dimensional Data Model. A dimensional data model is a logical database design which optimizes the data structure to make it easy to use in access and use of the data for management decision support, i.e. easy to access, fast responsive query performance. There are fact tables, which hold the measurements; and dimension tables which describe exactly what is known about those measurements, e.g. products, times, etc., related to the measurement of the transaction in question, say the sale of a grocery item. Because of the structure of the single *measurement table* to many surrounding *dimension tables,* this model is often called a *star schema.* There may be multiple copies of the data attributes (data descriptors), i.e. lots of redundant data. Therefore, dimensional data models are unlike the normalized data model, where there are strict mandates against redundancy of the data.

More Audit Considerations.

Data Platform and Modeling Design Issues. There are two major architecture philosophies for the Data Integration Platform, i.e. the Enterprise Data Warehouse. These have been discussed in more detail in Chapter 12.

Source Data Systems. The audit team should specifically find out if there are logical data models available for the source systems? These are necessary in order to identify, locate and extract the data. These are also necessary for all the preliminary design and testing, including the profiling of the data to ensure content and accuracy before actual implementation of the new Business Intelligence application.

Other Data Modeling Assessment Factors. Some of the other data modeling considerations which need to be addressed and reviewed are:

- Integration features: Are the local Business Process or Departmental data models tied into an enterprise wide data model? How is this validated? Is the Kimball Bus architecture used which counts on 'conformed' dimensions and facts? If so, how is conformity validated.
- What CASE (Computer Assisted Systems Engineering) tools are being used? Do they allow for all standard modeling features, including normalized and dimen-

sional models and is the physical database automatically derived?

Training and Communications

Sometimes the importance of training and communications aspects of Business Intelligence are overlooked. The Business Intelligence assets of the organization should be marketed to the whole organization. This is the only way to make sure that these assets are used to obtain the most value. The central Presentation Library of information contains information which can be of use to everyone in the organization. Even those whose needs are not met by the current data need to be aware of the potential of this invaluable information source. How else will they be able to ask for and define their own requirements - if they do not know what is possible.

There should be special programs for introducing people to the data warehouse and business intelligence functions and capabilities. There should be a full range of classes and training from simple, online introductions to class room and CBT training for full 'power user' analytical functions. The communications, e.g. a website or an enterprise portal, should be widely available and marketed. The training should be both online, with people able to interact from their work station, as well as some formal classes, which are instructor led.

Without these training and communications efforts, the data warehouse and Business Intelligence efforts will remain the parochial interests of only a few. People are usually too intent on doing their 'regular' jobs to find out how they can do things better. It is the job of those in charge of the Business Intelligence arena to market the services. These are services which will improve the overall operations and management of the organization. Auditors: Make sure they are spreading the word -- and giving the needed training and support.

Standards, Guidelines, and Procedures

What are the standards, guidelines and procedures to be audited? What should be identified and assessed? Some examples are:

- data naming, abbreviations, quality
- data stewardship
- data certification
- development methods
- change control and other issues and operations
- testing
- auditing
- data integration standards and governance
- development and maintenance of logical data models and architecture
- service level agreements
- development and enhancement methods, standards and guidelines (see chapter 16)

In review and assessment of these crucial blocks in the non technical framework for Business Intelligence, we need to look for and consider several factors:

> *What standards, guidelines and procedures are documented and readily available? How are these communicated? Have they been made an integral part of the Business Intelligence development and operations? What kinds of governance methods and teams are in place? How often do the teams meet and what kinds of decisions do they make? Who are the team members - i.e. what are their roles in the organization and responsibilities within the Business Intelligence arena?*

Service Level Agreements

Service Level Agreements have been included as a Key Assessment Feature in several other Business Intelligence components. It is important to mention these important contracts here because they are part of the glue which fuses and creates the foundation for Business Intelligence. These are agreements between any two parties, usually the user community and those who are responsible for creating and delivering the Business Intelligence. They should be written documents which are treated as formal contracts between the two parties. There should be some form of measurement and management of these contracts. Also, both sides should understand exactly what the commitments and expectations mean in terms of cost and value to the organization. If the users expectations are set too high, no one is happy, including those who are trying to satisfy the commitments. There should be careful and complete dialog prior to setting the expectations and writing of the Service Level Agreement. These contracts may be written at any time, including well after the development process has occurred. However, they work best and are most effective when the expectations and commitments are part of the design and development of the Business Intelligence application process. Regular measurement, reporting and common discussions, including revised expectations and commitments are necessary in order to make the process work.

Special Initiatives

There are numerous programs which benefit the organization and are not necessarily tied to a single department or function. Look for these and see how well they are accomplishing their mission. In particular, the following two initiatives and programs should be identified and assessed . Find out, for example, are they present? What is being accomplished? What are the stated objectives?

Master Data Management. This is a program initiative which concentrates on the identification, recognition, management and common use of the data across an organization. Master Data are a set of core data elements, along with all their attributes and hierarchies which are common across the whole of the organization. These Master Data are not transaction data - which essentially is data which describes the activities, or transactions, of the business. The Master Data are those core data elements which are used to categorize, aggregate and describe the transaction data, e.g. product, customer, employee, account. These are the Dimension values which populate the Dimensional Data Models. The primary focus of a Master Data Management initiative is the accomplishment of what Ralph Kimball describes as Conformed Dimensions. The ultimate goals are to standardize and effectively manage the common data across the organization.

Some of the objectives and results from an effective Master Data Management coupled with the Kimball Data Warehouse Bus are:

- Data Integration,
- 'Control' data which enables users to have a 'common' understanding of the data,
- Assist in the achievement of timely, accurate, consistent information
- Facilitates referential integrity across the system - which, in turn, supports alignment of information and decision making.

The Master Data Management initiative is, in effect, a 'bottom-up' attempt at creating an integrated enterprise data architecture.

Quality Data Initiative. A Quality Data initiative is the result of a recognition by the organization that consistent, accurate, timely data is key to the organization success. A Quality Data initiative or a quality data management program includes the review, careful monitoring and management of data creation and use within the organization. Some of the key elements of any effective program are:

- data stewardship programs - which assign a responsible party to ensure the accuracy, timeliness and other features of the data;
- data certification programs - which ensure that data will have a core 'source of truth' or a single element (out of multiple source copies) which can be accepted as the 'true, accurate data'. Only this data may be used for management decision and reporting.
- Common Data Definitions.

Monitoring and Governance

In every case where there is a rule or standards which have been set in place, then there should be documentation. The nature of the business and development arena for Business Intelligence requires that these rules and standards be followed. The audit team should look for some form of monitoring and governance for each and every one. This may be in the form of regular reviews, during development, automatic via software or manually performed. The consequences when the rules or standards have been violated should at least lead to enforcement of the standardization. If, for example, a system is to go into production, then it should be well known that it must first pass the reviews.

Audit Guidelines

Use the information in this chapter, as well as the metrics descriptions, i.e. Key Performance Indicators If there is little or no evidence of the Key Assessment Feature, rate it as 0 or 1. Highest level should be 4, with a level 5 rating given only in outstanding circumstances, i.e. auditor is particularly impressed with the comprehensive and/ or creativity of the organization. A rating of '5' for the whole of the nonTechnical Infrastructure requires a rating of '5' for each of the Key Assessment Features. Overall rating should include all the features and may be an average or some features may be given more weight, depending on subjective or objective reasons.

Business Intelligence nonTechnical Infrastructure

Rate each Key Assessment Feature for each of the KPI's. Rating should be 1 to 5, with 5 as highest rating. See the appropriate chapter for audit and rating guidelines.	KEY PERFORMANCE INDICATORS											
KEY ASSESSMENT FEATU…	Mangment Support	BUSINESS ALIGNMENT	PARTNERSHIP	Business Goals	Scalability	INTEGRATION	ADAPTABILITY	PERFORMANCE	USER FRIENDLY	COMPREHENSION	QUALITY	VALUE
Enterprise Architecture												
Data Architecture												
Data Models												
Training and Communications												
Standards and Guidelines												
Service Level Agreements												
Special Initiatives												
[illegible]												

$$Y = f(X) + E$$

The Six Sigma *Breakthrough* **Formula**

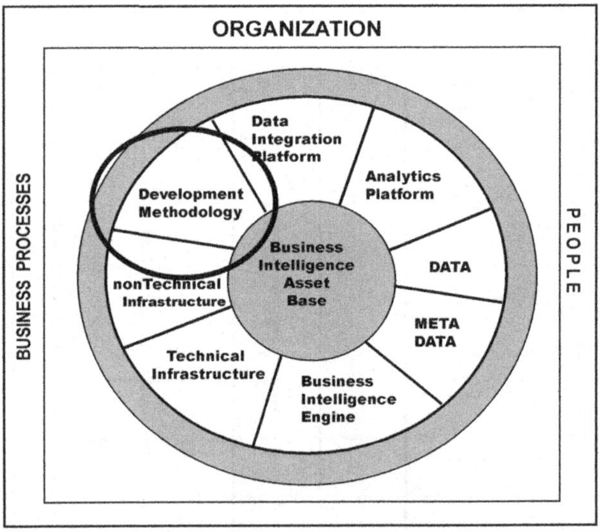

Business Intelligence
Product, Causal and Impacting Factors

CHAPTER 19

BI Continuing Improvement Model 68

Defining the Causal (X) Factors

Business Intelligence

Asset Base:

Development Methodology

The way that the applications are designed and developed is critical to the success of Business Intelligence in any organization. There should be well documented and communicated methods and processes for development of Business Intelligence applications. There should be a program which defines the development process - step by step. The process can be complex. The process needs to be repeatable and all the standards and system components need to be included with every application development project.

The Information Base which is the focus for any new business intelligence development project is, most often, an active, existing library. Development methods need to be consistent and should incorporate safeguards for the current information. There are numerous other requirements which should be incorporated into the development process in order to meet the organization needs for a continuing base of quality Business Intelligence. An important first step is to ensure the application team understands the complexities of the Business Intelligence Asset Base for the organization.

> ***Note:*** *The information provided here should help in assessing this X component. However, the audit team should include business and information technical specialists who have a clear understanding of the organization and accepted business practices. The team should also include a Six Sigma knowledgeable resource.*
>
> *The goal is not to make the reader a Business Intelligence expert. The goal is to introduce the X Components and provide some helpful information and guidelines for those who are not experts.*
>
> *The primary objectives for this chapter are:*
>
> 1. *to identify the specific relevant constructs and features and assist in the process of analyzing those X factors which cause and/or impact the quality of the Business Intelligence product; and*
> 2. *to enable and guide the use of those X factors and metrics in a process for improvement of the Business Intelligence product.*

The purpose of this chapter is not to define the development process. However, there are a number of principles and constructs which we need to ensure are present, i.e. included in the methodology, in order to provide for and protect the quality of Business Intelligence assets. Any audit of the Business Intelligence assets for the organization requires a close review of the existing development process. This chapter will define some of the more critical points which should be analyzed.

The Audit Wheel - the Key Assessment Features

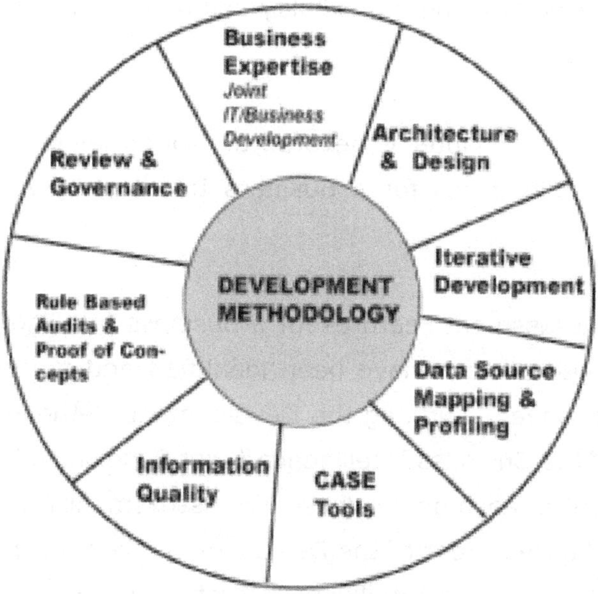

Any audit should begin with the question of whether there is a documented set of processes for Business Intelligence design and development. There are some guidelines which should be recognized by the development teams and the management of the organization. These should be documented somewhere or there should be answers for each item if put in the form of a question to the project managers and sponsors. Some of the '50,000 foot level type of observations' are noted here. Most of these are described in the Key Performance Indicators

Is the project aligned to business goals?

Does it have complete management support? What are the management expectations? What are the organiza-

tion impacts and political ramifications?
Is there joint business and IT management and participation?
Are we building in flexibility and adaptability into the application?

The rest of the chapter is devoted to ground level observations and integral features for a Business Intelligence development project.

The Key Assessment Features for a Business Intelligence development methodology have been identified and are included in the Audit Wheel. Auditing the Development Methodology component of the Business Intelligence Asset Base should include an assessment of each one of these Key Assessment Features, plus an overall assessment of the Development Methodology component of the Business Intelligence Asset Base. The materials in this chapter should provide some understanding of the features and the basic descriptions.

Key Assessment Features

Business Expertise

It is important that the business users (i.e. people who understand and use the business intelligence product) understand and are involved in the whole development process. These business people should be full members of the design and development team. They need to be involved in the daily decision making and activities. Any audit should check out the amount of time and number of end user resources which are usually assigned to a

Business Intelligence application development project.

One of the major benefits of the Kimball philosophy of Data Warehouse architecture is that it seems easier to involve the business/end users from the initial stages of design and throughout the development process.

> *The inherent star pattern structure of the dimensional model parallels the user requirements and optimizes the process of accessing and using the information. The primary alternative to the dimensional model is the normalized data model, which is architected to reflect the organization structure and to optimize the creation and update of the transaction data. The design and development of a normalized relational database requires database experts. It is not so easy for the business user to understand the design and process.*

In auditing the Business Intelligence Development process, take a look at who is assigned to the projects (i.e. roles and organization job responsibilities), what kinds of teams are formed, and how many specialists like the business experts and data architects, modelers and ETL specialists are available. Lack of resources certainly can impact the development success rate.

Management Support. The need for management support is so pervasive and well recognized that it is commonly written into any planning documentation. The need for management support for the Business Intelligence application development process is just as important. Resources, funds and other tangible signs of management support should be apparent.

Architecture and Design

The integration of data is of primary importance in building a successful Enterprise Data Warehouse. A well established, uniform architecture is one of the primary constructs. The architecture should include such features as incorporation of master data and quality data precepts. There should be review and governance to ensure that the architecture patterns and rules are upheld.

The primary architecture models for the Enterprise Data Warehouse have been discussed in previous chapters. The important considerations in the audit of the Business Intelligence development methodology are:

- Has an architecture been clearly defined for the Enterprise Data Warehouse?
- Is there a strong conceptual understanding of that architecture and the designs and processes required to create a consistent infrastructure using the architecture concepts?
- Is the architecture used as the pattern for design and development in a consistent manner?

The two most prominent architectures and philosophies for the design of an Enterprise Data Warehouse are those presented by Inmon and by Kimball.
The auditor should research how well and how consistently the organization developers adhere to the required methods for the chosen architecture.

Disagreement and ambiguity about the architecture foundation of the Enterprise Data Warehouse are not unusual and can be devastating to the integrity of the data warehouse library(s).

Iterative Development

The Big Bang theory of Data Warehouse development has been proven to create a big history of failures. Iterative design and development provides for the design and development of small pieces of an application at a time. Since there are fewer and less complex parts to go wrong or be misunderstand, this approach allows an easier management process. This iterative development concept is also known as the 'don't bite off more than you can chew' philosophy. Both business and information technology people can easily visualize the design. Everyone sees the results faster. They can see and use and change, as necessary, the resulting information faster, in more easily understood small 'chunks', and in a more informal, less stressful, manner. The information can be made to conform to the real needs of the business user, as those needs are recognized. The final results are more likely to fit the exact requirements and the overall costs should be much lower. These are just a few of the reasons for the recognition by the industry that iterative development of applications is the most successful approach. Look for prototypes and pilot stages in the development methodology.

There are a number of formal development methodologies available on the market today. The auditor should identify any in use within the organization and explore the following questions: Do the developers understand and use the formal methodology? How well does it work for them? Are the results consistent and successful? Ask the developers and look at the documentation and some of the development project documentation and results.

Data Profiling

Sampling the source data and ensuring that it is as defined in the documentation and data models is important to success. The source data may reflect the documentation, may not have integrity and/or may not be accurate and up to date. It is best to find this out well before the development work begins. Any changes to the source data needs to be recognized and dealt with as soon as possible in the Business Intelligence Application project. The data sampling should be done early, before a lot of costs have been sunk into the project. If there is just no way to obtain data with integrity and accuracy - i.e. if the data source is corrupted and unfixable - then the project should be abandoned until the data can be found or created. This is a hard lesson and almost never learned without some rough experience. These guidelines and steps should be written into the methodology documentation.

Source Mapping

As part of the design process, the Business Intelligence data requirements are identified. Exact locations of the data, formats, how to extract them -- these are all key parts of the Business Intelligence application design. The auditor should make sure that the development documentation includes the requirement for maps which pinpoint the source data. There should also be a requirement and descriptions of all the documentation which is needed for the source data. This should include business meta data, e.g. definitions, as well as technical meta data, including, for example, formats and database structures.

The data profiling should match the data values found against the expectations based on the documentation. The design and development of the extraction process requires that the source data be mapped and matched with the target data.

In addition to the data source maps, there should be documentation and identification of available meta data.

Case Tools

Automated, easy to use and to understand software (CASE - Computer Assisted Software Engineering) should be available for each of the design and development steps and functions. This includes, for example, the design of the logical data models and the design, development and runtime processing of the Extract, Transform and Load processing. In addition, it is just as important that there are team members who understand the information requirements, the development process, and how to use the CASE tools.

In the audit process, look for CASE tools which are well established and are being used within the organization. Check that these tools meet industry standards. This usually means a review of the web site and technical descriptive literature. Also, check with the developers. How well are the tools accepted? Do they like the tool and why? Are there any specific issues and how critical are they?

Prototypes and Rule Based Audits

There is a significant amount of risk associated with any Business Intelligence application development project. Some of this risk comes from unknown factors in the source data and the source applications. We have discussed activities to mitigate some of these risks, i.e. data mapping and data profiling. There are some other major methods which the organization should be using as standard practice. With a little research, the auditor should be able to determine whether these are a part of the project development methodology. The practices should be well documented and understood by any of the project teams. The following practices should be included in the standard development process:

- Rule based Audits allow for testing of sample source data. (Data profiling is also an up front testing of source data - but differs slightly in that it is checking the validity and accuracy of the data.) This allows the determination that source data along with the known business rules would allow the creation of the desired target data.
- A Proof of Concept or pilot/test with a set of data which is considerably smaller than the final production data volumes can also assist in reducing the risk for the whole project.

Information Quality

All the requirements which are necessary for data quality must be built in - during the development process. There should be parts of the formal or informal Development Methodology which specifically addresses the data quality issues. This should include comprehensive meta data. In addition, during the design and development process, data stewards should be identified and assigned the responsibility for specific meta data and data. The project documentation should include the identification of these data stewards. There should also be some method for certification of data and other data quality constructs which enforce the integrity and accuracy of the data. These features should be integral to the development process.

Auditors should look for specific documentation related to incorporation of data quality into the design and development process. There should also be some indication that these are included in the governance and review process.

Review and Governance

Application development projects should have consistent and regular reviews at various points in the process. The reviews should include resources external to the development team. There should be a documented review process. The contents should include review of all the audit points, including, for example, follow-up on information quality, profiling, and mapping results.

Audit Guidelines

Use the information in this chapter, as well as the Key Performance Indicators. If there is little or no evidence of the Key Assessment Feature, rate it as 0 or 1. Highest level should be 4, with a level 5 rating given only in outstanding circumstances. This might mean, for example, that the auditor is particularly impressed with the comprehensive and/ or creativity of the organization. A rating of '5' for the whole of the Development Methodology component requires a rating of '5' for each of the Key Assessment Features. The Overall rating should include all the features and may be an average. However, some features may be given more weight, depending on subjective or objective reasons by the auditor.

Business Intelligence Development Methodology

KEY ASSESSMENT FEATURES	KEY PERFORMANCE INDICATORS											
Rate each Key Assessment Feature for each of the KPI's. Rating should be 1 to 5, with 5 as highest rating. See the appropriate chapter for audit and rating guidelines.	Mangment Support	BUSINESS ALIGNMNT	PARTNERSHIP	Business Goals	Scalability	INTEGRATION	ADAPTABILITY	PERFORMANCE	USER FRIENDLY	COMPREHENSION	QUALITY	VALUE
Business Expertise & Resource Utilization												
Design and Architecture												
Iterative Development												
Data Source Mapping & Profiling												
CASE Tools												
Rule Based Audits & Proof of Concepts												
Information Quality												
Review & Governance												
Development Methodology												